The Skill and Art
of Business Writing

The Skill and Art of Business Writing

An Everyday Guide and Reference

HAROLD E. MEYER

QUORUM BOOKS
Westport, Connecticut • London

Library of Congress Cataloging-in-Publication Data

Meyer, Harold E., 1920–
   The skill and art of business writing : an everyday guide and reference / Harold E. Meyer.
      p.   cm.
   Includes bibliographical references and index.
   ISBN 1–56720–457–0 (alk. paper)
   1. Business writing.   I. Title.
   HF5718.3.M48   2002
   808'.06665—dc21   2001018028

British Library Cataloguing in Publication Data is available.

Library of Congress Catalog Card Number: 2001018028
ISBN: 1–56720–457–0

First published in 2002

Quorum Books, 88 Post Road West, Westport, CT 06881
An imprint of Greenwood Publishing Group, Inc.
www.quorumbooks.com

Printed in the United States of America

∞™

The paper used in this book complies with the
Permanent Paper Standard issued by the National
Information Standards Organization (Z39.48–1984).

10 9 8 7 6 5 4 3 2 1

To Irma

Contents

How This Book Will Help You Write Clearly

The Purpose

Communication is many things. It is talking face to face, it is talking on the telephone, it is writing letters, it is sending radio messages, it is electronic mail, it is the way you stand, it is the way you walk, it is the way you approach a person, it is your facial expression, it is your voice, it is your body movements; and it is the nonoccurrence of these things.

In written communication, flat words on a sheet of paper must convey the same feelings and impressions that may be readily seen and felt when meeting a person face to face.

Writing, however, has the advantage of review and editing; you can rewrite until the message is clear, be it a detailed report on a business project, a birthday letter to your mother or a note to your postal carrier. Whatever your intent, this book will show you how to write what you mean.

The purpose of this book is to show you how to write phrases, sentences, paragraphs and complete compositions that your reader will understand after the first reading.

Practically all the ideas, suggestions and examples presented here can be applied to speaking as well as to writing. By using the book's recommendations you can make your "speeches" to a colleague, a client or a group of any size more interesting and purposeful.

The Need

The need for improved writing ability can be illustrated with a few quotes from Harvey Mackay in an article written for United Features Syndicate.

Mackay says, "I have never walked into the office of a corporate executive and found a dictionary, thesaurus, encyclopedia or any other accouterments of the writer's trade anywhere in sight. After all, what do these people do for a living?" He further states, "In real life, when we're not polluting, exploiting or discriminating, we don't make speeches. We attend meetings. We make phone calls. And we write memos. In fact, if you're like most of us who earn a living behind a desk, you are judged as much by your ability to convey your ideas as the quality of those ideas themselves." Mackay concludes, "If you sit at a desk, you probably write for a living."

I once belonged to a group in which we analyzed each other's writings. The senior person there had spent some forty years as an office worker with Texaco, the oil company. He told us that whenever he was asked about his position, he replied, "I'm a writer." As an accountant, I too spent much of my time writing.

Here are a few more items that point out the need for clear writing.

A New York-based writing consultant, Gary Blake, said the most common business-writing mistakes were poor organization, wordiness, antiquated or overblown phrases and sloppiness.

In a cartoon, a secretary, having just taken dictation from her boss, says, "Would you like me to read that back so you can hear how silly it sounds?"

A quote from Lewis Carroll's *Alice's Adventures in Wonderland* illustrates a problem common to writing as well as to speaking:

"Then you should say what you mean," the March Hare went on.

"I do," Alice hastily replied: "at least—at least I mean what I say— that's the same thing, you know."

"Not the same thing a bit!" said the Hatter. "Why, you might just as well say that 'I see what I eat' is the same as 'I eat what I see'!"

A short item in the July 1993 *Reader's Digest* quotes Russell L. Ackoff in *Management in Small Doses*, published by John Wiley & Sons:

"I once had a brilliant student, now a well-known professor, who wrote a highly technical thesis. I asked him to assume that I was an ordinary corporate manager. Would he explain his thesis briefly?

"He went to the blackboard and began to cover it with mathematical symbols. I stopped him to remind him that I was an ordinary manager, not a mathematician. After a long pause, he said, 'I don't understand what I've done well enough to explain it in nontechnical language.' "

To avoid the mistakes suggested above, put a little time into looking over, perhaps even studying, *The Skill and Art of Business Writing*. Both job and social positions require a certain level of education, and your writing and speaking skills are the best indicators of that level.

A Practical Approach

This book demonstrates *practical* approaches to improving your language skills. It is based on my over thirty years in various businesses reading and writing memos, letters, procedures, proposals and reports and twenty years devoted to writing business communication books.

In this book, the topic explanations are short and clear, and the examples are numerous. This format is a welcome contrast to many books about the English language, which offer long explanations and few illustrations. Some topics in this book have as many as thirty examples, making it easy to determine if your sentence is clearly written and will communicate your intended thought.

What This Book Will Do for You

Treat every word as a precious emotion. This is an allusion to a quote of jazz trumpeter Wallace Roney, a protégé of Miles Davis. Roney said of Miles Davis, "He taught me to treat every note like a precious emotion."

The need to use words that have the proper emotional meaning to your reader can be illustrated in this brief summary of a newspaper article written by Jay M. Kaplan for the *Arizona Republic* on April 3, 1994: Jay Kaplan was buying real estate for a limited partnership. He found a likely apartment building, but the owner wanted more than the current market value. Kaplan proposed a "joint venture" to finance the transaction. At the sound of that phrase, the seller balked. Kaplan's boss suggested that the term "joint venture" conjured up hostile memories in the mind of the seller. From then on, Kaplan avoided such phrases as "lease option" and "joint venture." Write with your reader's background, knowledge and possible biases in mind.

The Skill and Art of Business Writing will show you how to clarify what you have written by rewriting. A composition is seldom "finished" after the first draft, but once you have started, write thoughts only. Concern yourself with punctuation and clear phrasing during the rewrite. This book provides numerous examples of rewritten sentences, paragraphs and complete compositions. Clarity is usually improved by shortening the writing to eliminate duplication and fuzzy arrangements of words and thoughts. A clear letter of information or request is answered more quickly than one that requires the reader to "plow" through it more than once.

What This Book Covers

This is a reference book that covers a large number of topics that explain how to construct clear sentences, paragraphs and compositions. In addition, this book includes chapters showing you how to spell, punctuate sentences, clarify confusing words, write reports and understand language terms you may have forgotten. If you have a particular problem, the Index will steer you to the solution.

Among the thirty topics related to sentences are these:

Outdated language

Agreement: subject and verb, noun and pronoun, noun and adjective

Familiar words

Overused words and clichés

Specific words for exactness

Logical order

Misplaced modifiers

Parallel word groups

Necessary words

Jargon

Variety

The subject of paragraphs is well covered with sixty-three topics, including:

Paragraph development

Outline and topic statement

Too-brief paragraphs

Detailed paragraphs

Parallel construction

The many types of transitions

Topic sentence

Summary paragraphs

Unity

Coherence

Bad news messages

Unusual paragraphs

Revised paragraphs

The treatment of complete compositions (Chapter 8) is titled "Tie It All Together." Coverage of this subject required a hundred topics. Some of them are:

Introduction to the whole composition

Types of outlines

Order of items placed in an outline

Twenty examples of outlines

Defining clarity

Examples of clear writing

Making requests specific

Stating the purpose of the composition

Learning about your audience

Examples of emphasis

Three ways to revise

Checklist—the final review

"Why Spelling?" (Chapter 10) points out the reasons for spelling correctly, why it is difficult and ways to overcome common problems. Various devices to make spelling easier are illustrated.

The chapter on punctuation (Chapter 11) explains why proper punctuation is necessary. The various marks are discussed and illustrated.

Chapter 12, on reports, provides three varied examples: a procedure, an accounting audit and solutions to financial losses in a manufacturing plant.

Chapter 13, "Confusing Words Clarified," explains the differences between words that are commonly misused: For example:

Accept/except	Disinterested/uninterested
Affect/effect	Error/mistake
All ready/already	Fewer/less
All right/alright	Its/It's
All together/altogether	Last/latest
Assure/ensure/insure	Principal/principle
Can/may/might	Who/whom
Capital/capitol	

The Glossary of Terms (Chapter 14) defines words the reader may have forgotten or never understood completely. The terms defined and explained include:

adverb	person
antecedent	predicate
case	preposition
conjunction	subject
gerund	voice

Easy-to-Use Index

In this reference book, double indexing is used. For example: *reader's view-point* is indexed under both *reader's* and *viewpoint*.

A Helpful Reference Book

Language changes, and that is recognized in this book. The latest changes are discussed and illustrated, and reasons for certain preferences are stated. *The Skill and Art of Business Writing* is a reference book that will be helpful for many years.

CHAPTER 1

Understandable Sentences

A sentence is many things, and that's why it needs all seven definitions.

Definition

The seven definitions of a sentence are:

1. A sentence contains a subject and a verb and expresses a complete thought.

In the sentence *Pepo hit the ball*, the idea is complete because we know exactly what happened. Also the sentence is emphatic because of the arrangement of words: subject, verb, object.

Pepo—subject; Pepo is the doer.

Hit—verb (and part of the predicate); what Pepo did.

Ball—object (and part of the predicate); what was acted upon (receiver of the action).

2. A sentence is a sequence of words that contains a subject and a predicate and conveys a complete thought.

The only real difference between this definition and the first one is the use of the word *predicate* rather than *verb*. A verb is a predicate, but a predicate can include a verb and any number of modifiers. In the sentence *Pepo hit the ball*, hit is the verb and part of the predicate. In the sentence *Pepo hit the ball so hard it cleared the center field fence*, Pepo is the subject and the remainder of the sentence is the predicate.

> 3. A sentence is a basic unit of language, a communication in words, consisting of at least one independent verb with its subject, giving the reader or listener the feeling that it is complete and independent.

This is a more complete or less clipped way of saying the same thing as the first and second definitions.

> 4. A sentence is one or more words conveying to the reader a sense of complete meaning.

Subject and verb are not mentioned in this definition. That is because they can be implied, and the meaning is still complete. In the one-word sentence, *Go!*, the subject *you* is implied, resulting in the sentence *You go!* The completely worded sentence could read *I want you to go now*, or perhaps *I order you to remove yourself immediately*.

> 5. A sentence expresses one thought.

This is a short, neat definition, but perhaps it needs a little elaboration. The essential components of a sentence, subject, verb and object, are assumed known by the writer or speaker. From this definition, we can expand our thinking to realize that several thoughts require several sentences, and then we have a paragraph, which can be defined as a complete idea or topic rather than a single thought. A single thought can be complicated, and that is the reason for the long sentences in literary, political and legal writings.

Here is an example:

> It is now explicitly found that the acreage minimums contained in the Land Use Element and Map of Sonoma County Agriculture, Orchards and Vineyards, and Agricultural and Residential do not authorize zonings, major or minor subdivision, or other entitlements for use in such designations that materially alter the stability of the overall land use pattern to the substantial detriment of these resource areas are inconsistent with the Sonoma County General Plan.

Ranchers, landowners and experts in land use matters were unable to understand how their property would be affected by this proposed Farmlands Initiative. I, too, have no idea what the sentence means. It seem to contain several thoughts.

6. Although not strictly a definition, one author writes, "Don't try to put too many ideas in a single sentence. Keep each sentence to one or two ideas. Write other sentences to add new thoughts."

What the author probably had in mind was a complicated or compound sentence. An example of a compound sentence is *The project promised to be interesting, and the team was eager to begin*. You may at first think of this as two thoughts, but they are sufficiently related and interdependent to be one thought.

Complicated sentences can be found in most legal documents and are often unintelligible to readers not versed in legal jargon. Here is an example:

Except as otherwise provided in this Agreement, the property now owned and hereafter acquired by either party, which by terms of this Agreement is classified as the separate property on one party, can only become the separate property of the other party or the joint property of both by a written instrument executed by the party whose separate property is reclassified.

After reading this sentence six times and then asking an attorney to explain it, I now understand what is being said. Clarity could be improved by dividing the statement into two or three sentences. Here is one possibility:

Unless provided for elsewhere in this Agreement, any property now owned or later acquired as separate property by one person shall remain the separate property of that person. However, a change in ownership may be made with a document written by the person who gives up his or her ownership.

7. A sentence is a single and complete thought.

This definition is probably the best because it is simple, straightforward and complete.

In the remainder of this chapter we will discuss and illustrate ways to make sentences understandable.

Agreement—Subject and Verb

You wouldn't want to write the following sentence even to your most forgiving friend:

Our *warehouse don't* have any number 5 golf clubs in stock now; *Jackson Golf Shop and Sportsmen's Outfitters* is your best bets.

You have communicated with your reader, and perhaps you are kidding, but if you received a note written like that your impression of the writer would be at rock bottom. Why is that statement so bad? Because the subjects and verbs do not agree in number, singular or plural.

In the first part of the sentence, the subject, *warehouse*, is singular and takes a singular verb, *doesn't* or *does not*. In the second half of the sentence, the compound subject, *Jackson Golf Shop and Sportsmen's Outfitters*, is plural and takes a plural verb, *are*, not the singular verb, *is*.

Here are more examples of singular and plural subjects and verbs that agree in number:

Singular: The clock strikes one.

Plural: The clocks strike one.

Singular: The cat is hungry.

Plural: The cats are hungry.

Singular: Our super engine runs better.

Plural: Our super engines run better.

As we saw in the first paragraph under "Agreement—Subject and Verb," compound subjects when joined by *and* take a plural verb. When joined by *nor, or*, or *not only*, and when one of the compound subjects is singular and the other is plural, the verb agrees with the *closest* subject.

Correct: Neither Bob nor the twins were ready.

Correct: Neither the twins nor Bob was ready.

Correct: Either Bob or the girls were qualified for jumping.

Correct: Either the girls or Bob was qualified for the pursuit.

Correct: The leader as well as the followers were wrong.

Correct: The followers as well as the leader was wrong.

Correct: Not only Jim but also his band members were dressed in red.

Correct: Not only the band but also Jim was dressed in red.

A compound expression used as a subject when considered to be a single unit takes a singular verb.

Singular: Corned beef and cabbage is my favorite dinner.

Plural: Corned beef and cabbage are best when served together.

Singular: *Amos and Andy* was a popular radio program.

Plural: Amos and Andy were star radio performers.

Collective nouns can be either singular or plural depending upon how their use is intended. Collective nouns include, among others, *army, band, class, committee, couple, crew, family, gang, group, jury.*

Singular: Our family has breakfast together.

Plural: Our family have separate bedtimes.

Better: Our family members go to bed at different times.

Singular: Sports is a game.

Plural: Sports are played by all the students.

Singular: The committee is tired.

Plural: The committee are disagreeing among themselves.

Better: The committee members are disagreeing.

Singular: The Sanders couple is a handsome pair.

Plural: The Sanders couple are handsome.

Better: The Sanders are two handsome people.

The following words are singular, even if many end in *s* and sound plural. When used as sentence subjects, they require a singular verb:

aerobics	everyone	news
another	everything	nobody
anybody	gallows	no one
anyone	geriatrics	nothing
anything	headquarters	one
athletics	herpes	phenomenon
billiards	it	physics
criticism	little	politics
datum	mathematics	radius
each	measles	robotics
economics	mechanics	somebody
either	medium	someone
electronics	molasses	something
ethics	much	stamina
everyone	mumps	whereabouts
everybody	neither	

We have seen that subjects and verbs must agree in number, singular or plural. Subjects and verbs must also agree in person: first person, second person or third person. First person is the person speaking, *I* or *we*. Second person is the person spoken to, *you*, whether singular or plural. Third person is the person or thing spoken about, *he, she, they* or *it*.

First person singular: *I am* happy now.

First person plural: *We are* happy now.

Second person singular: *You are* happier now. (Referring to one person.)

Second person plural: *You* all *are* happier now. (Referring to more than one person.)

Third person singular: *It is* a balmy night.

Third person singular: *He* (or *she*) *enjoys* a balmy night.

Third person plural: *They enjoy* a balmy night.

Be careful not to shift from one person to another, as in the following example (from third to second person).

Wrong: *People* work better before a heavy meal because *you* don't get drowsy.

Right: *People* work better before a heavy meal because *they* don't get drowsy.

Verb tense (past, present, future) must be consistent.

Wrong: We *examined* the circuit breaker then *fix* it.

Right: We *examined* the circuit breaker then *fixed* it.

Wrong: We *run* to the ocean beach and *looked* at the breakers.

Right: We *ran* to the ocean beach and *looked* at the breakers.

Right: We *will check* the error then *(will) correct* it.

Long sentences can separate the verb from the subject and make subject-verb agreement easy to overlook.

Wrong: A *manager* who is successful *gives* occasional praise to his employees, especially to those who show promise, and *use* various motivational devices that encourage them to work even harder.

The second verb, *use*, should be *uses*, to agree with the subject, *manager*. In essence, the manager *gives* praise and *uses* devices.

Better: A successful manager praises and motivates his employees.

Inverted sentences—the subject follows the verb—can cause agreement confusion.

Wrong: With poverty *comes* hunger and discouragement.

The compound subject is *hunger and discouragement*, not poverty. Thus the verb should be plural, *come*.

Correct: With poverty *come* hunger and discouragement.

Not inverted: Hunger and discouragement *come* with poverty.

Wrong: *Does* Witness and Outreach (sections of a department) take a summer holiday at this church?

Right: *Do* Witness and Outreach take a summer holiday at this church?

The subject is *Witness and Outreach*, a compound subject, taking the plural verb *do*.

Connective or transitional phrases in a sentence can signal a parenthetical phrase that must be ignored when checking subject-verb agreement. Some of the transitional phrases are these:

along with	in addition to
also	including
as much as	more than
as well as	rather than
but not	together with

Wrong: John, along with the whole pizza gang, *like* to walk to pier 49.

Right: John, along with the whole pizza gang, *likes* to walk to pier 49.

Wrong: Her preference, rather than similar alternatives, *were* not acceptable to the others.

Right: Her preference, rather than similar alternatives, *was* not acceptable to the others.

Wrong: The pair of ostriches *were* one of her favorite exhibits.

Right: The pair of ostriches *was* one of her favorite exhibits.

The subject is *pair*, not ostriches. In this usage, *pair* is a single unit and therefore is a singular subject, taking the singular verb *was*.

Many sentences start with the word *there*. Technically that is an *expletive*, a fill-in word usually signifying that a meaningful subject will follow. For example: *There* will be no dessert for *you* tonight. In other words, *you* will be without dessert tonight.

The word *expletive* was made popular during the time of President Nixon's impeachment with the phrase, "expletive deleted." This phrase uses another definition of the word and means an exclamation that is obscene or profane.

When a sentence starts with the word *there*, the verb must agree with the true subject.

Wrong: There *is* several *players* arguing at third base.

Right: There *are* several *players* arguing at third base.

Wrong: There *is* not any *totals* shown, just the heading.

Right: There *are* no *totals* shown, just the heading.

Wrong: There *is Doctors* Justin and Jordan.

Right: There *are Doctors* Justin and Jordan.

Right: There *is* the *office* of Doctors Justin and Jordan.

Sentences using numbers or mathematics can be confusing. The key is whether the subject is intended to be one unit or more than one unit: Three and four is seven. Three and four are seven. Both are correct. In the first sentence, *three and four* is intended to be a single set of numerals. In the second sentence, *three* and *four* are intended to be two separate units, thus requiring a plural verb.

The following examples illustrate when the verb should be singular or plural:

Five dollars was once a high daily wage.

Three hours at the airport *is* a long wait.

Four quarts of oil *is* all the reserve we need.

Seventy miles were covered on our Saturday bicycle ride.

Seventy miles was a normal daily ride for Andy.

Seven coins were laid out on the table.

Ten days was a long hospital stay.

Ten days were required for full recuperation.

Twenty divided by two *is* ten.

Two goes into twenty ten times.

Seven from thirteen *is* six.

The last half of the *project is* unfinished.

The last half of the *projects are* unfinished.

Agreement—Noun and Pronoun

Pronouns must agree with the noun to which they refer. This agreement must be in number, singular or plural; in person, first, second or third; in case, subjective, objective or possessive; and in gender, feminine, masculine or neuter.

Number:

Singular: Each *employee* may contribute up to 5% of *his* or *her* salary.

Plural: Eligible *employees* may contribute up to 5% of *their* salaries.

Singular: The *foreman* took *his* coffee break.

Plural: The *mechanics* took *their* coffee break.

Singular: Every *hiker* must bring *his* or *her* own lunch.

Plural: All *hikers* must bring *their* own lunches.

Wrong: Nothing is worse than looking at *a parent* and telling *them* their child is going to be blind.

Right: Nothing is worse than looking at *parents* and telling *them* their child is going to be blind.

Right: Nothing is worse than looking at *a parent* and telling *him* (or *her*) *his* (or *her*) child is going to be blind.

Wrong: It was an opportunity for *each* of the contributors to order *their* own copy for $35.

Right: It was an opportunity for *each* of the contributors to order *his* or *her* own copy for $35.

Better: All *contributors were* encouraged to purchase a copy for $35.

If there are two or more nouns to which a pronoun refers, the pronoun agrees with the closest noun.

Would the family or the *daughter* have *her* say about his becoming a part of the family?

Would the daughter or the *family* have *their* say about his becoming a part of the family?

Either John or his *brothers* will have *their* opportunity next year.

Either his brothers or *John* will have *his* opportunity next year.

The relative pronouns *who, which*, and *that* are substitutes for nouns they relate to. Here again the noun and pronoun must agree in number, singular or plural. Relative pronouns also connect parts of sentences while showing their relationship.

Singular: Hans is the *one who trims* our sumac tree.

Plural: Hans is one of the *men who trim* our sumac tree.

Singular: Fresh water on a hike is *one item that is* essential.

Plural: Fresh water is one of *several items that are* essential on a hike.

Person:

First person singular pronouns, are *I, me, mine, my*. First person plural pronouns are *we, our, ours, us*.

I ran the race for *my* benefit; it helped *me*.

We bought the house; it is *ours* and is right for *us*.

Second person pronouns are the same for singular and plural uses.

You appear comfortable with *your choice*.

You people appear comfortable with *your choices*.

Third person singular pronouns are *he, him, his, she, her, hers, it, its*. Third person plural pronounds are *they, them, their, theirs*.

Wrong: *Carpenters* must bring *your* own tools. (Shifts from third to second person.)

Right: *Carpenters* must bring *their* own tools. (Third person noun and pronoun.)

Case:

The three *cases* of personal pronouns are subjective, objective and possessive.

Subjective pronouns are used as subjects of a sentence: *They* walked along the seashore. Other subjective pronouns are, *I, we, you, he, she, it, who*.

Objective pronouns are objects of a verb: Please *help her* over the large log. Objective pronouns are also objects of a preposition: This boat is right *for them*. Other objective pronouns are *me, us, you, him, it, whom*.

The possessive pronoun is used to show ownership or possession: The dancer raised *her* arms. The dog raised *its* paw to "shake hands." Other possessive pronouns are *my, mine, our, ours, your, yours, his, hers, their, theirs, whose*.

Compound subjective and objective pronouns can be confusing until you identify the true subject or object. The key is to test the compound subjects or objects separately.

Right: The surveyors, *Jim* and *I*, worked last Sunday. (*Jim* worked last Sunday. *I* worked last Sunday.)

Wrong: The cement finishers, *Tom* and *me*, worked overtime. (*Tom* worked overtime. *Me* worked overtime.)

Right: The foreman asked *Jim* and *me* to work Sunday. (The foreman asked *Jim*. The foreman asked *me*.)

Wrong: The foreman also asked *Tom* and *I* to work overtime. (The foreman asked *Tom*. The foreman asked *I*.)

Right: *Tim* and *I* will work with you.

Wrong: *Tim* and *myself* will work with you.

Right: Please do this for *Joan* and *me*.

Wrong: Please do this for *Joan* and *myself*.

Right: *I, myself*, will do the task. (Emphasis added.)

Right: I am not *myself* today. (Abnormal physical or mental condition.)

A possessive pronoun should be used before a gerund. A *gerund* is a verb ending in *ing* that is used as a noun. For example: *asking, being, running, swimming, waiting.*

Right: *His running* away from home was anticipated.

Right: *Your going* to work early is a good idea. (Not *you* going . . .)

Right: *Their owning* a new car made the trip easier. (Not *them* owning . . .)

Gender:

The English language recognizes three genders or sex differences: feminine, masculine and neuter. In most instances, which pronoun to use is not difficult.

The *girl* raised *her* hand.

The *boy* raised *his* hand.

The *dog* raised *its* paw.

The *house* looks nice with *its* new paint.

The *corporation* raised *its* profit goal.

Confusion arises when using the classically standard masculine singular pronoun, *his*, with subjects that can be masculine or feminine or both and that may sound plural. These subjects include *anybody, anyone, everybody, everyone, nobody, no one, one, somebody, someone*, and they all take singular pronouns.

Wrong: *Everyone* forgot *their* manners that day. (Language experts regret that this usage, especially in speech, has become standard in recent years.)

Right: *Everyone* forgot *his* manners that day.

Right: *Everyone* forgot *his* or *her* manners that day.

Better: *They* all forgot *their* manners that day.

Agreement—Noun and Adjective

That nouns and adjectives should agree in number, as do nouns with verbs and pronouns, did not occur to me until I received a letter from a corporation that included this sentence:

The ABC publishers would like to bring to your attention the *numerous amount* (my italics) of mail we have received from your readers.

The letter was a form letter, meaning that probably hundreds of copies had been mailed over a period of time. Perhaps the word *amount* was mistyped and should have been *amounts*. But *numerous amounts of mail* for one person who is not a celebrity doesn't seem logical, although both words would be plural. *Numerous* is defined as "consisting of great numbers of units or individuals."

The sentence would be more understandable if the writer had said, ". . . the large amount of mail we have received . . ." or ". . . the numerous letters we have received . . ."

Verb Tenses

The purpose of verb tenses is to indicate the time of a verb's action: present, past or future, but present perfect, past perfect and future perfect tenses are frequently useful.

The queen of the Portland, Oregon, Rose Festival in 1994 read in her speech opening the festival, "I declare it officially begun!" She should have said, "I declare it *has* officially *begun!*"

This statement was repeated many times during the day on television newscasts. The writer of the declaration should have known that *begun*, the past participle of *begin*, needs the helper or auxiliary verb *have* or *has*. The verb *has begun* is in the present perfect tense, tying it to the present tense of the main verb, *declare*. The present perfect tense describes a period of time after the simple past but before the present—after *began* but before *begin*.

The proper use of tenses has been argued for centuries. Millar Burrows, in his 1955 book *The Dead Sea Scrolls*, points out that two historians differed over which tense was used shortly before 63 B.C. The question was whether the Kittim (probably the Romans, but the evidence is not clear) arrived before, during or after the time of the writing. One historian stated that the commentary was in the "perfect" tense, indicating completed action. The actions of the Kittim, however, indicated that the "imperfect" tense should have been used, which might refer to the future, but also might not.

A second historian disagreed, stating that the "imperfect" tense was frequently used for repeated actions in the present or in the past. Thus the Hebrew tenses did not clarify if the Kittim (Romans) had arrived, were arriving or would arrive.

Other oddities of tenses are mentioned by Mario Pei in his book *The Story of Language*. In Chinese, a verb does not express tense. To express *write* in the present, past or future tense, you must use the root word for *write* and precede it with *now, yesterday* or *tomorrow*. A Pacific Northwest Indian language distinguishes between recent past, remote past and mythological past. An Australian aborigine language has five future tenses, two for today and three for later happenings.

As strange as these facts about tenses seem, the English language has over thirty tenses. The *Harbrace College Handbook* lists thirty-two. The tenses vary from the simple present, *I see*, to the indicative mood in the passive voice of the future perfect tense, *they will have been seen*. This is also referred to as the progressive form of the future perfect tense.

Do not despair, however. In the business world, the three simple tenses will cover most of your written communications:

Present	*Past*	*Future*
go	went	will go
am, is, are	was, were	will be
send	sent	will send

At other times, the perfect tenses will be needed:

Present Perfect	*Past Perfect*	*Future Perfect*
have gone	had gone	will have gone
have, has been	had been	will have been
have sent	had sent	will have sent

Here are examples of sentences that illustrate these six most common tenses:

Simple present:

I *see* the blue bird.

He *sees* no difficulty.

Our classes *begin* (or *are beginning*) right now.

He *writes* free verse.

Simple past:

I *saw* the blue bird.

He *saw* no difficulty.

Our classes *began* yesterday.

He *wrote* free verse.

Simple future:

I *will see* the blue bird.

He *will see* no difficulty.

Our classes *will begin* next week.

He *will write* free verse.

Free verse *will be written* by him.

Present perfect: Refers to a time in the past up until now.

I *have seen* the blue bird.

He *has seen* no difficulty.

Our class *has begun* today.

He *has written* free verse.

Past perfect: Refers to a past action completed before another past action.

I *had seen* the blue bird when Pete arrived.

He *had seen* no difficulty before the fire started.

Our class *had begun* then was canceled.

He *had written* free verse until he discovered the beauty of rhyme and
  rhythm.

Future perfect: Refers to a future action that will be completed before
another future action.

I *will have seen* the blue bird by tomorrow.

He *will have seen* no difficulty before next winter.

Our class *will have begun* next week before the snow thaws.

He *will have written* free verse by the time he graduates.

A few illustrations will indicate sentences that can cause problems and how
to overcome those problems.

Universal, habitual and historical truths are stated in the present tense:

The world *is* round.

Water *freezes* at 32 degrees Fahrenheit.

The morning newscast *starts* at 9:00 A.M.

The bus *leaves* at midnight.

A farmer *rises* early, *milks* and *feeds* the cows, and *feeds* the chickens and horses, all before breakfast.

Tense sequence must be logical and state your intended meaning.

Wrong: I would *have* liked to *have* run.

Right: I would *have* liked to *run*.

Right: I would *have* liked to *have* run *before* the major event.

Wrong: When the coach *talks*, the players *listened*.

Right: When the coach *talks*, the players *listen*.

Wrong: The plants *died* after the gardener *watering* them.

Right: The plants *died* after the gardener *had watered* them.

Wrong: The architects *had surveyed* the landscape before they *design* the building.

Right: The architects *had surveyed* the landscape before they *designed* the building.

Right: When I *lost* my earring, I *was running*.

Right: I *want* to visit my uncle Tom.

Right: I *was driving* my car when I *smelled* smoke.

Right: I *drove* my car home before I *smelled* smoke.

Right: After *having run* two miles, he *walked* home.

Wrong: He *caught* the pass and *runs* for a touchdown.

Right: He *caught* the pass and *ran* for a touchdown.

Wrong: *Have* you *spoke* about this to your father?

Right: *Have* you *spoken* about this to your father?

Right: When I *had been employed* two years, I *learned* that my retirement program *had been* started.

Wrong: I *would have* liked *to have lived* in the days of the Old West.

Right: I *would have* liked *to live* in the days of the Old West.

Right: *Sliding* into second base, he *skinned* his knee.

Right: *Having slid* into second base, he *felt* warm blood on his knee.

Right: He *assumes* she *is* bright.

Right: He *assumed* she *was* bright.

Right: He *assumed* she *is* bright.

The timing of each of these last three sentences is different.

Right: She realized he *had left* the house and *gone* to the bank.

Right: She realized he *had left* the house and *went* to the bank.

In the last sentence above, *she* went to the bank. In the interest of clarity, the last sentence should read: She realized he had left the house, then she went to the bank.

Familiar Words

Clarity in communication requires that the writer use words familiar to the reader. Only in the classroom should the reader be encouraged to "look it up" in the dictionary. Business writers all too often use the biggest words that come to mind. The reason is ostensibly—(There, I'm doing it myself. I mean what is implied but not necessarily true. Let's start over.). The writer wants to think he is impressing the reader favorably, but really the writer is insecure and tries to overcome that insecurity through the use of impressive-sounding words.

The result of this style of writing is a document the reader puzzles through two or three times before phoning the writer for an explanation. Also, using the less familiar words puts more distance between the writer and the reader, and the formality of big words tends to create a coolness in the message.

During a high school teachers' strike, a parents' club member wrote a letter to the school board. Here is part of that letter:

> We, the concerned parents of ABC High School, in order to effect an immediate reunion, establish justice, promote the general welfare on our campus and secure the blessings of quality welfare for our children do hereby petition, direct and order our duly elected school board representatives and their administrative staff to take the following affirmative actions on our behalf:
>
> Re-examine the 19__–19__ district budget. It is imperative that the present impasse be broken, and the responsibility for the next step lies with the district. . . .
>
> Stop using the students as pawns or statistical abstractions indicating positionary [*sic*] advantage in this dispute. . . .

No, these big words did not get big results.

In the opinion of some newspaper readers, the champion user of obscure words is William F. Buckley, Jr. in his columns written for Universal Press

Syndicate. He reportedly used these words in his articles: anfructousity, adumbrated and phogistonic. In articles published in August 1994, he used the following words: fettering, promulgate, querulous, acronymic, contavens, hectoring, pestiferous and eudaemonia.

Also in August 1944, *Time*, the weekly news magazine, ran an article using the words: quotidian, solipsims and pusillanimity.

In a book submitted to a major publisher, I included the following paragraph to illustrate the importance of goodwill in collection letters:

> You *must* retain the goodwill of your clientele. One seller found ignoring that truth detrimental to his reputation. He sold and installed some decorative iron work. The buyer, when making payment, held back a small amount because of a dispute over part of the installation. Within a week the supplier phoned, called the buyer a cheat, and threatened to file a lien against the property and even to tear out the installed iron work. The purchaser eventually settled, but he had already spread the word about that *mingy* (italics added) vendor. This is an extreme example, but when you write a collection letter, keep in mind the profits to be derived from goodwill.

The editor circled the word *mingy* and commented in the margin of the manuscript, "What does this mean?" Being a senior editor of a large publishing house, she likely thought that if she didn't know the meaning the readers wouldn't either. I changed *mingy* to *mean and stingy*, quoting *Webster's Collegiate Dictionary*.

Outdated Language

One of the surprises encountered when reading business letters is the amount of old "business English" that is used. You still see such expressions as:

Your request regarding the above

We are herewith enclosing

As we discussed telephonically,

. . . which remittance will go forward to you momentarily.

Trusting to hear from you in the near future regarding this matter, we remain

Here to serve,

We will anticipate his payment at that time.

If you have any questions, please advise.

Enclosed please find

Please be advised that

Please be advised the same was issued

. . . deduction of subject credit is not in order.

I remain, yours faithfully,

Thanking you in advance

Thanking you for past courtesies, I beg to remain

. . . in this regard

With a firm desire to work further with you on this project, I remain,

These expressions should have disappeared with the buggy whip and high buttoned shoes. This stilted or "business" style of writing originated in England when business was looked upon as a craft beneath the dignity of the well educated who went into government service or the professions. Thus when a letter was required, a highly educated person, often a lawyer, was hired to do the writing. Much of the language was borrowed from the courts and the flowery expressions of the aristocracy. Style seemed to be emphasized more than substance.

Overused Words and Clichés

The word *basically* is overused by adults almost as much as *like* and *you know* by teenagers:

"Then, you know, we saw a great movie, and she was, like, 'wow!'"

"Basically, there are seven steps to this operation."

"Basically, our searching for a better approach is the reason for the change."

"That is basically why we do the task this way."

I find myself wanting to start sentences with *basically*, and wonder why. Apparently I use the word to make my writing seem fundamentally sound; or, to use another overused expression, it implies that I have gone "back to the basics," and therefore know what I am writing about. In spite of all that, *basically* is a word whose use should be strictly limited.

Many overused words become clichés, trite words, phrases or expressions that have been used so much they become overly familiar. Clichés should not be used in formal writing and should be used in casual writing only for special effects.

Some clichés last only a short time, while others hang on for years. Here is a sampling of both:

Age of innocence

Ado about nothing

Any port in a storm

At a loss for words

Ballpark estimate

Between a rock and a hard place

Bird in the hand is worth two in
the bush

Bite the dust

Bitter end

Bolt from the blue

Bottom line

Breath of fresh air

Bright and early

Brown as a berry

Buzzwords

Can of worms

Catch the competition

Competitiveness

Could care less

Cut the mustard

Dead to rights

Early bird gets the worm

Easier said than done

Established belief

Feathering his nest

Few and far between

Filthy lucre

Fly in the ointment

Gentle as a lamb

Grandstand play

Grim reaper

Grist for the mill

Hand-me-downs

Hang one on

Hit a sour note

Hit pay dirt

Hope springs eternal

Impact

In full swing

In group

In store for us

Interface

In the ball park

Light-years away

Like a duck out of water

Live it up

Mad as a wet hen

Make hay while the sun shines

Mother nature

Nipped in the bud

Offer you can't refuse

One fell swoop

Passing years

Playing second fiddle

Poor as a church mouse

Price of fish in China

Raining cats and dogs

Real thing

Rebellion in the ranks

Road to Hades is paved with good
intentions

Road to ruin

Rolling stones gather no moss

Rotten in Denmark

Roundhouse estimate

Sauce for the goose is sauce for
the gander

Selling like hotcakes

Ship of state

Shot in the arm

Shun like the plague	Tongue in cheek
Smelled a rat	Throw caution to the winds
Sour grapes	Viable
Strange bedfellows	White elephant
Swing of the pendulum	Whole new ball game
Take a back seat	With a ten-foot pole
Take down a peg	With bated breath
Tender mercies	With our pants down
Test of time	Worked like a Trojan

Other words commonly overused, or at least used in the wrong places, are *of, to, to be, up* and *that.*

Poor: I kind *of* like it this way.

Better: I like it this way.

Poor: She has a sister by the name *of* Ivy.

Better: She has a sister named Ivy.

Poor: Some *of* the helpers *of* the bricklayers were *of* Irish descent.

Better: Some of the bricklayers' helpers were Irish.

Poor: I gave the water *to* the gardener *to* drink.

Better: I gave the gardener a drink of water.

Poor: Peggy gave the cat *to* Alice.

Better: Peggy gave Alice the cat.

Poor: Jim seems *to be* the faster runner.

Better: Jim runs faster.

Poor: Andy found Alice *to be* polite.

Better: Andy found Alice polite.

The word *up* is tacked onto so many words that the combination is often considered standard. For example: *round up*, which can be either one or two words. We round up the cattle, but cannot round the cattle; we round up a handful of pencils, but don't round them. We could, however, gather them.

More about the excessive use of *up* is discussed in the section on Redundant Words, but here are some examples of words that could do well without the "follow up" word *up*:

stir up

speak up

fix up

lock up

Please stir up the egg batter.

Why not speak up at the meeting?

John will fix up the dripping faucet.

Lock up the house when you leave.

The word *that* is often used when it is unnecessary.

Poor: I worked at a job *that* I hated.

Better: I worked at a job I hated.

Poor: Selling is a type of work *that* I like better.

Better: Selling is work I like better.

Better: I like selling better.

Poor: The minivan is a style of car *that* I like.

Better: The minivan is a style of car I like.

Better: I like the minivan style.

Poor: The problem *that* she has seems so difficult *that* she cannot overcome it.

Better: The problem she has seems so difficult she cannot overcome it.

Better: The problem she has seems too difficult to overcome.

On the other hand, in some sentences, a well-placed *that* is essential to the
reader's understanding on the first reading. This occurs when the relationship
between two parts of the sentence must be made clear.

You read this far into a sentence:

Remember the early bird . . .

At this point you try to recall which bird you should remember. Then, starting
over, you read the complete sentence:

Remember the early bird gets the choice of cabins.

The sentence should read:

Remember *that* the early bird gets the choice of cabins.

Here is another example:

He felt her bottom . . .

Is this a risqué statement? In anticipation you read the whole sentence:

He felt her bottom kitchen shelf needed stronger support brackets.

The sentence should read:

He felt *that* her bottom kitchen shelf needed stronger support brackets.

Pompous Words

An advertising manager, after going through the company files of letters to customers, is reported to have said, "I've been worried about the English language for twenty years, but I never knew there were so many ways to say nothing in three-syllable words."

An article advertising a musical group read, "They have concertized nation-wide and in Europe, South America, Australia. . . ." The word *concertized* is used correctly in this sentence. For a sophisticated musical audience it is appropriate, but for a general audience the word sounds stuffy. Instead of writing "They have concertized," write, "They have given concerts."

Business people seem prone to use pompous words. This is possibly because the writers are more concerned with self-promotion than with clear communication with their readers. Any written document should be directed, not to the writer, but to the audience. Use words you know the meaning of, and state the facts in plain English.

Here is an example of pompous business writing:

> Due to the fact that many minority vendor representatives have had minimum exposure and experience in the arena of big business—and they may even be overawed by the environment of large office buildings, ostentatious reception areas, and private offices—it is reasonable to expect that the buyer will have to exert special effort to arrange an interview for constructive exchange of information.

How much more effective it would have been for the writer to have said:

> When minority vendor representatives call, buyers must do their best to make those sales people comfortable.

Flowery language, while different from pompous language, is just as ineffective when you are trying to communicate facts. The result is often humor rather than information. Look at this example:

Basketball, especially at the professional level, now is an elegant, cerebal, fluid, vocal, cocky, reckless sport, played with a new, swaggering intelligence, with its urban-street-playground roots unearthed and burnished to a mesmerizing shine for all to see.

I like to watch professional basketball, not because of all the above razzmatazz, but because it is a fast-moving game.

Effective communication requires clarity, clarity requires brevity, and brevity requires simplicity: simple and usually short, direct words.

The following is a list of some pompous words and their clear or direct alternatives:

Pompous	*Direct*
accompany	go with
accomplish	do
advise	tell
anticipate	expect
approximately	about
ascertain	find out
assist	help
benefit	help
conclude	end
concur	agree
commence	begin
complete	fill in
cooperate	help
deem	think
demonstrate	show
desire	want
determine	find out
disclosure	show
elect	choose
employ	use
endeavor	try
ensue	follow
ensure	make sure
exhibit	show

Pompous	*Direct*
experience	have
facilitate	help
finalize	end
forward	send
furnish	give, send
furthermore	also
however	but
identical	same
impact	affect
implement	do
inception	start
indicate	show
initial	first
initiate	begin
legislation	law
locate	find
location	place
maintain	keep, support
maximize	increase
minimize	decrease
modify	change
monitor	watch
negative	no
notify	let me know
numerous	many
observe	see
obtain	get
perform	do
permit	let
presently	now
personnel	people
prioritize	rank
procure	get, buy
purchase	buy

Pompous	*Direct*
qualify	measure
request	ask
require	need
requirement	need
residence	home
retain	keep
reveal	show
review	check
state	say
submit	send
sufficient	enough
supply	send
terminate	end
transmit	send
transpire	happen
utilize	use
viable	workable
witnessed	saw
whereas	because, since

CHAPTER 2

Action in Sentences

Specific Words for Exactness

Chapter 13, "Confusing Words Clarified," explains the different meanings and usages of words that are often confused, such as *assure, ensure*, and *insure* and *lay* and *lie*. Specific Words deals with the selection of the *exact* word or phrase that best expresses your intended meaning.

When writing, why not use the exact word you want rather than dashing off the first close-enough word that comes to mind? Most likely because there are too many words meaning the same or nearly the same as the exact word. Suppose you write the word *fix*, to be used as a verb. *Fix* has many meanings including *repair*, as in, "I am going to *fix* my bicycle," and *locate*, as in, "Will they get a *fix* on the old oak tree?"

Here is a list of words with nearly the same meaning as *fix*. Which one is the *exact* word for your purpose?

Locate—To determine or indicate the place

Establish—To institute permanently

Direct—To manage the affairs

Circumscribe—To trace a line around

Quantify—To indicate the extent

Form—To give shape to

Perforate—To make a hole or holes through

Kill—To cause the death of

Resolve—To break into separate parts

Accustom—To make familiar or habitual

Bribe—To obtain influence over

Perfect—To bring to completion

Settle—To put in order or place firmly

Repair—To put back in good condition

Prepare—To make ready for a specific purpose

Defect—To forsake a party or cause

Prescribe—To set down a rule or direction

Arrange—To put into correct order

Revenge—To inflict damage, injury or punishment

Punish—To cause to undergo pain

Harmonize—To make into a pleasing whole

Fasten—To join securely

Dispose—To place in a certain order or to throw away

Organize—To arrange in an orderly manner

Define—To determine or set boundries

Specify—To describe in detail

Decide—To make up one's mind

Prove—To establish as true

Prearrange—To arrange beforehand

Assure—To give confidence to

If this example seems overwhelming, here is a shorter example, but the need to be specific remains the same. You are asked to give a speech before an association of condominium chairmen. Your *speech* can express ideas, feelings or a specific stance on a subject; provide information; be serious or entertaining; be prepared or off-the-cuff. Perhaps you will deliver an *address*, a carefully prepared speech about the advantages of condominium ownership. Perhaps you will give an *oration*, an eloquent address intended to stir the emotions of the audience so they will give generously to your favorite charity. You may feel the need to *harangue* the audience about the sloppy yard maintenance many of the condominium chairmen are allowing. Perhaps you will present a *discourse* on the procedures for and the advantages of each condominium unit becoming incorporated. You may *lecture* the chairmen on the reasons for establishing a Block Watch program to become aware of strangers in each condo's vicinity. Unless you are a clergyman, you probably will not deliver a *sermon* on the advantages to the community of church attendance, or a *homily* on the ethics of obedience to the law.

To understand the effect your choice of words has on your reader you need to know what *denotes* and *connotes*. A denotation is a straightforward dictionary definition. A connotation is a feeling of what the word implies.

I once worked for an income tax accountant who hated using the word *house-wife* to describe a woman who did not work outside her home. When he saw the word *housewife* on a tax form, he ran out of his office to the preparer and ranted, "She is not a *housewife*, she is a *homemaker!*"

The denotation and connotation of a word can be vastly different. For example, in 1995, after criticizing the Republicans for supporting a welfare plan that promoted orphanages, the Secretary of Health and Human Services, Donna Shalala, conceded that President Clinton's Democratic administration's plan could lead to poor children being taken from their mothers. She refused, however, to use the word *orphanages* when questioned by Representative Bill Archer, a Texas Republican at a House Ways and Means Committee hearing.

An orphanage is an institution for the care of children who have lost one, or usually both, parents. That is the denotation. For many, the connotation is a place dark and dreary where many bewildered and underfed children are warehoused and disciplined by strict, uncaring, unconcerned and impersonal guards. Shalala did use the words *foster care* and *group homes*. For many people, foster care connotes unfriendly supervision by people who are concerned only with their monthly checks from the welfare department.

Now for a less emotional example. The word *dark* means *black* and also *evil* or *wicked*. To say a person is dark may describe his or her skin color, but the connotation is a person who probably has an African heritage. To say a person is dark may also imply that he is "dark and sinister" or "dark in his ways" or evil. In either case, the word *dark* is not the exact word.

As well as having denotation and connotation, words are specific and general, and it is more informative and interesting to your reader to use specific rather than general words in a sentence:

General: I like my professor.

Specific: I like Dr. Warren.

General: I have a new car.

Specific: I have a new, red Toyota Camry V6.

General: He runs fast.

Specific: John Halstrom runs the 100-yard dash in 3.8 seconds.

General: She has a new job.

Specific: Joan Watson is now Director of Personnel at Arlington Manufacturing Company.

General: It sounds like a piece of metal sliding across the bottom of my car's glove compartment.

Specific: The noise sounds like a one-inch metal washer sliding across the
bottom of my car's glove compartment.

Many examples of poor and inexact word choices exist. The following are a
few that illustrate the confusion that can result from inexactness:

The directive, "Take one tablet twice daily" on a drug prescription bottle is
easily understood because we are used to this type of "shorthand," or abbreviated
expression. Literally, the statement could mean that only one tablet is taken
twice during the day, which raises the question, "How?" An exact statement
requires more words: "Take one tablet in the morning and one tablet in the
evening," or "At two separate times during the day, take one tablet," or "Two
times during the day, take one tablet."

"If you have any questions, please contact me at (000) 000-0000." Because
a phone number is provided, it is better to say ". . . *phone* me at . . ." rather than
". . . *contact* me at . . ."

"Could Smith Publishers *handle* another book on space travel?" It would be
more specific to ask, "Could Smith Publishers *sell* another book on space
travel?"

Stated about a seminar: "Simply the best. Something just clicked when they
presented it." What clicked? It would be better to be specific, for example, "I
finally understood what a living trust is," or "The causes of my anxiety became
clear to me."

General statements communicate only an inkling of your message:

"What is your line of work?"
"I'm a teacher."

That is informative, but vague. How much better to be specific and say, "I
teach high school math, physics and biology, and after school I coach the boys'
baseball team."

"What do you like best about teaching?"
"Coaching."

We could have guessed that, but what we really want to know is why.

"I like to watch the changes that come over the boys, not only their
improvement in batting and ball handling, but also their increased level
of confidence as their physical strength and mental alertness improve."

Now we know what the teacher-coach likes and why.

Using the exact word means the reader interprets the word the same way the
writer intends. Does a "long coat" reach to the thighs or to the ankles? Does a
"fun party" mean becoming inebriated or having an interesting discussion with

a new acquaintance? What is "democracy" to a United States citizen? to a Russian citizen? A dictionary is a great help, but you must remember that definitions change with time, so use a current dictionary. A happening that was once "hot" is now "cool"; "humorous" once meant "humid"; it now means "amusing"; "illness" once meant "wickedness"; it now means "sickness"; "let" once meant "hinder"; it now means "permit." One word that is undergoing change is the word *unique*. It once meant only one of a kind. Now it has evolved so that it can be used to mean unusual or distinctively characteristic. For example: That is a *very unique* pen. We are a *fairly unique* group.

Numbers used to represent opinions, thoughts or even facts are seldom as accurate as they are intended to imply. The following is from *Time* magazine (June 6, 1994, p. 11):

> When President Clinton visited Capitol Hill last week for closed-door meetings on health care, he didn't make his usual threat to veto any bill that fails to provide "universal coverage," according to Representative Jim Cooper. Instead, Clinton used the phrase "full coverage." Cooper and other lawmakers have been arguing that "full coverage" is like "full employment—it doesn't mean 100%; it means roughly 95%." Some members of Congress feel that with this latest very Clintonian semantic shift, the President may be giving himself room to compromise.

The list below is a sampling of absolute values given to common phrases. These values are by Michael Wisenberg, reprinted in the *San Jose Mercury News* from *InfoWorld*.

A couple	2 to 4
Many	3 to 8
Half a dozen	5 to 7
A lot	6 to 10
A whole lot	8 to 17
A bunch	8 to 15
About two dozen	21 to 27
Two or three hundred	175 to 270
Most	10% to 20%
A vast majority	52% to 60%
Absolutely all	86% to 90%

The word *that* as a pronoun is usually considered applicable to things, not persons:

This is the project that I worked on.

That is the right screw for this hinge.

There is the barn that my grandfather built.

Since the twelfth century (that's the 1100s), *that* can properly relate to persons, things or ideas:

That is my grandmother.

Are you the one that took my pen?

That is the tool I need.

After that we were completely satisfied.

In this same vein, *whose* can relate to animals and things as well as to persons:

Whose book are you reading?

Whose finger prints are these?

This is the dog whose ears were recently clipped.

This is the cat whose milk the dog lapped up.

We loved the dark red roses whose scent reminded us of our childhood.

Here is the first paragraph of a direct-mail sales letter addressed to an office manager:

> We would like to introduce the services available to you at 1000 Main Street, City, California. We are conscience and provide a high level of service for a variety of mail and personalized direct mail applications.

The word *conscience* is defined as a knowledge of right or wrong with an urge to do right. The writer should have known the word she wanted was *conscientious*, meaning meticulous, careful and scrupulous.

More examples of poor word choices: Ask Jean and Ellen how they like their job and they'll tell you! They'll *infect* you with their enthusiasm.

Infect is a poor word choice. *Infect* connotes contamination with a disease. However, *Webster's Collegiate Dictionary* lists one definition as "to work upon or seize upon so as to induce sympathy, belief, or support, for example: trying to infect their sales people with enthusiasm." Despite the fact that *infect* may be technically correct, a more appropriate word is *inspire*.

"We will have a Father's Day dinner at North Beach Park on June 20, maximizing at 100 persons."

A more specific word replacing *maximizing* is *limited*: ". . . on June 20, *limited* to 100 persons.*"

"Jo Ann and the children opened a huge pile of gifts."

This sentence should read: ". . . a *large number* of gifts."

The word *just* is sometimes used as a substitute for *only*: I just gave you the original document. This sentence is ambiguous; it could have more than one meaning. It could mean: I gave you *only* the original document. In speech, he or she would have said, "I *only* gave you the original document," which is acceptable—but only in speech—or the statement could mean: At this instant I gave you the original document.

A tendency to exaggerate can lead to the usage of words you hope will support your viewpoint but in reality will make you look silly. Here are two examples from newspaper reports:

> The *stunning* defeat for President Reagan came on a 50-49 vote.
>
> It was the worst setback Reagan had suffered in the Senate since his presidency began 2½ years ago.
>
> It was a *tremendous* victory for President Bill Clinton Thursday night, when the Senate voted 50-49, with Vice President Al Gore the deciding vote, that was more like reductions in increases than cuts.

Similies, metaphors, hyperboles and personifications can be effective in painting word pictures:

> Sightseers flocked around the TV crew like vultures around a dead lamb.
>
> Viewed from outer space, the earth is a child's blue and white ball.
>
> The mosquitoes in those weeds strike with the speed of an automatic riveting gun.
>
> The third hurricane of the season slashed through the Florida swamps as though God were punishing the whole wicked world.
>
> She was as self-confident as a rooster crowing at daybreak.
>
> Constant bickering is as cruel as murder.
>
> Her eyes looked as blue as the waters of Lake Louise.

The correct relationship between words and phrases requires the proper prepositions and conjunctions:

> Wrong: There were other applicants, *and* Joe got the job.
>
> Right: There were other applicants, *but* Joe got the job.
>
> Wrong: He crossed the infield and went *in* the dugout.
>
> Right: He crossed the infield and went *into* the dugout.

Wrong: Wait *on* me if I don't get there by 5:00 P.M.

Right: Wait *for* me if I don't get there by 5:00 P.M.

Wrong: He bought the used bike *off* Timmy.

Right: He bought the used bike *from* Timmy.

Wrong: I don't know *as* I can run with you tomorrow.

Right: I don't know *that* I can run with you tomorrow.

Wrong: She is angry *at* me.

Right: She is angry *with* me.

Wrong: I heard *where* you got a raise.

Right: I heard *that* you got a raise.

Wrong: We are also looking for a new coordinator *of* this group. Please call Mrs. Ashwood *and* volunteer.

Right: We are looking for a new coordinator *for* this group. Please call Mrs. Ashwood *to* volunteer.

Incorrect punctuation can change the meaning of a sentence, because you are unsure what words to pause between. A few examples:

"In a dream I had a wolf come to me and say how he's tired of his followers being killed." Is the first phrase, after which the reader pauses, *In a dream* or *In a dream I had*? After reading the sentence twice, the reader decides that *come* and *say* are correct, and that a comma is needed after *In a dream*.

"As I ran the course became more rocky." After reading *As I ran the course* as the first phrase, *became more rocky* didn't fit. The reader expected something like, *As I ran the course, I found it more rocky than expected.* A comma is needed after *As I ran*. The sentence would then read: As I ran, the course became more rocky.

A missing apostrophe can cause similar confusion in the reader's mind, as seen in this magazine quote:

Bay Area Association of Realtors Executive Vice President, Joan Mason, pictured at right above . . .

On the first reading, the reader paused after the word *President*, thinking it should be Presidents (plural). Reading on, only one vice president was mentioned. The first reading was wrong. What was right? Could it be that Joan Mason was the sole Executive Vice President? That seemed likely. In that case the organization's name would be Bay Area Association of Realtors, to which the Executive Vice President belonged (possessive). An apostrophe after the *s* in the word *Realtors* would have indicated the possessive case of the proper noun, Bay Area Association of Realtors, and forestalled all this confusion.

One June morning while I was driving up the hills toward Washington's Mt. St. Helens, I spotted a road sign that read:

CHAIN-UP
PARKING
HERE ONLY

Not knowing what *chain-up* meant, I asked my brother, who lived in the area. He said, "That's where you put your chains on." (Oh!)

It would have been more clear to have printed:

CHAINS-ON
PARKING
HERE ONLY

Later, as we drove down the hill, I saw a sign that read:

CHAINS-OFF
PARKING
HERE ONLY

That I understood.

How to Use Phrases and Clauses

Dangling phrases can be humorous because they don't clearly modify—limit or restrict—a particular word or subject. They seem to modify two subjects or none at all, and readers are amused as they try to decide which. Here are a few old standards:

The evening passed very pleasantly eating candy and playing the piano.

The car swerved off the road hitting a concrete wall going at a terrific speed.

I was unable to stop in time and my car crashed into the vehicle. The driver and passenger then left immediately for a vacation with injuries.

I had been driving my car for forty years when I fell asleep at the wheel and had an accident.

I was thrown from my car and it left the road. I was later found in a ditch by some stray cows.

Also, misplaced phrases can be humorous: Our piano was used during the wedding that had to be tuned first. Misplaced phrases are discussed in the section on misplaced modifiers.

What exactly is a phrase? A phrase is a related group of words that modifies another word in the sentence and has no subject or verb. Phrases are classified by how they are used in a sentence.

Noun—The *sad, old man* hobbled on slowly.

> *Sad, old man* is a noun phrase used as the subject of the sentence.

Verb—The bird *had been plucking* yarn from the old rug.

> *Had been plucking* is a phrase used as the verb of the sentence.

Gerund—*Making the team* was Gerry's goal.

> *Making* is a verbal that ends in *ing* that is used as a noun, and in this sentence the whole phrase is the subject.

Prepositional—He was called *for jury duty*.

> *For* is the preposition. It links *was called* to *jury duty*. The prepositional phrase, *for jury duty* includes the object, *duty*.

Infinitive—He decided *to run home*.

> The infinitive, *to run* is a verbal that modifies the verb, *decided*.

Participle—My daughter, *walking from school*, saw the first spring robin.

> A participle is a verb form that may modify a noun or adverb and here modifies the noun, *daughter*. Past participles usually end in *ed* or *d*.

Subject Complement—Carol's hobby is *raising rabbits*.

> The phrase *raising rabbits* completes the meaning of the linking verb, *is*, which refers to the subject, *hobby*.

Absolute—*The rain having increased*, we decided to stay home.

> The absolute phrase is not an integral part of the sentence, but it modifies the balance of the sentence.

Appositive—John introduced her to Pete, *his cousin*.

> The appositive phrase modifies, explains or identifies the preceding word, here, *Pete*.

The following sentences illustrate dangling phrases, inappropriate phrases that have been tacked onto the end, along with suggestions for making them into understandable sentences.

Wrong: The grinder was used by other kitchens that needed sharpening.

Right: The grinder was used to sharpen knives in other kitchens.

Wrong: While drinking orange juice, the toast burned.

Right: While I was drinking my orange juice, the toast burned.

Wrong: When baked to a golden brown, she called her guests to dinner.

Right: When the chicken was baked to a golden brown, mother called her
    guests to dinner.

Wrong: Scraping the boat, the barnacles were thick.

Right: The boat had a thick layer of barnacles. We scraped them off.

Right: We scraped a thick layer of barnacles from the boat.

Wrong: Having purchased the boiler, the room was too small.

Right: The large boiler was too big for the room.

Wrong: While writing the report, his experience became obvious.

Right: As I wrote the report, I became aware of his experience.

Right: His experience became obvious to us while he was writing the
    report.

Wrong: Having finished the run up the mountains, a cold drink was re-
    freshing.

Right: Having finished the run up the mountains, we were refreshed with
    a cold drink.

Wrong: Entering the club, the bandstand is on the right.

Right: As you enter the club, the bandstand is on the right.

Unlike phrases, clauses have subjects and verbs. A sentence also has a subject
and a verb, for example, *John walked*. However, in the statement, *When John
walked*, complete sense is lacking. We want to know what happened when John
walked. Because he walked home rather than rode the bus, John arrived home
late. The complete sentence is *When John walked, he arrived home late*. This
sentence contains two clauses, *When John walked* and *he arrived home late*.
The first clause is dependent upon the second clause for clear meaning, thus the
labels *dependent* or *subordinate* and *independent* or *main*.

Unless there is a specific reason for doing otherwise, put the independent
clause last. It is more emphatic in that position.

Never punctuate or use a subordinate clause as a sentence.

Wrong: The playground was dedicated. By the newly elected mayor.

Right: The playground was dedicated by the newly elected mayor.

Right: The newly elected mayor dedicated the playground.

In informal writing, however, phrases and clauses and single words may be
punctuated as sentences to add emphasis.

One person is primarily responsible for our new playground. He worked diligently. Spent long hours. Finally persuaded the city council to approve the Garden Playground.

Who?

A dedicated public official.

Our new mayor!

Jim Allen!

Ideas of equal value are best expressed in parallel form. This written form adds rhythm and emphasis to statements. With phrases and clauses, parallel parts must repeat the same form of construction.

The supervisor mentioned a new procedure for meeting deadlines; she suggested the new procedure, she discussed the new procedure, she promoted the new procedure, she dictated the new procedure, and then she demanded adherence.

The three of us walked into the desert, observed the cacti, scared a rabbit and picked a handful of spring flowers.

The number of words can sometimes be reduced and clarity improved by turning clauses into phrases, or even into single words.

Clause: The major *who was friendly to our family* visited frequently.

Phrase: The major, *friendly to our family*, visited frequently.

Clause: The old bell tower, *which was once a thieves' hiding place*, was recently dismantled.

Phrase: The old bell tower, *once a thieves' hiding place*, was recently dismantled.

Clause: *When the summer season arrives*, we go swimming every day.

Phrase: *In summer* we swim daily.

Clause: I want to try on my new hat *so that I am sure it fits right*.

Phrase: I want to try on my new hat *to make sure it fits*.

Clause: We had a special send-off for the *people who got up* early.

Word: We had a special send-off for the early *risers*.

Clause: A special trip was planned for *those who were up in years*.

Word: A special trip was planned for the *elderly*.

Clause: Mr. Johnson was a driver *who was intent upon being especially careful*.

Word: Mr Johnson was a *careful* driver.

Clause: I sent my supervisor the budget, *which I had to do over again*.

Word: I sent my supervisor the *reworked* budget.

The Moods of Verbs

I wish I were rich. I wish I was rich. Which is correct?

After you win one of the large state or regional lotteries, you won't care which is correct. But in the meantime, you want to appear properly educated so you can get or keep a well-paying job or position.

To answer the question above, both are acceptable in the United States when used in appropriate situations. In informal conversation, *was* is okay. In formal conversation or any but the most casual writing only *were* is correct.

The above refers to the *subjunctive* mood, which expresses ideas that are contrary to fact, hypothetical, doubtful or wishful. The subjunctive is also used to express necessity, command, demand, possibility, a formal motion and recommendations.

Here are examples of sentences in the subjunctive mood:

If I *were* a rich man, I would buy a mansion.

If Johnny *were* to come home this week, we could celebrate at Tim's place.

If I *were* you, I'd go today.

I wish I *were* at Tim's place now.

If I *had arrived* sooner, we would be there tomorrow.

Had he *arrived* earlier, we would be there tomorrow.

Bill's wife demanded that he *stay* home tonight.

It is necessary for Bill to *stay* home tonight.

Bill's wife wishes he would *stay* home this week.

Bill wishes that this week *were* over.

It is important that Bill *finish* his production report this week.

Bill's wife asked that he *be* home this week.

Bill's wife asked if he *were* leaving.

If Bill *were* more sensitive, he would stay home this week.

Bill's supervisor recommended that he *stay* on the job this week.

Be careful on the way home, and peace *be* with you.

He would go first, *come* what may.

Long *live* the Queen.

Heaven *help* us!

Far *be* it from me to stop you.

I make a motion that we *seek* a new custodian.

Suppose he *were* to abdicate.

Bonnie asked that she *be* allowed to take another ride.

We urged that Jane *take* immediate action.

He talks as if he *were* correct.

He walks as though he *were* in a hurry.

It is important that he *be* there.

The other two verb moods are *indicative* and *imperative*. These are common in normal writing and speech and don't offer real problems. The *indicative* mood refers to straightforward actions or facts or questions. For example:

Alan *was* the better of the two.

We *will go* to school.

He *ate* his spinach.

Is that the correct procedure?

That *is* the correct procedure.

The clock *stopped*.

Did the clock *stop*?

We *need* help.

He *has come* home.

We *will take* care of the baby.

The *imperative* mood refers to commands or requests. We are introduced to this form early in life:

Don't touch.

No, no.

Come here right now.

Eat your peas.

Think big.

Do stop by soon.

Please *slow* down.

Watch the road.

Sharpen the old saw this morning.

A word of caution: do not shift moods within one sentence.

Wrong: Last summer I *would ride* my bike in the mornings and *walked* in the evenings.
   (Subjunctive to indicative)

Right: Last summer I *would ride* my bike in the mornings and *would walk* in the evenings.
(Subjunctive)

Right: Last summer I *rode* my bike in the mornings and *walked* in the evenings.
(Indicative)

Wrong: If he *were* absent yesterday, he *is* behind in his class work.
(Subjunctive to indicative)

Right: If he *were* absent yesterday, he *would be* behind in his class work.
(Subjunctive)

Right: He *was* absent yesterday, and he *is* behind in his class work.
(Indicative)

Verbs of Action

An active verb expresses action. It tells what the subject does:

Pedro *hit* the ball.

The president *examined* the document.

The Lions Club *distributed* the newsletter.

He *ate* the peanut butter sandwich.

Arve *watched* the baseball game.

The morning shift *set up* the printing machine.

Jason's mother *patched* his torn pants.

The auditor *reconciled* the bank statement.

Each of these sentences has an object, what the verb acted upon. In the last sentence, *auditor* is the subject doing the action, *reconciled* is the action verb and *statement* is the object that received the action.

Not all action verbs have objects. Those without objects are called *intransitive* verbs. The words following such verbs describe the verb rather than receive the action:

Alison *played* hard.

Mother *went* shopping.

The new bush *grew* rapidly.

She always *walks* fast.

When using active verbs, the subject of the sentence performs the action stated by the verb. In contrast, when using a passive verb, the subject receives the action.

Active verb: The supervisor *wrote* the report.

Passive verb: The report *was written* by the supervisor.

Passive verbs are discussed in the next section, "Nonactive Verbs." Although overused, passive verbs have their proper place in written communication.

The use of active verbs is emphasized because they add energy, spirit, spark and vitality to written messages. This is especially true when the subject-verb-object progression is followed. The first sentence in this section, *Pedro hit the ball*, is as straightforward, specific and dynamic as you can get.

Other reasons for using active verbs include these:

The sentence is more convincing.

John helped the plumber. (Active and positive.)

The plumber was helped. (Passive and weak.)

The sentence is more personal.

I believe the third article is better. (Active and strong.)

It is believed that the third article is better. (Passive and impersonal.)

The sentence is shorter.

We ate all our peas. (Active and snappy.)

All of our peas were eaten by us. (Passive and longer.)

Responsibility can be specified.

The class voted you out of office. (Active and definite.)

You were voted out of office. (Passive and responsibility avoided.)

The reader's attention can be focused.

The lead man arranged the printing plates in sequence by color. (Active and direct.)

The color plates for the printing machine were arranged in the same order as the color would be applied by the rollers. (Passive and roundabout.)

The above examples show that the use of active verbs will make your writing more forceful, more concise, more lively and your meaning more directly accessible to your reader.

Although passive verbs have their place and often make the task of writing easier, vigor can be added by turning passive sentences into active sentences. Here are some examples:

Passive: The phone was installed by Jim.

Active: Jim installed the phone.

Passive: Investigation was begun by Detective Ashford.

Active: Detective Ashford began the investigation.

Passive: Nurse Jean will be oriented tomorrow.

Active: Supervisor Alice will orient Nurse Jean tomorrow.

Passive: The checks were put in the mail.

Active: We mailed the checks.

Passive: Help will be given to our city's homeless.

Active: Our church will help our city's homeless.

Passive: Nursing is studied by Laura.

Active: Laura studies nursing.

Passive: Tim is inclined to work faster than Al.

Active: Tim works faster than Al.

Passive: The new reports will be started tomorrow.

Active: The Personnel Department will start its reports tomorrow.

Passive: A beautiful picture was taken.

Active: Betty took a beautiful picture.

Passive: Receipt of your letter of April 4 is acknowledged.

Active: We received your letter dated April 4.

Whole paragraphs can be written in the passive voice using passive verbs. This may be easier than using active verbs because the identity of the people involved can be omitted, direct blame or credit can be skipped and the writer can hide behind his or her vague statements. Writers sometimes assume that this passive, impersonal tone sounds dignified and professional. A couple of examples:

Passive: Because of recent computer changes in our accounts payable system, it is required that each of our locations be identified by a "customer number." The customer number, located on the above mailing label, has been assigned to identify all invoices you send to this location. Also, invoice numbers should continue to be listed on payment checks sent to Headquarters.

Active: We recently made changes in our accounts payable computer system. We now identify each of our locations with a number, which is on the above mailing label. Please put this number on all invoices you send to this location. Also, continue to list the invoice numbers on all your payments sent to Headquarters.

Passive: For the forseeable future, it will not be necessary to submit the quarterly tax reports to James & James as was done in 19__ and 19__. The accumulation of monthly data should be continued, however, so that preparation of the annual tax reports can be done quickly.

Active: For the forseeable future, you will not have to submit your quarterly tax reports to James & James as you did in 19__ and 19__. Please continue to accumulate monthly data, so you can prepare your annual tax reports quickly.

Nonactive Verbs

Nonactive verbs are called *passive* verbs. They have two basic characteristics: First they always use some form of the verb *to be* (such as *is, am, are, was, has been, will be, were* and *will have been*) along with a past participle, for example, *prepared, existed, inspected, sent, approved* and *warned*. Second, the subject of the sentence is not the doer of the action but the recipient of the action.

In the sentence *Mark married Judy*, Mark is the subject and the doer. *Married* is the active verb; the sentence is in the active voice. Judy, however, may object and declare that the sentence should read, *Judy married Mark*, another active sentence. A third party might try to smooth over the disagreement with a passive sentence, *Mark is married to Judy* or perhaps, *Judy is married to Mark*. In either case the subject is acted upon rather than creating the action. *Is* has become the verb and *married* has become the past participle. Our third party has succeeded in making the sentence more tactful—one of the reasons for using a passive sentence.

I would probably say, *Judy and Mark are married.*

A second reason for using the passive voice is that the writer does not know who performed the action, the doer is of little importance to the subject matter of the writing or the actor is clearly understood.

Joe's suggestion was tabled.

The earth was found to be more round than flat.

The program was scheduled for an inappropriate time.

Three years of English are required for graduation.

Johnson was fouled twelve times during the basketball game.

Seven false fire alarms were recorded last night.

Contributions of $2,000 were collected.

Another snorkeler was rescued at Drake's Bay.

The watch was stolen while Mr. Emerson slept in the overstuffed chair at his lodge.

A third reason for using the passive is to protect the doer or actor, or the audience does not need to know.

The robber was later identified.

The computer hacker's felonious actions were uncovered by electronic surveilance.

The embezzler's technique was brought to light.

All the cash was stolen while the manager stood helplessly outside the vault.

All conceivable alternatives have already been examined.

Incorrect data were recorded during the last two experimental runs.

A fourth reason to use the passive voice is to avoid responsibility. This passive device is a favorite of politicians and bureaucrats.

Active: Our committee chairman will not release your bill this term.

Passive: Your bill will not be released to the floor this term.

Other political examples:

These Summary Annual Reports have been filed with the IRS as required under ERISA.

It has been decided that your amendment will not be voted on.

House Bill 2218 has been introduced to regulate roller rink operators.

A House bill is being prepared that will require parents to attend the tatooing of their children.

The fuselage of the B-29 that dropped the bomb on Hiroshima will be exhibited without much comment by the Smithsonian Museum.

A committee was chosen to review the anti-American exhibit.

The conclusion was reached that certain right-wing brethern were suffering from a neurological disorder.

A fifth reason for using the passive voice is that a formal and impersonal tone is desired.

Your report was received yesterday.

The amount for which your account is insured is now $100,000.

Your presence is requested at the Johnson reception at the Borden House at 3:00 P.M. on Thursday, July 6.

Mr. Alber's promotion to executive vice president was approved today.

The appointment of Mr. Wilshire to the Board of Directors was announced today by BoTech, Inc.

A sixth reason for using the passive voice is that one point of view can be maintained through several sentences. This can avoid awkward shifts in the point of view.

Awkward shifts from Lila to Jason to reporter to Lila:

Lila was decorating her Christmas tree. Jason, her new boyfriend, called and wanted to go for a walk with her. The television weather reporter had forecast blizzard-like winds. Lila decided to continue her tree decorating.

Lila's viewpoint only:

Lila was decorating her Christmas tree when she was interrupted by Jason, her new boyfriend. She was asked to go for a walk but had heard from the television weather reporter that a blizzard-like wind was coming soon. Lila declined Jason's invitation and continued with her tree decorating.

A word of caution about the use of the passive voice: Do not shift from passive to active or from active to passive in the same sentence or paragraph.

Active to passive: Our group at last finished the long trek to the summit where we were provided with a much-needed lunch.

Consistent, active: Our group at last finished the long trek to the summit where we ate a much-needed lunch.

Consistent, passive: The long trek to the summit was ended at last and we were provided with a much-needed lunch.

Whole paragraphs can be more effective in the passive than the active when the sequence of events is more important than the person performing the action. Two examples:

In order to do the best purchasing job possible, the responsibility for control of major raw materials, process chemicals, maintenance, and capital equipment is vested in the Headquarters Purchasing Department. The purchasing of materials and services is done at the division, mill, plant or office closest to the point of ultimate use. This is a system of decentralized buying with centralized control.

The passive voice is appropriate in this case because headquarters personnel changes from time to time, and no one person or group is responsible for the corporate policy, which is applicable to all employees now and in the future. There is no need to personalize this policy statement.

Modern wastewater treatment is generally divided into three phases: primary, secondary, and tertiary. Primary treatment, or plain sedimentation, developed in the early 1900's, removes only the settleable solids from wastewaters. This process is considered to be the absolute minimum of treatment that every community must afford. (Taken from the 1974 edition of *Encyclopedia Americana*, vol. 28, p. 424g.)

In this example, the procedure described is in general use, a series of events is described and the emphasis is on the operation not the operators.

One final comment about the use of the passive voice in any writing: Language experts agree that unless there is a definite reason for using the passive, use the active voice because it emphasizes the doer of the action and makes your writing more lively and interesting to your reader.

Verbs as Nouns and Adjectives

Verb forms called *verbals* consist of *gerunds*, *participles* and *infinitives*. In essence, a participle is a verb form used as an adjective, while gerunds and infinitives are verb forms used as nouns.

Some examples of how gerunds are used as nouns:

Swimming is fun and also good exercise.

> *Swimming* is a form of the verb swim and is used here as a noun, which is the subject of the verb *is*.

Do not confuse *swimming* as used in the above sentence with *swimming* in the following sentence: *The girl swimming backstroke will come in first.* Here *swimming* is a *participle*—discussed next—and is used as an adjective describing the noun subject *girl*. Also, as a verb it takes the object, *backstroke*.

Eating has become an enjoyable social event.

> *Eating* is a gerund that acts as a noun and is the subject.

The auditor liked *finding* mistakes.

> *Finding*, a gerund, is the noun object of the verb *liked*.

Winning the race was the start of his career.

> *Winning the race* is a gerund phrase serving as as noun subject.

Crying all day and *sobbing* half the night wore her to a frazzle.

> *Crying* and *sobbing* are gerunds creating a compound subject.

Brother Bob uses my garage for *storing his old "78" records.*

> *Storing his old "78" records* is a gerund phrase and the object of the preposition *for.*

A rule is that the subject of a gerund must be in the possessive case.

Wrong: I appreciate *him going* to bat for me.

Right: I appreciate *his going* to bat for me.

Wrong: *Irene refusing* the promotion was surprising.

Right: *Irene's refusing* the promotion was surprising.

Because of our English idiom, there is some disagreement about how wrong it is to say, *We experienced the car stalling* instead of *We experienced the car's stalling.* The meaning is the same and also clear in both sentences, but why not be correct rather than merely acceptable? Another example of acceptable rather than correct is, *Is there a reason for both of us going?* rather than *Is there a reason for our both going?*

You may start a sentence that requires the possessive before the gerund but that has become awkward by the time you finish. For example:

Wrong: We old timers object to a person who was fired for cause's being hired again.

In cases like this, start over again and recast the sentence.

Better: We old timers object to re-hiring a person who was fired for cause.

Better: When a person has been fired for cause, we old timers object to hiring him again.

Better: When a person has been fired for cause, we old timers object to his being hired again.

The gerunds in the first two sentences that follow are *having won* and in the next two sentences are *winning.* Note that the tenses of the gerunds do *not* relate to the tenses of the verbs.

First: Having won the race *pleases* her father.

Second: Having won the race *pleased* her father.

> The first sentence is in the present tense, the second in the past tense. Otherwise the meanings are the same. However, the following two sentences have a different meaning.

Third: Winning the race *pleases* her father.

Fourth: Winning the race *pleased* her father.

> The tense in the third sentence is present and in the fourth past. The meanings are otherwise the same.

Sentences first and second do not mean the same as sentences third and fourth. Sentences first and second refer to the *fact* of having won while sentences third and fourth refer to the *activity* of winning.

A *participle* is a verb form functioning as an adjective, which describes a noun or pronoun.

The present participle ends in *ing*: walking, speaking, reading, acting, throwing. The past participle ends in *ed, e, g, t, en, k, n*, or *d*: asked, come, stung, brought, arisen, sunk, begun, paid.

Adjective describing a noun:

She wore a *red* dress (noun).

Participle describing a noun:

Running so fast, Peter (noun) passed a rabbit.

Improving prospects (noun) for employment brought him to Denver.

Estimated costs (noun) were out of line.

The *spoken* word (noun) is more effective.

The *bent* wheel (noun) is here.

Participle describing a pronoun:

Running faster, he (pronoun) outraced the overweight policeman.

Always *speaking so harshly* (phrase), they (pronoun) were disliked.

Hoping for a better job, he (pronoun) resigned.

Having waited, they (pronoun) did not participate.

Tense is important when using participles. You must be careful to word your sentences to clearly indicate the sequence of time you intend to reveal.

To describe things happening at the same time, use a *present participle*.

Walking down Seventh Street, Alex *sees* the accident.

Walking down Seventh Street, Alex *saw* the accident.

Although seemingly strange, both sentences indicate simultaneous action. In the first sentence, Alex walks and sees at the same time: now. In the second sentence, Alex saw at the same time he was walking: in the past. But in both sentences the *present* participle is used.

To show action occurring in the past *before* the time indicated by the main verb, use the *past perfect* tense of the participle, which is the past participle with the helper *had* or *have*.

Having been forgiven by his wife, he *hurried* home.

In May we *burned* the branches that *had been* cut during the winter.

She *revealed* that she *had been* happier during her first marriage.

Joan *had talked* to me before she *wrote* the paper.

Their home *had been* for sale for three years before they *sold* it last June.

Having been broken in spirit, he *dragged* himself to a Mission home.

Having become pleased with the club he joined, he now *works* hard to be accepted.

An *infinitive* is a verb form used primarily as a noun but can be used as an adjective or an adverb. The infinitive is usually preceded by the word *to*, although the *to* is sometimes omitted as in these examples:

She said (to) *let* him go first.

We all helped (to) *make* him happier.

They wouldn't dare (to) *go* past the graveyard in the dark.

The infinitive's most common use as a noun is illustrated in these sentences.

The infinitive can be the object of the verb:

He hates *to arrive* after dark.

We tried *to finish* organizing the procedure.

Pedro wanted *to ride* the horse.

The infinitive can be the subject of the sentence:

To read is to enjoy the observations of others.

To try is the first step.

To swim was John's objective.

Used as an adjective, infinitives can modify nouns:

We told Pedro this is the *horse* (noun) *to ride*.

This is a better *book* (noun) *to read*.

This is the *proposal* (noun) *to accept*.

Used as an adverb, infinitives modify verbs, adjectives or other adverbs.

Infinitives as adverbs modifying verbs:

The gate *opens* (verb) *to let* the lake water flow out.

The mechanic *rushes* (verb) *to finish* by noon.

The ball *was thrown* (verb) *to put* the runner out.

He *closed* (verb) the accounting books *to end* the business year.

Infinitives as adverbs modifying adjectives:

Cy was *kind* (adjective) *to visit* her this week.

She was *pleased* (adjective) *to meet* Fred.

Fred was *happy* (adjective) *to see* her.

Infinitives as adverbs modifying other adverbs:

Early (adverb) *to awaken* was her daily habit.

Slow (adverb) *to arise* he stood straight and tall.

Knowingly (adverb) *to falter* fooled no one.

An infinitive phrase includes the infinitive plus any modifiers or objects:

To tell the truth, we were late.

To prepare for the final event, we need your help.

She wanted *to drive the new car*.

Alvin decided *to study German*.

Sharon hopes *to join a new firm soon*.

Awkward sentences can result from dangling infinitives or inappropriate clauses. For example, in the sentence, *To enjoy playing tennis proper shoes must be worn*, the infinitive phrase, *To enjoy playing tennis*, refers to the person who might play tennis, while the phrase that follows, *proper shoes must be worn*, refers to wearing the shoes but does not refer to the tennis player who will wear the shoes. This inconsistency in parts of the sentence causes the infinitive to "dangle." An improved sentence would be, *To enjoy playing tennis, one must wear proper shoes*, or *Wearing proper shoes helps one to enjoy playing tennis*, or *A person can enjoy playing tennis only if he or she wears proper shoes*.

A few more examples:

Dangling: Unable to work, the doctor told me my knee cap was broken.

Better: After the doctor told me my knee cap was broken, I could not return to work.

Dangling: To get high grades, good study habits are necessary.

Better: To get high grades, a student must have good study habits.

Dangling: To play a musical instrument well, it must be practiced several hours each day.

Better: To play a musical instrument well, a musician must practice several hours daily.

Better: Several hours of daily practice are required if you wish to play a musical instrument at the professional level.

Parallel, or equal, construction contributes to the smooth flow of a sentence. This is discussed more in the section on Parallelism, but its application to infinitives is briefly illustrated here. The key is to repeat the infinitive.

Wrong: Betty learned to stand, then walk and now she can run.

Better: Betty learned to stand, to walk and to run.

Wrong: Alex strove to become rich and he wanted to be famous.

Better: Alex strove to become rich and to become famous.

Wrong: We were asked to wake up early, pack our bags and board the bus at 6:00 A.M.

Better: We were asked to wake up early, to pack our bags and to board the bus at 6:00 A.M.

Here is a common mistake when using an infinitive:

Wrong: They wanted Alice and *I* to work together.

Wrong: They wanted Alice and *myself* to work together.

Right: They wanted Alice and *me* to work together.

In these sentences, although *Alice* and *me* are subjects of the infinitive *to work*, the objective case is required. Also, the objective case is used for objects of an infinitive.

Wrong: They tried to destroy Frank and *he.*

Right: They tried to destroy Frank and *him.*

Here, *Frank* and *him* are objects of the infinitive *to destroy.*

Splitting an infinitive, placing a word or words between *to* and the verb of the infinitive, used to be considered an error in English usage. But now there are acceptable exceptions. Splitting the infinitive with one word in these acceptable exceptions tends to emphasize the inserted word.

Acceptable: Joan wants to *really* see her long lost sister.

Acceptable: I hoped to *properly* learn computer programming.

Acceptable: We were asked to *quickly* leave the accident scene.

Acceptable: For him to *always* complain seemed unreasonable.

Wrong: For him to *always, especially when we were trying to meet a deadline,* complain seemed unreasonable. (Awkward sentence)

Right: For him to complain all the time when we were trying to meet a deadline seemed unreasonable.

The rule is: do not split an infinitive unless there is a good reason for doing so.

Making verbs into nouns often makes a sentence wordy, awkward and weak.

Weak: Your cooperation is respectfully solicited.

Strong: Please cooperate.

Weak: Consideration should be given to the deadline.

Strong: Consider the deadline.

Weak: The need for action is immediate.

Strong: We must act immediately.

Weak: An investigation will take place tomorrow morning.

Strong: We will investigate tomorrow morning.

Weak: We encourage your preparation for the event.

Strong: Prepare for the event.

Weak: (Football game) I believe blocking that kick is essential.

Strong: Block that kick!

Weak: (Basketball game) Shooting the ball toward the basket should be a priority at this time.

Strong: Shoot, shoot!

When you tend to ease into a passive sentence using a word that ends in *tion*, pause and consider rewriting the sentence in subject-verb-object order.

Passive: Application of the new paint should be started tomorrow.

Active: Andy will use the new paint tomorrow.

Making nouns into verbs is another common abuse of the English language. Some examples:

I will *xerox* a copy of this report.

We may have to *laymanize* this government pamphlet.

I wish to *dialogue* with you.

We should *target* the retired groups.

The applicant must be able to *interface* with management.

I find it difficult to *decouple* myself from my previous work.

In my opinion you have not *contexed* that correctly.

This is a *customer-installable* device.

Two-party checks will be accepted by our bank for deposit or *encashment*.

(Ad for seat belts) Have you *belted* your kids today?

The B-1 bomber would have *obsoleted* the B-52.

She *enthused* over her guest's emerald necklace.

I promise not to *jargonize* my writing.

CHAPTER 3

Order in Sentences

Objects in Sentences

It is important to know how to use *objects* properly in sentences. They are used for:

Direct object of a verb
Indirect object of a verb
Subject of an infinitive
Object of a preposition

To make this meaningful, here are examples and illustrations of these uses of *objects*:

Direct object of a verb—receives or is affected by the verb's action.

Wrong: Father sent *Peter* and *I* to England.
Right: Father sent *Peter* and *me* to England.
Wrong: I like *he* (*she*) better.
Right: I like *him* (*her*) better.
Right: Julia threw the *bouquet.*
Right: Pedro hit the *ball.*
Right: Andy and Alice robbed a *bank*, then stole a pickup *truck.*
Right: The man offered her a *bribe.*

Right: The clerk sold the *diamond*.

Right: They all blamed *me*.

Right: I raked the *leaves*.

Right: They didn't know *where I live*.

Right: We saw *him* looking at our new car.

Right: The view amazed *her* and *me*.

Right: The visitors offered *money*.

Right: At this school we teach *English*.

Right: Jean hid the *books* behind the sofa.

Right: *What* did Theresa say?

Right: I see *what you believe*.

Wrong: Did you watch *Jim* and *I*?

Right: Did you watch *Jim* and *me*?
  When in doubt, omit the first part of the compound object, *Jim and*, to determine which sounds correct.

Wrong: At the party I asked *she* for a dance.

Right: At the party I asked *her* for a dance.

Indirect object of verb—states for whom or to whom the verb acts.

Right: I gave *Susan* the flowers.

Right: I told *him* my story.

Right: Please tell *me* your story.

Right: Mother bought *her* a new doll.

Right: The mechanic gave the *machine* a high polish.

Right: He gave *Tim* the accounting report.

Right: They sold *him* a "bill of goods."

Right: I bought *Sally* a new computer.

Right: John sold *his friend* a bicycle.

Wrong: Wally sold *Terry* and *she* a ticket.

Right: Wally sold *Terry* and *her* a ticket.

Subject of an infinitive—always an object. An infinitive consists of the preposition *to* (usually) plus a verb: to go, to come, to work, to eat, to have gone, to have been seen.

An infinitive phrase consists of the infinitive plus its modifiers: to go home, to come to my party, to work hard all day long, to eat too much just before bedtime.

Example: I asked *him to visit me.*

> *Him* is the object of the verb *asked.*

> *Him* is also the subject of the infinitive *to visit.* The subject of an infinitive is in the objective case rather than the subjective case.

Wrong: We expected *she to go* home.

Right: We expected *her to go* home.

Right: We saw *her go* home.

> *Go* is an infinitive without *to.*

Example: Our supervisor expected Pete and *me to best* Mark and *her.*

> *Me* is the subject of the infinitive *to best* and *her* is the object of the infinitive. Both are in the objective case.

Right: I didn't want *them to succeed.*

Right: *To watch* her joy was a pleasure.

Right: For *me to watch* her joy was a pleasure.

Right: It was a pleasure for *me to watch* her joy.

Right: *To watch* her joy was a pleasure for *me.*

Object of a preposition—a noun or pronoun that relates to another word in the sentence. A preposition always has an object. A prepositional phrase consists of the preposition and the object plus its modifiers.

Examples:

We were *at* the *concert.*

He worked *about* the *house.*

She went *around* the *corner.*

Jim studied *for* the *exam.*

With regards to our last *letter*, please ignore the last paragraph.

Without a *doubt*, he is more able than Tad.

What was Mark so excited *about*?

> *What* is the object of *about.*

He hired a detective *with vast experience.*

> The phrase modifies *detective.*

He ate *with much gusto.*

> The phrase modifies *ate.*

Give help to *whoever is in need.*

> The clause is the object of the preposition *to. Whoever* by itself is not the object of *to.*

Wrong: Have patience, sir, everything comes to *them who wait*.

Right: Have patience, sir, everything comes to *those who wait*.

> *Those who wait*, not the single words *those* or *them*, is the object of the preposition *to*.

Ending a sentence with a preposition is a subject much debated in the last fifty years. The current wisdom is that it is acceptable to end with a preposition if the emphasis thus provided is reasonable. Finding the object of a tacked-on preposition may be difficult, but it is there. In the following sentence from a newspaper article, the object of the preposition *with* is *disclosures*.

> Talking about work-family issues may involve more disclosures than some students feel comfortable with.

Alternate sentence:

> Talking about work-family issues may involve more disclosures than some students feel comfortable revealing.

The alternative sentence is specific, while the first sentence requires the reader to search to connect *with* to *disclosures*.

Here is a list of some common prepositions:

about	before	during
above	behind	except
according to	below	except for
across	beneath	excepting
after	besides	for
against	between	from
along	beyond	in
along with	but	in addition to
among	by	in back of
apart from	by means of	in case of
around	by reason of	in front of
as	by way of	in lieu of
as for	concerning	in place of
as regards	despite	in regard to
at	down	inside
because of	due to	in spite of

instead of	outside	unlike
into	over	until
like	past	up
near	regarding	upon
next	round	up to
of	since	with
off	through	within
on	throughout	without
on account of	till	with regard to
on top of	to	with respect to
onto	toward	with reference to
out	under	with the exception of
out of	underneath	

Adverb-Adjective Confusion

Our purpose here is to dispel the confusion that exists between adverbs and adjectives; they both modify, that is change, describe or limit other words. Briefly, adjectives modify nouns or pronouns—persons, places, things or ideas, while adverbs modify verbs, adjectives, other adverbs and complete sentences.

Adjectives can be studied and classified in many ways such as direct, descriptive, word endings, compound, possessive, indefinite, demonstrative and others, but an examination of the following illustrations will serve you better:

He owns a *blue* car.

Your plants are *beautiful*.

The *pink* roses are *healthy*.

That bike belongs to Andy.

Those workers dug *that* ditch.

Few samples are available today.

Each person is welcome.

One quart is required.

They walked a *rocky* path to the *muddy* river.

The *faithful* followers turned *sinful*.

That wooden board is *rotten*.

Jones got *favorable* treatment.

James tells *credible* stories.

It was a *marvelous* trip paid for by a *generous* man.

She is *fortyish* and loves *Danish* pastries.

The *experimental* procedure is *optional.*

He passed the *primary* and *secondary* tests.

She thought him *handsome* although *tiresome.*

Joan has an *artistic* bent.

She is a *tireless* worker.

That was a *fast-paced* demonstration.

Betty made a *long-term* commitment.

He edited a *twelve-page* newsletter.

There is the *old, weathered, dilapidated* barn.

Adverbs usually tell how, how much, how often, when, where and why.

Adverbs that modify adjectives:

We are *nearly ready* to go home.

The down pillow is *very soft.*

This is the *most important* report.

The *too-often neglected* boy has become *almost hopelessly delinquent.*

We got up at a *reasonably early* hour to go camping.

Wrong: My father was *real glad* to see me.

Right: My father was *really glad* to see me.

Wrong: That was *awful good* of you.

Right: That was *awfully good* of you.

Better: That was *very good* of you.

Wrong: That was a *sturdy constructed* shed.

Right: That was a *sturdily constructed* shed.

Wrong: He ran *plenty fast.*

Right: He ran *very (exceptionally) fast.*

Adverbs that modify verbs:

Wrong: I *improved* my tennis *considerable.*

Right: I *improved* my tennis *considerably.*

Wrong: Dawn *talks clever.*

Right: Dawn *talks cleverly.*

Wrong: He *drives* a car *good.*

Right: He *drives* a car *well.*

Wrong: He *speaks abrupt.*

Right: He *speaks abruptly.*

Wrong: *Plan* your activities *careful.*

Right: *Plan* your activities *carefully.*

Adverbs that modify other adverbs:

Wrong: Tom ran *considerable faster* than Tim.

Right: Tom ran *considerably faster* than Tim.

Wrong: Walk to the bedroom *very quiet.*

Right: Walk to the bedroom *very quietly.*

Wrong: My pulse is *serious slower* than last month.

Right: My pulse is *seriously slower* than last month.

Wrong: His proposal was *definite best.*

Right: His proposal was *definitely best.*

Wrong: Bart drives *real well.*

Wrong: Bart drives *really good.*

Double Wrong: Bart drives *real good.*

Right: Bart drives *really well.*

Adverbs that modify whole sentences:

Fortunately, people are eating smaller quantities of high-cholesterol foods now.

Unrelentlessly, he pursued the Sando gang.

Knowingly, Arvid let her continue with the rejected project.

Here are some adverbs ending in *ly* that are not included in the illustrations above:

badly	richly
certainly	sadly
dashingly	slowly
differently	soundly
happily	subsequently
loudly	surely
normally	

Some adverbs not ending in *ly*:

almost	moreover
also	nevertheless
besides	next
deep	meanwhile
early	nonetheless
fast	right
furthermore	still
here	then
however	there
indeed	therefore
instead	thus
likewise	too
little	well-nigh

The difference between adjectives and adverbs is not determined by the ending but by the use to which the word is put in a sentence. Some words are either adjectives or adverbs depending upon how they are used. Examples:

Adjectives:

He is in a *deep* sleep.
She took the *early* train.
John is a *fast* walker.
Bob wore a *hard* hat.
She is a *kindly* grandmother.
He crossed the *little* stream.
Sue knew the *right* route.
He walks a *straight* path.
She will be *well* soon.

Adverbs:

He dug *deep*.
He rose *early*.
She drives too *fast*.
Bill worked *hard*.
Sam talks *kindly* to seniors.
It was a *little* closer.
That didn't go *right*.
Keep the line *straight*.
Tom is *well* prepared.

On the other hand, some adverbs have two forms, for example, the word *slow* can be an adverb or an adjective, but *slowly* cannot be an adjective.

Wrong: She *slow* walked. (Adverb)
Right: She *slowly* walked. (Adverb)
Right: She walked *slowly*. (Adverb)

Right: She walked *slow*. (Adverb)

Wrong: She is a *slowly* walker. (Adjective)

Right: She is a *slow* walker. (Adjective)

Here are a few other adverbs with two forms. They are not always inter-changeable. When in doubt about a word used as an adverb that seems to be an adjective, check a dictionary to find out if the word can be an adverb. An example: *The knot was tied loose*, meaning in a loose manner or loosely. As used here, *loose* is an adverb. Other adverbs:

bright/brightly	loud/loudly
close/closely	near/nearly
deep/deeply	real/really
high/highly	right/rightly
late/lately	sound/soundly

When a word modifies a verb of the senses—*feel, look, smell, sound* and *taste*—the adjective form of complement is used:

I *feel bad*.

You *look beautiful*.

The gardenia *smells sweet*.

The speech *sounded raucous*.

The apple *tastes sour*.

Other linking verbs, those that indicate a state of being or condition, are also followed by adjective complements. A few examples:

JoAnn *appears happy*.

I shall *be pleased*. (Other forms of *be* are: been, being, am, is, are, was, were: I *was* pleased)

Then Alice *became sullen*.

Ellen *grows happy* when visitors arrive.

Ellen *remains happy* after her visitors leave.

The report *proved accurate*.

Pete *seems right* for the job.

The ground must *stay wet*.

The juice *turned rancid*.

Related to these linking verbs that are followed by adjectives that describe the subject of the sentence are object complements. They are also followed by adjectives. However (a big *however*), if an object complement is followed by an adverb, the meaning of the sentence is changed. For example:

Jean *called* Anne *happy.* (*Happy* is an adjective describing the noun direct object *Anne.*)

Jean *called* Anne *happily.* (*Happily* is an adverb describing the verb *called.*

We *consider* him *regular.* (*Regular* is an adjective describing the pronoun direct object *him.*)

We *consider* him *regularly.* (*Regularly* is an adverb describing the verb *consider.*)

Mom *makes* chicken soup *different.* (*Different* is an adjective describing the noun direct object *soup.*)

Mom *makes* chicken soup *differently.* (*Differently* is an adverb describing the verb *makes.*)

Many adjectives and adverbs change form to indicate degrees of comparison by adding *er* for comparative and *est* for superlative:

big	bigger	biggest
slow	slower	slowest
wise	wiser	wisest
happy	happier	happiest

Some adjectives and adverbs indicate degrees of comparison by adding *more* and *most* or *less* and *least*:

believable	more believable	most believable
eager	less eager	least eager
likely	less likely	least likely
wisely	more wisely	most wisely

Several adjectives indicate degrees of comparison in irregular ways:

bad	worse	worst
badly	worse	worst
good	better	best
little	less	least

many	more	most
much	more	most
well	better	best

Do not use double comparisons:

Wrong: That was the *most worst* performance I ever saw.
Wrong: This method is *more better*.
Wrong: Mary is *least happier* now.

Some adverbs can be used as conjunctions, joining two independent clauses.

Common conjunctions:

We ate our lunch, *and* we later watched a movie.
John sat alone, *but* Jerry sat with two old friends.

Adverbs as conjunctions:

John sat alone; *nevertheless*, he was happy.
Jerry sat with two old friends; *however*, he wished for new friends.

Other conjunctive adverbs:

consequently
then
nonetheless
therefore

A dependent clause, one that cannot stand alone as a separatee sentence, can serve as an adjective or an adverb.

Adjective clause:

Peter, *who runs daily*, is the leanest teammate. (The clause *who runs daily* modifies the noun *Peter.*)
Sandy, *who overuses cosmetics*, really has a poor complexion. (The clause modifies the noun, Sandy.)

Adverb clauses:

Tad is overweight *because he eats too much*. (The clause modifies *overweight* and shows the cause.)

You may leave *when the report is finished*. (The clause modifies *leave* and states the time.)

Every window is barred *so burglars cannot enter*. (The clause modifies *barred* and indicates the purpose.)

She is stronger *than I am*. (The clause modifies *stronger* and makes a comparison.)

The boy cried *before he was hit*. (The clause modifies the verb *cried*.)

Fragmented Sentences

A sentence fragment is a group of words punctuated as a sentence—starts with a capital and ends with a period—but which is lacking a subject, a verb or an independent clause. Also, if a group of words has these three elements but is introduced by a word that makes the word grouping dependent upon other words to form a complete thought, the word group is a sentence fragment.

To illustrate these four elements:

Asked for help with the report. (no subject)

Judith asking for help. (no finite verb)

Without expecting help. (no subject and no verb)

When Judith sought help with her report. (no independent clause; this is a dependent clause)

Common errors involving sentence fragments:

Subject missing:

Wrong: Walking his dog at night.

Right: Joseph was walking his dog at night.

Wrong: Singing loudly all the way home.

Right: Beth was singing loudly all the way home.

Wrong: Worked hard for his father.

Right: Fred worked hard for his father.

Wrong: Included the Sears report.

Right: Her presentation included the Sears report.

Wrong: The testing ended for the class A students. Continued for another week for the others.

Right: The testing ended for the class A students, but it continued another week for the others.

Wrong: And for weeks helped me with the computer.

Right: For weeks Sue helped me with the computer.

Verb missing or incomplete:

Wrong: Water trickling along the creek.

Right: Water was trickling along the creek.

Wrong: The extension cord with three wires.

Right: The extension cord has three wires.

Wrong: The path that we took.

Right: The path that we took was the difficult one.

Wrong: The doctor who examined Joan.

Right: The doctor who examined Joan was new to us.

Wrong: The new doctor smiling at Joan.

Right: The new doctor was smiling at Joan.

Wrong: Bob swimming in the new pool.

Right: Bob was swimming in the new pool.

Wrong: Whoever arrived early.

Right: Whoever arrived early received two door-prize tickets.

Appositives—nouns placed near other nouns to explain or rename or supplement their meaning—used as sentences:

Wrong: I drive my old jalopy. Once Grandpa's pride and joy.

Right: I drive my old jalopy, once Grandpa's pride and joy.

Wrong: The club members respect their new president. A woman with many years experience.

Right: The club members respect their new president, a woman with many years experience.

Right: The club members respect their new president. She has many years experience as a leader.

Wrong: Alan longed for a new car. Especially one with a low maintenance record.

Right: Alan longed for a new car, especially one with a low maintenance record.

Right: Alan has longed for a new car. He wants one with a record of low maintenance.

Verbal phrases used as sentences:

Wrong: Without looking further.

Right: Without looking further, he accepted his first job offer.

Wrong: He wants to help with this project. And to work on the next project.

Right: He wants to work on this project and to work on the next project.

Right: He wants to work on this project, and he also wants to work on the next project.

Right: He wants to help with this and the next project.

Wrong: They left home at an early age. Returning only after their mother died.

Right: They left home at an early age, returning only after their mother died.

Wrong: They arrived home. Some grieving openly.

Right: They arrived home, some grieving openly.

Right: When they arrived home, some grieved openly.

Wrong: John was accepted into membership. And was made vice chairman.

Right: John was accepted into membership and was made vice chairman.

Wrong: Now the children to wait for supper.

Right: Now the children had to wait for supper.

Prepositional phrases used as sentences:

Wrong: Marty returned home. In record time.

Right: Marty returned home in record time.

Wrong: Our sales manager stopped to talk. For no particular reason.

Right: Our sales manager stopped to talk, for no particular reason.

Right: Our sales manager stopped by for no particular reason.

Wrong: I started a running program. First by myself then with Peggy.

Right: I started a running program, first by myself, then with Peggy.

Wrong: I planned to succeed. With help from Alex.

Right: I planned to succeed with help from Alex.

Dependent clauses used as sentences:

Wrong: When he tried to ride his bike backwards. He fell down.

Right: When he tried to ride his bike backwards, he fell.

Wrong: The whole department volunteered. When a new manager was appointed.

Right: The whole department volunteered when a new manager was appointed.

Right: When a new manager was appointed, the whole department volunteered.

Right: The whole department volunteered because a new manager was appointed.

Right: A new manager was appointed. Then the whole department volunteered.

Right: A new manager was appointed, causing the whole department to volunteer.

Right: The whole department volunteered following the appointment of a new manager.

The words you choose to use and their order in the corrected sentences depend on which thought you wish to emphasize. For the strongest emphasis, start with the dependent clause and end with the independent clause.

Wrong: While Jim twisted his ankle on the way to work.

Right: Jim twisted his ankle while he was on the way to work.

Wrong: Because Andy had a car accident coming home late.

Right: Andy was late coming home because he had a car accident.

Intentionally fragmented sentences—questions and their answers can appear as sentence fragments, but the missing words are implied:

Where is the office?

Second door on your left.

Is Jason here?

No.

Where'd he go?

Home.

Why?

Toothache.

Commands also are not true sentence fragments:

Come back here!

Please open the door. Now!

Drive carefully. Slower.

Comments not written in "grocery list" form are permissible fragments. This technique is used to impart emphasis. Note: do not use this style of expression in formal or business writing.

It was a pleasant walk through the woods. Autumn. Maple leaves turning red and yellow. Blackberry vines pricking my ankles. A rabbit darting out. Woops! Stuck my foot into a beaver hole after stepping over a log. Sun slowly dropping behind the Olympic Mountains.

Awkward Sentences

In an effort to reduce our pallet costs, the purpose of this letter is to establish a pallet control procedure effective immediately which will be as follows:

Experience: Has served two terms, one two year and three year term involved with traffic and security.

While the committee knows there were requests for this worthwhile course to be given on a different night, the available space for this large class (fifty to seventy people) is Monday night.

Did you find these examples confusing and awkwardly written? Sometimes this sloppy writing is a result of slovenly thinking, but in most cases it is carelessness caused by haste. The writer's haste in turn is often caused by procrastination: the deadline is suddenly here! The writer, and also editors, have not taken the time to correct obvious faults, especially the lack of clarity.

In the first example above, two separate thoughts are jammed into one sentence, and a phrase dangles from the end. A suggested improvement:

We must reduce our pallet costs. The following procedure will take effect immediately.

In the second example, the reader is thoroughly confused by the phrase, "one two year and three year term." Probably, the writer meant to say, "He has served one two-year and one three-year term, both involved with traffic and security."

The third example appears clear after the second or third reading, but to write, "the available space for this large class is Monday night," makes *space* the subject, *is* the verb and *night* the subject complement. Then we have, "Space is night," but the writer no doubt meant, "Space is available on Monday night." Let's rewrite to eliminate the fuzziness:

While the committee knows there were requests for this worthwhile course to be given on a different night, the space for a class of fifty to seventy people is available only on Monday nights.

The following are further examples of awkward sentences:

Bad: At four in the morning you roll out of bed, stiff, sore, dead tired and with the miserable memory of having only four hours of sleep.

Better: At four in the morning, you stumble out of bed, stiff, sore and dead tired; you recall going to bed at midnight.

Bad: He describes in a realistic way about the things he experienced in the slums of the big city.

Better: Because of his experience in the big city slums, he can provide a realistic description of their horrors.

Bad: John and Jo Ann, in a romantic mood, literally waltzed on air all evening.

Better: John and Jo Ann, in a romantic mood, waltzed the evening away.

Bad: Jo Ann loves music as much as John.

Better: Jo Ann loves music as much as *him*.
(Jo Ann loves music as much as she loves John.)

Better: Jo Ann loves music as much as *he*.
(Jo Ann loves music as much as he loves music.)

Bad: Maximum refunds in this first distribution are $2,500 of the amount that customers had in their escrow accounts at the time the company was seized.

Better: In the first distribution, customers will receive no more than $2,500 regardless of the amounts in their escrow accounts at the time the company was seized.

Bad: The company made the following allocations: Community Center, to sponsor a newly formed basketball program—$500. ($400 of this donation came from a personal gift designated to this project.)

Better: The company made the following allocations: The Community Center basketball equipment program was allocated $500. Of this amount, $400 was a personal gift.

Bad: A special service of about one hour will be prepared and performed by the staff.

Better: A special service lasting about one hour will be conducted by the staff.

Bad: I think my dissatisfaction with your consideration of my viewpoint should be reported to the Owners Association.

Better: Because I am not satisfied with your efforts, I think I should report that to the Owners Association.

Bad: We will have an opportunity of learning about your new program.

Better: We will have an opportunity to learn about your new program.

Bad: It is my belief that this new process will bring new life to this adaptation of the original process.

Better: It is my belief that this adjustment to the process will bring new life to the original process.

Bad: We receive aid from other charitable organizations. That means our friends from all over the country help make possible through their giving our work with immigrant farmers.

Better: We receive aid from other charitable organizations. That means our friends from all over the country help support our work with immigrant farmers.

Bad: But don't bet on anybody starting building until a franchise is in hand.

Better: But don't bet on anybody starting to build until a franchise is in hand.

Bad: The picture shows Mavis Stewart helping Edith Calveras, who lost her hair after chemotherapy, with a head covering.

Better: The picture shows Mavis Stewart helping Edith Calveras with a head covering. Edith lost her hair after chemotherapy.

Bad: An article headline states, "Val Vista Lakes caters to families with amenities." (This states clearly that families have amenities. It should state that Val Vista Lakes has amenities.)

Better: Val Vista Lakes' amenities please families.

Better: Val Vista Lakes provides amenities for families.

Bad: Our new parking lot clearly is relieving the congestion we otherwise would have following our first and preceding our second Sunday morning worship service.

Better: Our new parking lot relieves the congestion we otherwise would have between our first and second Sunday morning worship services.

Bad: The program will be given by Ben Casey, a retired school principal, an outstanding photographer on hummingbirds. (What is the program about?)

Better: The program, Hummingbirds, will be given by Ben Casey, a retired school principal and an outstanding photographer.

Bad: The flowers today are given by Jane Doe in memory of her and her late husband John's wedding anniversary.

Better: The altar flowers are a gift from Jane Doe on the 49th anniversary of her wedding to John Doe who died in 19__.

Bad: The property is adjacent to where a post office will be built this year.

Better: The property is adjacent to the site of a post office that will be built this year.

The following is from a questionnaire prepared by a graduate college student:

If you were to move to an assisted living retirement community, at what age would you anticipate yourself to be? Please write in an exact age that is your best exact estimate.

Exact age is ___.

I was appalled that a person who had graduated from four years of college and now is doing graduate work could write so poorly.

It can't be said that the phrase, "at what age would you anticipate yourself to be," is technically wrong, but *to be* is passive rather than active, and the question contains an unnatural arrangement of words. It suggests a person tiptoeing through a muddy field rather than walking briskly along a dry, defined path.

Here is a straightforward way of asking the question:

At what age would you expect to move into an assisted living retirement community?

The second sentence, "Please write in an exact age that is your best exact estimate," indicates too much effort put into trying, unsuccessfully, to write precisely. Referring to a "best exact estimate" of an "exact age" does not add more precision but "muddies the water"—and we are again tiptoeing through our muddy field. The writer apparently was trying to prevent readers from answering, "after retirement" or "over 70" or some similar phrase.

A simple and clear statement would be better, for example:

Please use a number for your age.

Reread the original question and compare its clarity to the following rewrite:

At what age would you expect to move into an assisted living retirement community? Please use a number for your age.

Age ___.

Logical Order

In the previous section, "Awkward Sentences," the emphasis was on word arrangements that are confusing, particularly on the first reading. Although many examples would be appropriate for either section, "Logical Order" emphasises the need for logic, or old-fashioned common sense, in arranging words in a sentence. The goal in both areas is a sentence clear to the reader after one reading.

Here is one hint for writing logical sentences: Arrange the parts by (1) cause and effect, (2) chronology, (3) order of importance, (4) steps in a procedure or (5) word arrangements that are logical. By following these steps, your sentences will flow smoothly from one phrase or thought to the next. Examples:

Cause and effect:

Fuzzy: He strode straight and tall into the meeting having received a friendly pat on the back from the president.

Logical: Having received a friendly pat on the back from the president, he strode straight and tall into the meeting.

Fuzzy: They parted friends, having reached a long sought after agreement.

Logical: Having reached a long sought after agreement, they parted friends.

Fuzzy: They are many types of boring people at formal gatherings, but I prefer a quiet evening at home with my books.

Logical: Because there are many types of boring people at formal gatherings, I prefer a quiet evening at home with my books.

Fuzzy: The electric power lineman can be a hero on a stormy night, and cowards are found in all walks of life.

Logical: Although cowards can be found in all walks of life, on a stormy night the electric power lineman is a real hero.

Fuzzy: Go west; it's better out here. (Slogan of a restaurant in the western United States.)

Logical: Come West; it's better out here.

Chronology:

Fuzzy: He walked away a happy boy after his perfect recitation.

Logical: After his perfect recitation, he walked away a happy boy.

Fuzzy: Sandra made plans for her vacation but waited until after supper to start them.

Logical: After finishing supper, Sandra made plans for her vacation.

Fuzzy: As soon as we correct our internal problems they will improve our profits.

Logical: After we correct our internal problems, we can expect higher profits.

Fuzzy: The team approach took four weeks to improve our production rate.

Logical: After using the team approach for four weeks, we improved our production rate.

Fuzzy: Your help is needed in the way of small or large donations to help pay for the new enhancements to our stage.

Logical: Your help is needed to pay for new enhancements to our stage. All donations whether small or large will be greatly appreciated.

Order of importance:

Fuzzy: Because of his superior education, Larry received the promotion.

Logical: Larry received the promotion because of his superior education.

Fuzzy: Cedric cut the base piece six inches long of oak already sanded smooth and only four inches wide from a piece one inch thick.

Logical: From a piece of smooth-sanded oak one inch thick, Cedric cut a base piece six inches long and four inches wide.

Steps in a procedure:

Fuzzy: You can solve this problem if you analyze it, study the situation and list the facts.

Logical: If you list the facts, study the situation, and analyze the possible conclusions, you can solve this problem.

Fuzzy: To pay an invoice you must have a packing slip, write a pay authorization voucher, find the purchase order, receive an invoice from the vendor, and match them all.

Logical: To pay an invoice you must have a purchase order on file, receive an invoice from the vendor, receive a packing slip from the Receiving Department, match all items on these three documents, and then write a pay authorization voucher.

Fuzzy: She turned the potatoes when browned after placing them in a non-stick skillet and spicing them with lemon pepper after slicing them.

Logical: She sliced the potatoes thin, placed them in a non-stick skillet, spiced them with lemon pepper and turned them when they browned.

Logical order:

Fuzzy: After columnist William Safire challenged the Central Intelligence Agency's view that the Soviet economy was weaker than the CIA estimate, Safire reported, "The assembled experts pooh-poohed this. When I challenged the evaluation, Director Webster looked toward Robert Gates who said, 'It's the same different view.' "

Logical: Robert Gates could have said, "There are different views, but we believe ours is correct."

Fuzzy: This church (on an Indian reservation) also has a large clothing room as well as providing worship, training and pastoral care throughout a widely scattered congregation in an area of small farms and camps.

Logical: This church has a large clothing room. It also provides worship, training and pastoral care for a widely scattered congregation in an area of small farms and camps.

Fuzzy: We heard two women tell of the needs of the area: poverty, alcohol, drug addiction, cult attraction among the youth, and most of all the need to build a church.

Logical: We heard two women tell of the problems of the area: poverty, alcoholism, drug addiction, and cult attraction among the youth. There is a great need to build a church.

Subordination and Coordination

The joining of two (or more) independent clauses with a coordinating conjunction or a semicolon results in a compound sentence.

The common coordinating conjunctions are:

Conjunction	Use
and	to join or add on
but	to contrast
for	to mean *because* or to show cause
nor	to indicate a second negative; use with *neither*
or	to suggest and alternative
so	to mean *therefore* or to show results
yet	to contrast
;	to separate slightly more than by using *and*, but less than by using two sentences

Examples:

The report was completed before the deadline, *and* it was submitted one day early.

The moon was bright, *and* the stars sparkled.

The sky was gray, *but* the sun broke through occasionally.

The machine was balky, *but* Tom could adjust it when he needed its output.

We worked late, *for* the overtime pay was good.

We listened intently, *for* we anticipated only a vague clue.

Neither of you will go, *nor* will I go.

Neither report was acceptable, *nor* was the third attempt we made to get to the root of the problem.

Will you spend this summer in Denver, *or* will you go somewhere else?

We can work on project A, *or* we can start project B if you wish.

We must finish before midnight, *so* let us start right now.

You know that procedure is wrong, *so* why would you want to use it?

This procedure is standard, *yet* the other procedure gets faster results.

Tim works slower, *yet* he always finishes on time.

No person was born educated; education must be learned.

Machines will not operate without preventative maintenance; they must be lubricated periodically.

Coordination can be effective as a device for emphasizing a point through repetition:

The accounting books had to be closed by noon the next day, and I needed help. I called Bob, and he had his own books to close, and I called Joe, and he had gone home sick, and I called Martha. She came to my rescue.

Be careful, however, not to overuse this device, or your reader will lose interest.

Bad: My car suddenly stalled, and I pulled off the road, and it wouldn't start, and either smoke or steam blew out from under the engine, and I didn't smell smoke, so I opened the hood, and the radiator was steaming, and I wondered what to do, and a man stopped across the road, and came to ask what he could do to help, and . . .

Better: My car suddenly stalled. My first thought was to pull to the side of the road. I tried to restart the car, but with no success. By this time white clouds were billowing out from under the engine. Not smelling smoke, I assumed the clouds were steam and thought it safe to open the hood. The radiator spewed out a strong hiss of steam, then suddenly stopped. While I pondered what to do, a motorist stopped and asked how he could help.

The paragraph immediately above contains seven sentences, rather than one; three coordinating conjunctions (but, and, and) instead of nine; and one dependent clause, introduced by *while*.

These devices make the paragraph more interesting and easier to read. This brings us to the subject of subordination or dependent clauses in sentences. A main or independent clause can stand alone as a sentence: The fire engine roared down the street. A subordinate or supporting or dependent clause cannot stand by itself: while we all stood with mouths agape. Subordination permits you to state your meaning precisely, and to provide the emphasis desired. The following is a list of some common introductory words to dependent clauses and what they indicate to the reader:

Condition:

if	so that
in order that	unless
once	when
provided	whenever
providing	whether

Reason:

because	whatever
how	whereas
since	which
than	whichever
what	whose

Time:

after	since
as	until
as soon as	when
before	while
once	

Purpose:

in order that	who
so that	whoever
that	whom
where	whomever
wherever	

Why:

although	even though
even if	though

Three of these introductory words, *as, since,* and *while,* can cause problems because each has several meanings. *As* can mean *because* or *when* or *while.*

Joe left at 10:30 P.M. *as* he became tired.

> Does this mean *when* he became tired or *because* he became tired?

John trudged on home *as* the rain and lightning began to subside.

> Does this mean *while* the lightning lessened or *because* the lightning lessened?

Since can refer to the passage of *time* or it can mean *because*.

Since he retired, Jonas has become a regular gadabout.

> This may mean *after* he retired, but equally, it could mean *because* he is retired.

While can relate to *time*, it can mean *but*, and it can mean *although*.

While Thompson was a police inspector, he indulged in the pleasures of marijuana.

> Here, *while* probably means *during the time that*, but it could mean *although*.

I prefer pinochle, *while* she prefers bridge.

> In this sentence, *while* means *but*.

With so many words available to introduce a dependent clause, the writer can use a word that states precisely the meaning he or she intends to convey. Here are examples of meanings changed by merely changing the introductory word:

Your department's ethics report must be brought up to date each year,

as a result of your writing the original report.

because you wrote the report.

although you wrote the report.

even though you wrote the report.

after you wrote the report.

if you wrote the report.

since you wrote the report.

provided you wrote the report.

unless you wrote the report.

once you wrote the report.

until you write the report.

when I write the report.

The independent clause receives more emphasis than the dependent clause. The emphasis can be changed by switching an independent clause to a dependent clause.

The manager refused to change the procedure until instructed by the president.

The president instructed the manager to change the procedure, which the manager had refused to change.

The accountant had great power although his was a junior position.

Although the accountant had great power, he held a junior position.

Another technique for indicating emphasis is to place the important idea in a prominent position. This is at the beginning or at the end of a sentence.

Professional basketball is a money-making venture even though thousands of fans eagerly look forward to each game, especially during the playoff series at the end of the season.

Even though thousands of fans eagerly look forward to each game, *professional basketball is a money-making venture*, which is most exciting during the playoff series at the end of the season.

Even though thousands of fans eagerly look forward to each game, especially during the playoff series at the end of the season, *professional basketball is a money-making venture*.

Misplaced Modifiers

A modifier is a word or phrase that describes, limits, restricts, defines, or explains another word or phrase.
For example:

Jose looked toward the red barn.

There stands a nun with a pretty face framed in white and black.

In the first sentence, *red* modifies the word *barn*. In the second sentence, *pretty* modifies *face*, and the phrase *framed in white and black* modifies *face*.

A misplaced modifier is a word or phrase that modifies another word or phrase that is so far removed, physically or intellectually, from the subject being modified that the message of the sentence becomes ambiguous or humorous.

With thanks to the cartoon *Wizard of Id*, from Creators Syndicate, Inc., the prison (a dark dungeon) doctor approaches the filthy prisoner and says, "I'm giving you a collar that will rid you of fleas and ticks for six months." The prisoner replies, "I like getting rid of the fleas, but why does it have to tick for six months?"

At a meeting the speaker said, "In a few moments I will have Bob Jones pass out among you (slight pause) some sign up sheets." The speaker chuckled and was echoed by the audience. Shortly the speaker repeated, "Now Bob Jones will pass out among you."

A printed guarantee: If you are not satisfied with any of our products, please return it and it will be replaced with a smile. (A smile will replace the product?)

Not all misplaced modifiers create humor. The remainder of this section illustrates numerous practical situations in which you must pay attention to the placement of modifiers.

Wrong: When twelve years old, my father built a brick house.

Right; When I was twelve years old, my father built a brick house.

Wrong: We just bought the cabin for summer use.

Right: We bought the cabin just for summer use.

Right: We bought the cabin only for summer use.

Wrong: There will be a cheese and wine tasting buffet hosted by our Board of Directors at which they would like to visit and become acquainted.

Right: There will be a cheese and wine tasting buffet hosted by our Board of Directors who would like to visit and become acquainted.

Wrong: I am sending you a copy of your check canceled because of insufficient funds that was sent to me from my bank on July 2nd.

Right: I am sending you a copy of your check that was sent to me from my bank on July 2nd and was canceled because of insufficient funds.

> The phrase *that was sent to me* modifies *check* and should immediately follow the word *check*, not *funds*.

Fuzzy: "A lot of people have offered to buy Riverside over the years," he said.

Better: "Over the years, a lot of people have offered to buy Riverside," he said.

Careless: "Seniors may pay a higher premium than they do now, those who can afford it!"

> A quote from Senator Pete Domenici (R-NM), talking about changes in Medicare.

Better: "Seniors who can afford it may pay a higher premium than they do now."

> Putting the phrase *those who can afford it* at the end of the statement reflects speaking before thinking—a common fault.

Wrong: She and her brother were thrown from their mother's truck as it crashed, landing under it.

> *Landing under it* modifies *truck* not *crashed*. The comma after *crashed* does not completely serve to move the last phrase back to the word *truck*, although it is intended to do that.

Right: She and her brother were thrown from their mother's truck, landing under it as it crashed.

> Now the phrase following the comma is placed to modify *truck*. Both *its* clearly refer to *truck*.

I was quite impressed with a newspaper advertisement that started this way:

> Your children learn much of what they're going to learn early, including the most important lesson of all—how to learn.
> That's why the formative years of pre-school and elementary school are so critical to their future.
> Now there's a new school with a philosophy of integrated learning, designed to give your children a high quality of early education and a critical edge in an increasingly competitive world.

Beautiful! But, I was glad my children were beyond first grade when I referred back to the ad's headline:

They Only Start First Grade Once

Only is probably the most frequently misplaced word in the English language. How could a school with such a concerned desire to educate children permit a headline with an obviously misplaced modifier? Someone at the school must have known where to place the word *only*:

They Start First Grade Only Once

The meaning is not that the children only start, but that they start only once. The word *only* must "hug" the word it modifies.

Wrong: We *only* ate supper that day.

Right: We ate *only* supper that day.

Wrong: We *only* walked one mile.

Right: We walked *only* one mile.

Wrong: Such policies *only* get you partway there.

Right: Such policies get you *only* partway there.

Correct: Right now *only* one percent of fathers take paternity leave.

Correct: I was *only* eighteen months away from tenure.

Wrong: When we arrived, we were told we could *only* have two pizzas.

Right: When we arrived, we were told we could have *only* two pizzas.

Wrong: I *only* draw $279 a week unemployment compensation.

Right: I draw *only* $279 a week unemployment compensation.

Wrong: Opportunity *only* rings once.

Right: Oportunity rings *only* once.

Correct: A Cuban jumps toward a raft he hopes will take him to the United States, but he may get *only* to Guantanamo.

Wrong: It *only* happens twice a year.

Right: It happens *only* twice a year.

Wrong: The ABCo can *only* be reached at 000-0000.

Right: The ABCo can be reached *only* at 000-0000.

Wrong: Cruise lines *only* provide complimentary overnight hotel rooms when it is required by the air schedule as part of their air/sea program.

Right: Cruise lines provide complimentary overnight hotel rooms *only* when it is required by the air schedule as part of their air/sea program.

Wrong: Baby Boomers *only* knew one Mormon leader.

Right: Baby Boomers knew *only* one Mormon leader.

Wrong: Winning is *only* possible when you have a strong team.

Right: Winning is possible *only* when you have a strong team.

Wrong: I had a favorite customer in Housewares who'd *only* let me help him.

Right: I had a favorite customer in Housewares who'd let *only* me help him.

Wrong: I'm sad to see any saguaro (one type of cactus) dying. Since they *only* grow about an inch a year, you know this one is an old timer.

Right: Since they grow *only* about an inch a year, you know this one is an old timer.

Wrong: The Suns signed Danny Ainge to a three-year deal, figuring he might *only* be able to help them for two.

Right: . . . , figuring he might be able to help them for *only* two.

Wrong: Braxton, 25, seems destined for pop "divadom," which is ironic, given that she, the daughter of a fundamentalist minister, was *only* permitted to listen to gospel music while growing up.

Right: . . . , was permitted to listen *only* to gospel music while growing up.

Wrong: This informational meeting should *only* take an hour or so.

Right: This informational meeting should take *only* an hour or so.

Wrong: We *only* got a one percent response.

Right: We got *only* a one percent response.

Wrong: Reservations *only* will be booked through travel agents.

Right: Reservations will be booked *only* through travel agents.

Wrong: "President Clinton is *only* making one stop," said Peter Jennings, ABC newscaster.

Right: "President Clinton is making *only* one stop," said Peter Jennings, ABC newscaster.

Wrong: You *only* pay interest on the unpaid balance of your loan.

Right: You pay interest on *only* the unpaid balance of your loan.

Wrong: It's always something supernatural, something dreamt, something you can *only* see in your dreams.

Right: . . . , something you can see *only* in your dreams.

Wrong: The authors *only* tell you how to analyze and select mutual funds. They are not selling anything.

Right: The authors tell you *only* how to analyze and select mutual funds.

Wrong: This call will *only* take a minute.

Right: This call will take *only* a minute.

Noting again that modifiers should "hug" the word they modify, various placements of *only* in a sentence can change the meaning of the sentence:

Only my headache was temporary.

My *only* headache was temporary.

My headache *only* was temporary.

My headache was *only* temporary.

My headache was temporary *only*.

As an adverb, *only* means *merely*, as: She could find *only* one shoe. It also means *solely* or *exclusively* as: We shopped *only* at the secondhand store. As a conjunction, *only* means *however* as: We talked to him, *only* he wouldn't accept the proposal. It can also mean *except* as: I would wrestle with John *only* he's too big.

The problem with the placement of *only* is not new. A quote from Johann Wolfgang von Goethe (1749–1832), "the greatest of all German poets and the outstanding figure of world literature since the Renaissance," according to *The Encyclopedia Americana:*

Venice can only be compared to itself.

Could it be the fault of the translator that Goethe was not quoted as saying, "Venice can be compared *only* to itself"? The word *only* should modify *to itself*, not *be compared*.

Discussions and arguments about the proper placement of *only* continue. Perhaps we can accept the conclusions of a widely recognized authority. The tenth edition of *Merriam-Webster's Collegiate Dictionary* states:

> The placement of *only* in a sentence has been a source of studious commentary since the 18th century, most of it intended to prove by force of argument that prevailing standard usage is wrong. After 200 years of preachment the following observations may be made: the position of *only* in standard spoken English is not fixed, since ambiguity is avoided through sentence stress; in casual prose that keeps close to the rhythms of speech *only* is often placed where it would be in speech; and in edited and more formal prose *only* tends to be placed immediately before the word or words it modifies.

Dangling phrases, those that hang too loosely at the end of a sentence, are discussed in a previous section titled "How to Use Phrases and Clauses." The following is a presentation of other misplaced modifiers:

Confusing: I don't know Mrs. Glenn as well as Mrs. Jones.

Better: I don't know Mrs. Glenn as well as Mrs. Jones knows her.

Better: I know Mrs. Jones better than I know Mrs. Glenn.

Confusing: We decided to study the reforms during lunch.

Better: We decided to study the reforms that would take place during lunch periods.

Better: We decided during lunch to study the reforms.

Fuzzy: Lifting weights often improves your muscles.

Better: Lifting weights often will improve your muscles.

Better: Lifting weights will often improve your muscles.

Fuzzy: Jean who is arranging tours presently needs a new assistant.

Better: Jean, the present tour arranger, needs a new assistant.

Better: Jean, the tour arranger, presently needs a new assistant.

Fuzzy: We tried on the next day to make the sale.

Better: On the next day we tried to make the sale.

Better: We tried to make the sale on the next day.

Fuzzy: Heated discussions had often occurred over technical points during the audit.

Better: Heated discussions over technical points had often occurred during the audit.

Fuzzy: No gene was harder to pin down than the one implicated in Huntington's disease—which was finally located after a decade-long search last year. (*Time*, January 4, 1994) (A decade-long search last year?)

Better: ... —which was finally located last year after a decade-long search.

Fuzzy: Carter's (former President) comment came at the end of a day of awards, grants and celebration of his 70th birthday at the State Department. (His 70th year at the State Department?)

Better: Carter's comment came at the end of a day of awards, grants and a celebration of his 70th birthday during a ceremony at the State Department.

Fuzzy: Remember to leave your summer address and dates you plan to be gone in the Church office.

Better: Please remember to leave your summer address with the Church office, and also give us the dates you will be away.

Fuzzy: He's been trying to figure out where the dog went for over an hour.

Better: For over an hour, he's been trying to figure out where the dog went.

Better: The dog has been gone for over an hour. He's been trying to figure out where it went.

Fuzzy: All pictures are for sale on the wall.

Better: All pictures on the wall are for sale.

Fuzzy: It seems we just bought this last week.

Better: It seems we bought this just last week.

Fuzzy: We did just buy it last week.

Better: We did buy it just last week.

Fuzzy: I just went to the grocery store yesterday.

Better: I went to the grocery store just yesterday.

Wrong: I like Jim my friend's bike.

Wrong: I like Jim, my friend's, bike.

Right: I like my friend Jim's bike.

Fuzzy: We began to lose our enthusiasm about painting the house after a while.

Better: We began after a while to lose our enthusiasm about painting the house.

Fuzzy: We were sorry to see the end of our vacation for several reasons.

Better: For several reasons we were sorry to see the end of our vacation.

Fuzzy: We found a bicycle at Sears with twenty-one gears.

Better: At Sears we found a bicycle with twenty-one gears.

Fuzzy: In the desert eating a rabbit I saw a coyote.

Better: In the desert I saw a coyote eating a rabbit.

Fuzzy: Sharon read a report on police dogs in the classroom.

Better: In the classroom, Sharon read a report on police dogs.

Sometimes it is better to omit such qualifiers or modifiers as *very, little, pretty, rather*, and *somewhat*. Note the following pairs of sentences and how much stronger the emphasis is when the qualifiers are eliminated:

This is a very high speed motor.

This is a high speed motor.

She is a pretty good worker.

She is a good worker.

She is a little better at volleyball.

She is better at volleyball.

Jim is a somewhat faster runner than Tom.

Jim runs faster than Tom.

CHAPTER 4

Positive Sentences

Place Pronouns for Clarity

A pronoun is a word that takes the place of a noun. For example:

Pedro hit a home run. (noun)
He hit a home run. (pronoun)

Common pronouns include:

all	myself	those
anyone	one	we
each	one another	what
each other	others	whatever
everyone	ours	which
her	ourselves	who
herself	such	whoever
himself	that	whom
I	themselves	whomever
it	these	whose
its	they	you
mine	this	yourself

Note: A pronoun must clearly relate to the word or words to which it refers. The word to which it refers is called the *antecedent*. If your reader cannot easily identify the antecedent, ambiguity results. With an ambiguous pronoun the reader is uncertain to which noun the pronoun refers. The result is vagueness rather than clarity. Here is one example:

Tom told Mike *he* was proud of his muscular body.

Does *he* refer to Tom or Mike? Some possible interpretations:

Tom is proud of his own body.
Tom thinks Mike is proud of Mike's body.
Tom thinks Mike is proud of Tom's body.
Tom is proud of Mike's body.

Possible revisions:

Tom told Mike, "I am proud of my muscular body."
Tom told Mike, "I think you are proud of your muscular body."
Tom told Mike, "I think you are proud of my muscular body."
Tom told Mike, "I am proud of your muscular body."

As noted above, a pronoun must clearly relate to its antecedent. The easiest way to do this is to place the pronoun adjacent to the noun. When this isn't feasible, place the pronoun as close as possible to its antecedent.

Right: Yesterday I met John Bartlett; *he* is a pleasant sort of a fellow.
Right: I met John Bartlett yesterday and found *him* a pleasant sort of a fellow.
    Four words away, but clear reference.
Wrong: The clerk reported to the salesman that *he* made an error.
    Who made the error, the clerk or the salesman?
Better: The clerk reported *his* own error to the salesman.
Better: The clerk reported that the salesman made an error.
Acceptable: Buy the *company's* finished products rather than *its* raw materials.
    Pronoun is five words from its antecedent.
Better: Rather than buying raw materials from the *company*, buy *its* finished products.
    Pronoun is two words from its antecedent.

Confusing: The *audit* will be undertaken in various steps, the first being an analysis of general ledger balances. *It* then proceeds to an analysis of cash activities.

> Pronoun is sixteen words from its antecedent.

Better: An analysis of general ledger balances is the first step in the *audit*. *It* then proceeds to an analysis of cash activity.

> Pronoun is adjacent to its antecedent.

Clumsy: Mother told her sister that she (mother) would be able to make the trip to visit her (sister) this year.

> Explaining a pronoun's antecedent in parentheses should not be necessary.

Better: Mother said to her sister, "I won't be able to make the trip to visit you this year."

Fuzzy: He reached for his gun, removed *it* from *its* holster, twirled the bullet chamber, and slowly returned *it*.

> The first *it* and *its* obviously refer to gun, but the last *it* could refer to *chamber* or *gun*.

Better: He reached for his gun, removed *it* from *its* holster, twirled the bullet chamber, and slowly returned the gun to *its* holster.

Fuzzy: You can do without flowers, fancy dress and cake, but you cannot be married legally without a license. You know that, but perhaps you don't know that, in many states, *it* must be at the site of the wedding.

Better: . . . , in many states, *the license* must be at the site of the wedding.

Fuzzy: The book is printed on fine acid-free paper and the binding is Smyth-sewn, so *it* opens flat on the table or desk.

> *It* could refer to *binding* but probably refers to *book*.

Better: . . . and the binding is Smyth-sewn, permitting the *book* to lie flat when open.

Fuzzy: Frank Carpenter called his cellmate Bongo, but *he* feared *him*.

Better: Frank Carpenter feared the cellmate he called Bongo.

Fuzzy: Prayers and sympathy of the congregation are extended to Jean Manly's family *who* died June 14.

> The family died?

Better: . . . are extended to the family of Jean Manly *who* died June 14.

Confusing: The congregation honored Pastor Sanders and his wife, Patty, recently retired as a private school principal, at the reception, and, on Sunday, June 25, *he* conducted his concluding worship service.

> Too many thoughts for one sentence, and the pronoun, *he* is eighteen words from its antecedent, Pastors Sanders.

Better: Pastor Sanders and his wife, Patty, who recently retired as a private school principal, were honored by the congregation at a reception on June 25. Earlier that morning *Pastor Sanders* conducted his final worship service.

Fuzzy: But it is Uncle Walty who inspires Lloyd to do something meaningful: *He* sews Lloyd a costume out of a silky bridesmaid dress and encourages him to become Super Tree Man.

> *He* does not refer back to the nearest noun, causing the reader to reread the sentence.

Better: . . . to do something meaningful: *Walty* sews Lloyd a costume . . .

Fuzzy: We are now preparing for out fifth program that is designed to strengthen communication between the church and its members, and to help *it* to be responsive to *their* needs.

Better: . . . communication between the church and *its* members, and to help the church respond to *its* member's needs.

Confusing: Toobin also reported that "this new and provocative theory" had been floated by O. J. Simpson's lawyers (one of whom, Alan Dershowitz, Toobin neglected to mention, was *his* professor at Harvard).

> To which person, Simpson, Dershowitz or Toobin, does *his* refer? Too many thoughts for one sentence.

Better: Toobin also reported that "this new and provocative theory" had been floated by O. J. Simpson's lawyers. (Toobin neglected to mention that one of the lawyers, Alan Dershowitz, was Toobin's professor at Harvard.)

Uncertain: Freud believed an ex-patient of Jung's named Sabina Spielrein had also been Jung's mistress; Jung in turn surmised that Freud had become involved with *his* sister-in-law, Minna Bernays.

> Whose sister-in-law? Research revealed that Freud had married Martha Bernays. Minna Bernays could be Martha's sister and Freud's sister-in-law.

Better: Freud believed an ex-patient of Jung's named Sabrina Spielrein had also been Jung's mistress. Jung thought no better of Freud because he felt sure Freud's sister-in-law, Minna Bernays, and Freud were involved.

Fuzzy: Ask the auto dealership to check the heat shields and if any of *them* are loose, have *them* reweld *them* for you.

> The three *thems* in the second sentence are more awkward than confusing. The first and third *thems* refer to *heat shields* and the middle *them* refers to *dealer*.

Better: Have the auto dealer check the heat shields and reweld any that are loose.

Fuzzy: Above all, invention is not innovation. *It* is a term of economics rather than technology.

> According to its placement, *It* should refer to *innovation*, but the reference in the remainder of the sentence to "economics rather than technology" suggests that *It* refers to *invention*.

Better: Above all, invention is not innovation. Innovation (or invention) is a term of economics rather than technology.

Fuzzy: *The Race of Meritocracy* is a little light on enlivening details, and it has no real characters except "Michael Young," who ends the book confidently predicting that there can be no effective rebellion against the meritocracy and then, we are informed in a footnote, is killed by *one*.

> The pronoun *one* is the fifteenth word after its antecedent, *rebellion*.

Better: . . . and then, we are informed in a footnote, it was a rebellion that finally killed Michael Young.

Fuzzy: I loved everything about *cars* and read everything I could get my hands on about *them*.

> The phrase "about them" modifies *cars* and should be as close to *cars* as possible.

Better: I loved everything about *cars* and read everything about *them* that I could get my hands on.

Pronouns with no antecedent can lead to humorous statements.

Wrong: The left leg became numb at times, and she walked *it* off.

Right: The left leg became numb at times, but she found she could walk the pain away.

Wrong: On the second day the knee was better, and on the third day *it* completely disappeared.

Right: On the second day the knee was better, and on the third day the pain completely disappeared.

Indefinite pronouns such as *it, such, that, these, they, this, those, which,* and *who* can cause awkward situations unless you review sentences in which indefinite pronouns are used.

Wrong: *Those* condo's *who* have their operating accounts at ABBank may notice a service charge on their account this month.

> A condo or condominium, as used here, is an association of apartments or housing units. *Those* and *who* refer to the association as though they were individuals rather than groups. (The plural of condo is condos, not condo's.)

Better: The condos that have their operating accounts at . . .

Correct: Murphy said he joined the league to improve his basketball skills. But if *that* doesn't happen, he at least will be able to spend Friday nights where there is air conditioning.

> *That* refers to the whole phrase "to improve his basketball skills." The antecedent of the pronoun is clear.

Wrong: *They* also provide a newsletter, "Medical Action."

> After mentioning topics to be presented at a medical seminar by two doctors and a nurse, the announcement continued with the "wrong" statement above. To what or whom does *they* refer? Investigation revealed that *they* was a regional medical center to which the nurse and doctors belonged.

Better: The Southern Regional Medical Center provides a newsletter, "Medical Action." You may obtain a copy by calling (000) 000-0000.

Fuzzy: If *questions* can be raised about an exclusive reliance on the whole language method (of teaching reading) in practice, *it* should not be surprising that *they* can also be raised about *it* in theory.

> Of the three distant pronouns, two are indefinite. The first *it* refers to all of the sentence preceding the word *it*. The second *it* refers to the same idea. *They* refers twenty-two words back to *questions*.

Better: Exclusive reliance upon the whole-language method (of teaching reading) is subject to questions about its theory as well as its practice.

Sometimes a pronoun should be left out.

Wrong: We incorrectly assumed that the public figure (House Speaker) Gingrich most wanted to rob of *his* power and influence, to humiliate and then destroy, was President Bill Clinton.

> *His* refers forward, not backward, to President Bill Clinton. The sentence is easier to understand if the pronoun *his* is omitted.

Wrong: Computer operators who work for hours with few or no breaks or changes in their daily routines are subject to the carpal tunnel syndrome. *This* reduces the number of documents processed daily.

> To what does *this* refer, long hours, few breaks, no routine changes, or carpal tunnel syndrome? The last noun before *this* is carpal tunnel syndrome, and that should be the antecedent. But then we wonder which of the conditions mentioned caused the syndrome. Actually, *this* refers to everything before the word *this*. Vagueness prevails. The second sentence could be written in different ways that are more specific.

Better: . . . carpal tunnel syndrome, thus reducing the number of documents processed daily.

Better: This syndrome reduces the number of documents processed
   daily.

Better: As a result, the number of documents processed daily is reduced.

Some uses of indefinite pronouns are so common they are acceptable when
used informally:

It's hot outside.

It sure is cold in here.

It's going to rain.

That was an exciting thunderstorm last night.

One learns to accept the bad with the good.

You learn to follow orders in the military.

When you see *it*, you'll know *it's* the right one for you.

The following four news items illustrate the problems writers can get themselves into when they fail to think ahead or to review what they have written:

A west Phoenix bridegroom who fired a shot that accidently killed *his*
father on *his* wedding day will be charged with second-degree murder or
manslaughter in the shooting, *his* brother said Wednesday.

The first sentence and paragraph in this article uses the pronoun *his* three
times. In the first part, "A west Phoenix bridegroom accidently killed *his*
father . . . ," the pronoun obviously refers back to the word *bridegroom*. Reading
on, "on *his* wedding day . . . ," *his* should refer to the closest noun, which is
father. Your mind pauses and wonders if the father is being wed when the
bridegroom fired the shot that killed the father. Going back and rereading the
sentence to this point, you decide that the second *his* really refers all the way
back to *bridegroom*. By now you decide that the bridegroom is also the one
who did the shooting. Thus you have no trouble realizing that the third *his* also
refers to *bridegroom* although the word *bridegroom* is twenty-five words back.
   Any time you have to read a sentence two or more times to understand it,
something is wrong with the writing: perhaps too many thoughts for one sentence, perhaps illogical flow of thoughts, or perhaps thinking details that are not
stated.
   Let's see what we can do to make this sentence clear:

A west Phoenix bridegroom, on his wedding day, accidently killed his
father. The bridegroom's brother stated on Wednesday that the bridegroom
will be charged with second-degree murder or manslaughter.

Two days later, the same reporter wrote a follow-up article. Someone must have pointed out the errors in her writing, and perhaps thinking.

The first sentence and paragraph of the subsequent article left no doubt in the reader's mind about who was to be wed. The sentence follows:

Steve Garcia, a bridegroom who unintentionally shot his father on the groom's wedding day last summer, has been charged with second-degree murder, Garcia's lawyer said Friday.

Here is the last sentence of a paragraph from an August 2, 1993 article in *Time*:

Hutton, a devoted adherent of Paglia's gender politics, has also asked the author to contribute to a book *she's* developing on the social history of fashion.

After two or more readings, you realize that the pronoun, *she's*, refers back to Hutton. "Back" is seventeen words back, too far for the pronoun to reach when another noun, Paglia, is placed between the pronoun and its antecedent.

Better: Hutton, a devoted adherent of Paglia's gender politics, is developing a book on the social history of fashion and has asked author Paglia to contribute to the book.

The following are the last three sentences of a paragraph from a *Time* magazine article of March 16, 1995. The pronouns are numbered so they can be referred to after the quote. Leopold was Mozart's father; Anna Maria was his mother:

Mozart's lifelong fear of *his* (1) father determined *his* (2) behavior. When on July 3, 1778, *his* (3) mother died in Paris, where Leopold, despite *her* (4) protestations of poor health, had sent *her* (5) to accompany Mozart as *he* (6) sought a high-paying position, *he* (7) could not bring *himself* (8) to tell the truth; *his* (9) letter home that day merely reported *she* (10) was very ill, and it was not until six days later that *he* (11) finally confessed that Anna Maria had died. Naturally, Leopold blamed *him* (12).

The first reading of these sentences went smoothly for me, but as I neared the end I began to realize I wasn't sure what I had read because I felt overwhelmed by the flood of pronouns that referred to three people. Which pronouns referred to Mozart, which to the father and which to the mother? After the third reading—it should have taken only one reading—I think I have solved the riddle.

Number 1 refers back to Mozart, that being the only noun already mentioned. Number 2 also refers to Mozart, although the noun *father* separates this pronoun from its antecedent noun. Number 3 again refers to Mozart. Having read the whole section, we know that Mozart's mother is the only mother mentioned, and that she is in extremely poor health. Number 4 refers to Mozart's mother. Number 5 also refers to Mozart's mother. After reading to the end, you will be aware of this. Number 6 refers to Mozart, because it is the closest preceding noun. This pronoun is properly placed. Numbers 7, 8 and 9 all refer to Mozart, but at this point the sentence becomes fuzzy; there are too many separate thoughts—and the sentence goes on. The need for revision has become obvious. Number 10 refers to Mozart's mother because she is the only female mentioned. Number 11 refers to Mozart because Mozart is with or near his mother when she died. Number 12 also refers to Mozart because Mozart is the only male mentioned whom Leopold could blame.

Here is a suggested rewrite. Five pronouns have been eliminated, and the message is more easily understood because the noun to which each pronoun refers is clear.

> Better: Mozart's behavior was determined by his lifelong fear of his father. Leopold sent Anna Maria, Mozart's mother, to Paris to accompany Mozart while the latter sought a high-paying position. Anna Maria had protested making the trip because of poor health, and when she died on July 3, 1778, Mozart could not bring himself to tell his father. In a letter home that day, Mozart reported that his mother was very ill. Not until six days later did Mozart confess that his mother had died. Naturally, Leopold blamed Mozart.

A former English teacher who had been fired by her school principal wrote a newspaper article about that experience. She discusses job dismissals with a fellow employee who was recently asked to resign from a company for which they both now work. The resigned attitude of her fellow employee awed the former English teacher. She writes:

> I could never have been as pragmatic talking with colleagues in the faculty lounge about my whiplash in the principal's office as this guy was being in mine.

The last word in this quote, *mine*, is a pronoun. But to what does it refer? After several readings, it seems to refer back to *office*. But then after reading the complete sentence and substituting *my office* for the pronoun *mine*, the sentence is still fuzzy. Some reworking needs to be done.

> Better: I could never have been as pragmatic talking with colleagues in the faculty lounge about my whiplash in the principal's office as this guy was while talking with me.

Parallel Word Groups

Parallel or balanced elements of a sentence are effectively used in lists and comparisons.

All the items in this list begin with a verb:

This week we must

>   Complete the maintenance budget

>   Start the accounting procedures outline

>   Review first-level salaries

>   Hire two salesmen

In the following three sentences, the elements being compared in the parallel examples use the same language structure:

Awkward: In her new position, Anne feels confident and she hopes she is secure in her job.

Parallel: In her new position, Anne feels confident and secure.

Awkward: Mr. Goldfab has a sharp mind, a wealth of experience, a prosperous business, and his feet are unusually large.

Parallel: Mr. Goldfab has a sharp mind, a wealth of experience, and a prosperous business.

Awkward: In college Martin plans to study hard, exercise regularly, and he hopes to find several pretty girls to date.

Parallel: In college Martin plans to study hard, to exercise regularly, and to date pretty girls.

Parallelism can improve readability, add emphasis, increase comprehension and stimulate interest in sentences and paragraphs. Do not, however, overuse parallelism.

One key to parallelism is to start each phrase or clause with the same part of speech: noun, verb, adverb, adjective, preposition or others.

More examples of parallel and non-parallel writing follow:

Wrong: Jake liked swimming, hiking, fishing, and enjoyed playing tennis.

Right: Jake liked swimming, hiking, fishing and tennis.

Wrong: Tommy liked sailing, water skiing and to comb the beaches for agates.

Right: Tommy liked sailing, skiing and beachcombing for agates.

Wrong: She runs and swims daily and has a low-fat diet.

Right: Daily she runs, swims and eats low-fat foods.

Wrong: The delay was caused by posting errors and adding the ledger balances wrong.

Right: The delay was caused by errors in posting and mistakes in balancing the ledger.

Wrong: The new cutter blade not only reduces energy costs but also the number of rejected boxes.

Right: The new cutter blade reduces not only energy costs but also the number of rejected boxes.

Wrong: The meeting included supervisors from production, the custodian and the accounting manager.

Right: The meeting included the custodian, the accounting manager and supervisors from the production department.

Wrong: First, let me congratulate you on your appointment and second, you have chosen an excellent department.

Right: Let me congratulate you first on your appointment and second on your choice of departments.

Wrong: She's both an exciting dancer and innovative.

Right: As a dancer she's both exciting and innovative.

Wrong: I do our condo's accounting and am editor of our church newsletter.

Right: I am our condo's accountant and our church's newsletter editor.

Here are a few examples of correct parallelism:

Right: We confess our pride in being prudent: controlled rather than unrestricted, economical rather than excessive, frugal rather than lavish and cautious rather than risky.

Right: The country's civil identity virtually disappeared with, "Peronists assassinating Peronists, the military assassinating the military, union members assassinating union members, students other students, policemen other policemen." (From *Time* magazine, June 15, 1981.)

> The first three comparisons repeat the word *assassinating*. The last two comparisons omit the word *assassinating* and use *other*, but the word *assassinating*, although omitted, is implied. The shift is good: three items in succession are forceful; more is tiresome.

Many examples of parallelism appear in the *Bible*, but to the modern mind they are somewhat difficult to follow. One example, however, of climatic parallelism that we can easily understand occurs in *Zephaniah* 1:15–16, Revised Standard Version. The passage is Zephaniah's description of the Day of the Lord, when the Lord said, "I will cut off mankind from the face of the earth."

> A day of wrath is that day,
> a day of distress and anguish,
> a day of ruin and devastation,
> a day of darkness and gloom,
> a day of clouds and thick darkness,
> a day of trumpet blasts and battle cry
> against the fortified cities, and
> against the lofty battlements.

A practical use of parallelism is in making lists. One bad example will make clear the need for parallelism.

Wrong: The purpose of this report is to discuss changes:

> In our accounting department
>
> Review production overtime
>
> Qualifications for a safety supervisor

Better: The purpose of this report is:

> To discuss changes in our accounting department
>
> To review reasons for excessive production overtime
>
> To establish qualifications for a saftey supervisor

The following is part of the list of categories of letters included in a how-to-write-letters book:

Thanking a person

> For being our customer
>
> For helping my career
>
> For doing a job well
>
> For accounting help

Collecting accounts

> By reminding gently
>
> By appealing to fear
>
> By taking legal action

Answering complaints

> About a misunderstanding
>
> About a faulty product
>
> About a foreign object in food

Selling

> A sales promotion book
>
> A loaf of bread
>
> An executive search service

Other examples of parallelism in lists:

The regional sales manager

1. Assists the corporate director of sales
2. Prepares sales forecasts and compares them to actual results
3. Supervises the field staff
4. Prepares sales and cost budgets.

Information for prospective temporary help:

> Pay will be on an hourly basis. Overtime rates will be paid after forty hours in one calendar week.
>
> The manager is the only person who can approve pay rate changes.
>
> A review of pay rates may be requested after four months employment.
>
> New positions will be added as needed. You may apply for these after three months employment.
>
> Temporary employees do not recieve medical and retirement benefits.

The Simplicity of Positive Statements

The following two statements have essentially the same meaning:

No smoking

Please smoke outside

One difference is that the first statement is negative, "No," while the second is positive, "Please smoke." The second statement is also more pleasant, not only because politeness is added by using the word *please*, but also because we humans find doing something easier than forcing ourselves to stay alert to actions we must avoid.

Here are a few other pairs of sentences in the same vein:

Negative: Don't go outside.

Positive: Stay inside.

Negative: Don't be so poky.

Positive: Please hurry.

Negative: Ellen hated symphony concerts. She had to sit still too long and couldn't keep awake.

Positive: Ellen hated symphonic concerts. She became restless and then sleepy.

Negative: I did not learn anything from Stewart's lecture.

Positive: I learned nothing from Stewart's lecture.

Negative: Do not distribute this notice to employees who did not sign the April 30 Agreement.

Positive: Distribute this notice only to those employees who signed the April 30 Agreement.

Negative: Don't negelect to sign in before 10:00 A.M.

Positive: Sign in before 10:00 A.M.

Confusing: Some vendors may *not* call, but *don't* use that as an excuse *not* to *avoid* making any payments at all.

> Four negatives in this sentence cause the reader to go over this several times until, in his mind, the reader arrives at what the "Better" sentence states.

Better: Even if vendors do *not* call, you should make partial payments.

> These last two sentences refer to your past due accounts payable.

The following three sets of sentences are suggested ways to change responses you make to customer complaints from negative excuses to a positive willingness to cooperate.

Negative: We can't make the adjustment.

Positive: We suggest you talk to your local dealer.

Negative: Your complaint arrived today.

Positive: Thank you for bringing this problem to our attention.

Negative: We don't know what is wrong.

Positive: We are investigating the problem and will let you know as soon as possible.

The following fuzzy sentence has four negatives: denounced, ban, against and discrimination.

Fuzzy: Gov. Fife Symington on Tuesday denounced a petition drive that seeks a ban on laws that would protect homosexuals against discrimination.

Better: Governor Symington in his typical strong style on Tuesday held to his belief that homosexuals should be protected from discrimination. He denounced a petition drive that would void the the current law.

Using two sentences and rearranging the words has made the meaning easier to understand.

It is usually better to use a positive rather than a negative statement, although the meaning, or at least the "feeling" of the statement, may be changed: the negative is often critical while the positive is intended to be helpful.

Here is a list of a few negative phrases and their positive equivalents. Use them where you can without changing your intended meaning;

Did not accept—rejected

Did not allow—prevented

Did not consider—ignored

Did not prevent—allowed

Did not remember—forgot

Did not stay—left

Did not succeed—failed

Does not have—lacks

Not able—unable

Not absent—present

Not certain—uncertain

Not clearly—unclear

Not different—alike/similar

Not many—few

Not old—young

Not possible—impossible

Not the same—different

Not unless—only if

Not until—only when

Some verbs are implicitly negative. If you use negative words with these negative verbs, you can easily find yourself writing double or triple negative sentences. For example:

We do *not reject* your position.

I *don't doubt* that you *didn't* do that.

She *can't reject* the possibility that you *abetted* that scheme.

Here are some of the negative verbs:

avoid	forbid	guard
contradict	inhibit	refuse
deny	lack	reject
doubt	muzzle	repress
enjoin	preclude	restraint
exclude	prevent	subdue
fail	prohibit	suppress

Below is a partial list of words one author suggested using in sales letters to stimulate a positive attitude toward the product being sold—and at the same time toward the supplier:

absolute	free	oldest
brilliant	guarantee	powerful
confidence	help	proved
controlled	impelling	quality
detail	instant	quickly
economical	know	results
emphasis	largest	stunning
expert	lowest cost	successful
fact	new	valuable
flair	now	you

You can slant or emphasize certain aspects of an article's content by the order you use to arrange the facts and by the connections you use to join the list of facts. As an example, after talking with Andy one afternoon, you learn these facts, which you plan to use in an article about swimming.

1. Andy started swimming at age three.
2. He has been swimming for twenty years.
3. He was his high school champion swimmer each of his four years.
4. He lost only one swimming contest in four years at college.

5. He served as a life guard for seven years.

6. He taught one-on-one CPR and water rescue for three years.

7. He has never taught a swimming class.

8. He wants to apply for the job of swimming coach at a college.

You can't put all those details into the first sentence, so you decide to mention items 1, 2, 4, and 7.

A strongly negative statement: Although Andy has swum for twenty of his twenty-three years, and lost only one college competition, he has no classroom teaching experience.

A less-strong negative statement: Andy has swum for twenty of his twenty-three years and won all but one of his college competitions, but he has no classroom teaching experience.

Minimizing the negative impact without omitting any facts: Although Andy has no classroom teaching experience, he has swum for twenty of his twenty-three years and has won all but one of his college swim competitions.

> In the first and second examples Andy's weak point is stated at the end. In the third example the first clause is dependent, the weak one, and the last two are independent and stronger. The strongest point is properly placed at the end.

Positive repetition is good, but there is a limit to how much readers retain. Let us look at a quote from Winston Churchill, who upon becoming prime minister of Britian in 1990, told the House of Commons:

I have nothing to offer but blood, toil, tears and sweat. . . .

Churchill mentioned four items he had to offer. We remember, because of numerous misquotes of this statement, only three items: blood, tears and sweat. The rhythm of three is easier to remember and to say than four or two groups of two.

To end this section on a positive note, here are two paragraphs from a 1994 annual report:

In my opinion ABC Corp. stood up to the challenge better than any other mortgage banker in America, which should give you a solid indication of how well we expect to perform once interest rates stabilize or decline.

Of great importance to me is the fact that during the worst year possibly ever for our industry our stategy did not necessitate laying off a single employee.

Redundancy

"Play it over again, Sam" is an intentional misquote of a phrase used by actor Humphrey Bogart to a pianist in the 1942 movie, *Casablanca*. It illustrates the meaning of redundancy: a phrase with an unneeded word that duplicates the meaning of another word. In the quote, the word *over* adds nothing to the clarity of the phrase. A common redundancy is *refer back* (refer), and another is *at this point in time* (then).

Do not confuse redundancy with repetition, which is often used to add emphasis. We might emphasize the above quoted phrase by writing: I love to hear you play it again and again, Sam.

A few "right" and "wrong" illustrations of how to handle redundant thoughts will prove helpful.

Wrong: During World War II, all sections of Civil Defense cooperated together.

Right: During World War II, all sections of Civil Defense cooperated.

Wrong: The house provided a dull and nonshiny background for the bright green, shiny, waxy leaves of the new plants.

Right: The house provides a flat background for the new, waxy, bright green plants.

Wrong: The holes drilled for the chair back had to be aligned in an accurate manner.

Right: The holes drilled for the chair back had to be accurately aligned.

Wrong: Street repair maintenance and sewer systems are taken care of by the county government.

Right: The county takes care of streets and sewers.

Wrong: At long last the package arrived; it was square in shape and inside was a blue bowl, pretty and beautiful.

Right: At last the package arrived; it was a square box and inside was a beautiful blue bowl.

Wrong: Several have indicated their desire to have the later class for various reasons such as health problems that prevent them from coming to an earlier morning class and schedules that make it difficult to come to an earlier class and some have an interest only in a later class.

Right: Several have indicated their desire to have the later class for various reasons such as health problems and scheduling difficulties.

Wrong: Joseph Roach is a partner and the managing partner of the Phoenix office of Random, Hall and Butterworth.

Right: Joseph Roach is the managing partner of the Phoenix office of Random, Hall and Butterworth.

Wrong: Mr. Smith will also be going into the hospital as well.

Right: Mr. Smith will also be going into the hospital.

Wrong: Please give me a full and complete report.

Right: Please give me a complete report.

Wrong: We first began this business in 1981.

Right: We began this business in 1981.

Wrong: Please give this new procedure your prompt and immediate attention.

Right: Please give this new procedure your immediate attention.

Radio and television announcers and commentators are notorious for bandying about the English language, apparently never bothering to correct obvious errors in usage. Here are some of their redundancies:

. . . subject to air strikes from the air.

You will enjoy our new furniture selections, especially the La-Z-Boy recliner in particular.

Details will follow later, at 12 noon.

You could pay twice as much for the exact same thing.

Searchers found more survivors still alive.

Phony counterfeit bills.

Police officers walking their beat on foot.

Minus 25 degrees below zero.

Let me reiterate what I said.

Adjacent cities next to each other.

Workers mingling together at this point in time.

Police estimated a crowd of about fifty to seventy-five demonstrators.

Slim, one-vote margin.

The Rams lost their first two games of the season in consecutive order.

A complete false lie.

I watched them personally myself.

Here is a sampling of common redundant words or phrases with suggested omissions or changes. Notice the clarity that is added when the redundancies are left out.

Redundant	*Better*
Abby is one of two twins	Abby is a twin
absolutely perfect	perfect

Redundant	*Better*
actual experience	experience
advance plan	plan
an asset on the plus side	an asset
any and all	any
as a general rule	as a rule
as usual as ever	as usual
athletic person	athlete
at this point in time	now
aware of the fact that	know
basic essentials	basics (or essentials)
being in good health	healthy
being redundant again	being redundant
chemotheraphy treatment	chemotheraphy
close proximity	near
close scrutiny	scrutiny
collaborate together	collaborate
combine into one	combine
component parts	parts
consecutive in a row	consecutive
consensus of opinion	consensus
contemporary writer of today	contemporary writer
continue on	continue
cooperate together	cooperate
correct amount of change	correct change
current status	status
dead corpse	corpse
died of fatal wounds	died of wounds
different choices	choices
different varieties	varieties
dislike very much	hate
due to the fact that	because
each and every one	all
enter into	enter
equally as well	as well as

Redundant	Better
estimate about	estimate
fellow classmates	classmates
final outcome	outcome
first and foremost	first
first introduction	introduction
first priority	priority
foreign imports	imports
free complimentary gift	gift
free gift	gift
future prospects	prospects
goals and objectives	goals
has the ability to	can
honest truth	truth
honor and privilege	honor
I may possibly	I may
in close proximity to	near
in this day and age	today
isolated by himself	isolated
joined together	joined
joint cooperation	cooperation
kills bugs dead	kills bugs
mental awareness	awareness
mingle together	mingle
mix together	mix
mutual cooperation	cooperation
necessary requsite	requisite
new breakthrough	breakthrough
new innovation	innovation
NRA Association	NRA
on a daily basis	daily
on a personal basis	personally
overall plan	plan
past experience	experience
past history	history

Redundant	*Better*
personal opinion	opinion
plans for the future	plans
point in time	time
potential hazard	hazard
range all the way from	range from
refer back to	refer to
repeat again	repeat
small in size	small
stands out the most	stands out
sworn affidavit	affidavit
take the place of	substitute
the color green	green
the final conclusion	the conclusion
the majority of	most
the month of June	June
the reason why	the reason
this particular instance	this instance
totally monopolize	monopolize
true facts	facts
tuition fees	tuition
utmost perfection	perfection
valuable asset	asset
very vital	vital
viable alternative	alternative
whether or not	whether

CHAPTER 5

Words in Sentences

Don't Omit Necessary Words

Words and phrases at times are omitted from a sentence, making it difficult or impossible for the reader to understand. In many cases, this omission is carelessness, which could be offset by proofreading. Sometimes the omission is intentional; to the writer the meaning is clear, while to the reader the meaning may be either clear or doubtful.

This section points out some of the most common types of omissions, and offers ways to rectify them.

Small words such as prepositions, conjunctions, articles, and pronouns are probably the most common omissions.

Prepositions:

Doubtful: I had no interest her computer proficiency but liked her individualism.

Clear: I had no interest *in* her computer proficiency but liked her individualism.

Doubtful: For more than a month, Johnson and Bell asked the administration conduct its own survey and weigh the implications.

Clear: For more than a month, Johnson and Bell asked the administration *to* conduct its own survey and weigh the implications.

Doubtful: I had never seen that type scarf before.

Clear: I had never seen that type *of* scarf before.

Conjunctions:

Doubtful: We noticed the man limping badly carried no cane.

Clear: We noticed *that* the man limping badly carried no cane.

Doubtful: He found the bottom quark, the latest subatomic particle discovered, and he oversaw the most powerful atom smasher in the world serving as director of the Fermi National Accelerator Laboratory.

Clear: He found the bottom quark, the latest subatomic particle discovered, and oversaw the most powerful atom smasher in the world *while* serving as director of the Fermi National Accelerator Laboratory.

Doubtful: The boys skated on the sidewalk then in the street.

Clear: The boys skated on the sidewalk *and* then in the street.

Clear: The boys skated on the sidewalk, then in the street.

Articles:

Doubtful: The meeting was held at campus lodge.

Clear: The meeting was held at *the* campus lodge.

Doubtful: Karen ran better race than Steve.

Clear: Karen ran *a* better race than Steve.

Doubtful: He saw opportunity at the trade school.

Clear: He saw *an* opportunity at the trade school.

Pronouns:

Doubtful: I know two people have computers like yours.

Clear: I know two people *who* have computers like yours.

Doubtful: He is the candidate I supported, but he was not elected.

Clear: He is the candidate *whom* I supported, but he was not elected.

Doubtful: He was elected president and CEO and later promoted to board chairman.

Clear: He was elected president and CEO, and *he was* later promoted to chairman of the board.

Ambiguity:

Doubtful: The attorney and city commissioner attended the first meeting. (One or two persons?)

Clear: The attorney and *the* city commissioner attended the first meeting. (Two persons.)

Clear: The city commissioner, an attorney, attended the first meeting. (One person.)

Small verbs are often omitted in speech, but in business and formal writing, all verbs should be written rather than implied.

Doubtful: As of the present writing, PORA services only for SCW residents.

Clear: As of the present writing, PORA services *are* only for SCW residents.

Doubtful: The plans are drawn and the project started.

Clear: The plans are drawn and the project *has* started.

Doubtful: Jane's present is wrapped and the packages mailed.

Clear: Jane's present is wrapped and all the packages *will be mailed.*

Doubtful: He either will or has already gone to work.

Clear: He either will *go* to work or has already gone.

Doubtful: He talked with the suppliers and purchases made that day.

Clear: He talked with the suppliers and purchases *were* made that day.

Avoid using adjectives and adverbs in ways that leave the reader to imagine the specific meaning or the balance of the sentence.

Fuzzy: She is *so* beautiful.

Clear: She has a flawless complexion.

Clear: She has deep, blue eyes.

Clear: I can't take my eyes from her.

Fuzzy: I am *too* far gone.

Clear: I am incapacitated.

Clear: I am unable to work any more.

Clear: I am too tired to continue eating.

Clear: I can't stay awake any longer.

Fuzzy: He is out of it.

Clear: He is intoxicated.

Clear: He took a drug overdose.

Clear: He has a hangover.

Clear: He had a nervous breakdown.

Another usage to avoid is making a verb serve two phrases or clauses that are not logically tied together.

Fuzzy: John never *has* and never *will like* the used tractor he bought.

Clear: John never *has liked* and *never will like* the used tractor he bought.

Clear: John never *liked* the used tractor he bought and never *will like* it.

Fuzzy: Garcia is *as fast* if not faster than Pedro.

Clear: Garcia is *as fast as* Pedro if not faster.

Fuzzy: Service industries are now *as important*, if not more important than manufacturing.

Clear: Service industries are now *as important as* manufacturing, if not more important.

Fuzzy: The signing of the Declaration of Independence was one of the greatest *if not the greatest* event in our history.

Clear: The signing of the Declaration of Independence was one of the greatest events in our history, *if not the greatest*.

The following are examples of various other confusions caused by the omission or misplacement of words.

Fuzzy: AT&T Phoenix Works, on Fifty-first Avenue, will be closed in September, sold to a group led by seven plant executives, and all of its 1,600 employees will be laid off.

Clear: AT&T Phoenix Works, on Fifty-first Avenue, will be closed in September. *The factory was* sold to a group . . .

Fuzzy: Broken drinking glasses around a swimming pool are more dangerous than the kitchen.

Clear: Broken drinking glasses are more dangerous around a swimming pool than *in* the kitchen.

Fuzzy: Sometimes counselors help a depressed person less than the rest of the family.

Clear: Sometimes counselors help a depressed person less than *they help* the rest of the family.

Clear: Sometimes counselors help a depressed person less than the rest of the family *does*. (A different meaning.)

Fuzzy: Nedder works harder *than any employee* in the the office.

Clear: Nedder works harder than any *other* employee in the office. (Nedder is one of the office employees.)

Sparse: He is *so* rich. (How rich?)

Informative: He is so rich he will never be concerned about money.

Sparse: Your speech was the greatest. (How great?)

Informative: Your speech was the greatest valedictory address in the history of this college.

Sparse: We enjoyed the party.

Informative: Jane, Alice and I enjoyed Beth's birthday party.

Informative: Jane, Alice and I enjoyed Beth's birthday party, especially the mind-twisting games.

Informative: Jane, Alice and I enjoyed Beth's birthday party, in particular the white cake with the blue frosting.

Fuzzy: The duties of an accountant are more complex than a bookeeper.

Clear: The duties of an accountant are more complex than *those of* a bookeeper.

Fuzzy: Being able to write clearly may mean the difference between securing and being turned down a job.

Clear: Being able to write clearly may mean the difference between securing a job and being rejected.

When I ordered a dashboard cover for my car, the sales clerk asked, "Does your car have an air bag?" I replied, "Yes." A few days later when the service man started to install the dashboard cover, he said, "This part doesn't fit; you don't have a passenger-side air bag."

The sales clerk should have asked, "Does your car have a passenger-side air bag?" The omission of a single adjective caused inconvenience and wasted time for the sales clerk, the supplier, the installer and me.

Too Many Words?

The section above covered examples of necessary words left out. This section covers the opposite: too many words left in.

It is usually easier to write long, flowing sentences, replete with adjectives, adverbs and excess explanatory words than to write concisely. Writing concisely requires more thinking.

Wordiness supresses the reader's understanding, for example, "Let me take this opportunity to inform you of a situation in the production department that I believe needs your prompt attention," instead of, "A bottleneck exists at the number 2 rotary cutting machine."

Does every word you use add meaning to your presentation, or can you omit some words without changing the meaning? A review and close editing of your writing can eliminate unnecessary words and phrases and improve both forcefulness and clarity. An example:

His (extravagant) courting of Diane with (a dozen) roses (daily, sumptuous) meals at (luxury) supper clubs, dancing at (exclusive) hotel ballrooms and expensive jewelry was the start of (his trip into) bankruptcy.

Short, precise sentences save the reader time. This is appreciated by business people, who read numerous letters and memos daily, and will put aside documents that appear too long to be absorbed readily.

On the other hand, at times the writer intentionally uses long sentences to slow the reader to achieve a calming effect, the opposite of using short sentences that create speed and excitement.

Brevity alone does not improve clarity. In descriptions, added words provide clarity, completeness and comprehension. For example:

Once in a lifetime there is a special place. Just beyond the gentle rise overlooking a flowering meadow you come upon a secluded setting of prestigious homes. The tree-covered slopes are fenced and guarded, ensuring protection and peace of mind.

A brief statement might be:

For a once-in-a-lifetime special, we offer prestigious homes in a secluded setting. The area is protected by a fence.

This is a factual statement, but not one to encourage sales because the mood has been changed.

The story and mood of a romance novel could be summarized in a thousand words or less, but readers prefer a thousand pages of intriguing detail.

Getting back to formal and business writing, the consensus of language experts is that short, clear sentences are more informative than long descriptions. The following are examples of how you can improve fuzzy sentences. They cover a wide variety of subjects and situations:

Fuzzy: You said I could pick out any kind of dress *that* I wanted.

Clear: You said I could pick out any kind of dress I wanted.

Fuzzy: The Eagles Group will meet at 2:30 P.M. on June 18, 19__. You are invited to join us *on that date* in Logan Hall.

Clear: The Eagles Group will meet at 2:30 P.M. on June 18, 19__. You are invited to join us in Logan Hall.

Fuzzy: This is true only *in the case* where supervision is lacking.

Clear: This is true only where supervision is lacking.

Fuzzy: Our experience has proved valuable in these *types of* cases.

Clear: Our experience has proved valuable in these cases.

Fuzzy: The problem is attributable to *various causes such as* low paid workers, lack of supervision and racism.

Clear: The problem is attributable to low pay, lack of supervision and racism.

Fuzzy: The potholes are located *in all portions* of the parking lot.

Clear: The potholes are located throughout the parking lot.

Fuzzy: The new form is for *your use in* reporting daily absenteeism.

Clear: The new form is for reporting daily absenteeism.

Fuzzy: This report must be completed *in advance* before we receive new computers.

Clear: This report must be completed before we receive new computers.

The next group of sentence revisions involves not only single words but also phrases and complete sentences.

Fuzzy: After reviewing details of your personnel records and interviewing new employees, as well as those who have been with us over two years, I conclude that your analysis of excess turnover of employees is correct.

Clear: Your analysis of our employee turnover rate is correct.

Fuzzy: It is my personal opinion, and only my personal opinion, based on my personal observations that worker fatigue increases and therefore efficiency decreases when workers are required to work twelve hours during each day.

Clear: A twelve-hour day reduces worker efficiency.

Fuzzy: It is requested that parts of this application that are marked confidential remain confidential for the reason that they contain confidential information.

Clear: The confidential parts of this application must not be released.

Fuzzy: Your check in the amount of $200.10 payable to the order of Cannon Company has been received.

Clear: Your check for $200.10 payable to Cannon Company was received January 10, 19__.

Fuzzy: Due to the fact that you arrived late, you did not get preferred seating.

Clear: Because you arrived late, no preferred seating was available.

Fuzzy: I would like to take this opportunity to congratulate you,

Clear: Congratulations!

Fuzzy: I will pay the time sales prices of items charged to my account, consisting of (a) the cash sales prices, plus (b) finanace charges computed by applying to the adjusted balance (the unpaid balance of the cash sales prices and the unpaid finance charges at the beginning of my monthly billing periods, less any payments and credits during the respective billing periods) monthly periodic rates of 1½% on the portion of the adjusted balance not exceeding $500 and 1% on any excess over $500 (subject to a minimum charge of $1.50 on an adjusted balance of $10 to $37).

This is *one* sentence. The only way to improve this confusing legal statement is to divide it into short, understandable sentences. Here is one possibility:

Clear: I will pay the "time" sales prices of items charged to my account. The "time" prices consist of the cash sales prices plus unpaid finance charges. Unpaid finance charges are those remaining at the start of each billing period less payments and credits during the billing period. A monthly charge of 1½% will be made on the unpaid amount due up through $500. A 1% monthly charge will be made on unpaid amounts above $500. The minimum monthly charge, however, is $1.50 on unpaid amounts due ranging from $10 to $37.

Fuzzy: This is to confirm our telephone conversation of December 1, 19__ wherein we notified your office of our desire for contacting this office prior to honoring Abbott's revolving fund V.O. No. 11721.

Clear: This is to confirm our phone conversation of December 1, 19__. Please contact this office before honoring our V.O. No. 11721.

Fuzzy: For our silent auction we need new items for this sale, like maybe a gift you received but it really doesn't fit in your house or it just isn't you. Also antiques or hand-made items. Any item would be appreciated.

Clear: For our silent auction we need new items, antiques or hand-made crafts.

Fuzzy: Fourteen of the group are dedicated to providing for caregivers of invalids, and they took a special training course given by another group so they can do the job well.

Clear: Fourteen of the group are dedicated and trained to provide help for caregivers of invalids.

Fuzzy: Our thanks to Jean who each month spends hours in the typing of this publication.

Clear: Our thanks to Jean who each month spends hours typing this publication.

Fuzzy: Awareness is the best tool in the battle against the polysyllabic fog which threatens to smother lucid prose. (*Waterbury Republican-American*)

Clear: Clarity in writing requires an awareness of your writing style.

Fuzzy: There is a library cart located in the social hall. The most recent books are on the shelves of the cart.

Clear: A library cart holding our most recent books is in the social hall.

Fuzzy: He is a cabinet maker. He specializes in refinishing kitchen cabinets.

Clear: He is a cabinet maker specializing in refinishing kitchen cabinets.

Fuzzy: We were watching the distant haze that resembled the color of smoke.

Clear: We watched the distant, smoke-colored haze.

Fuzzy: Mr. Roberts is the supervisor in the department of finance.

Clear: Mr. Roberts is the financial supervisor.

Fuzzy: The thing that caused the accident was the water on an oil-slicked road.

Clear: The accident was caused by a wet road.

Fuzzy: A visit to the halfway house was made by the president of our youth-charities group.

Clear: The president of our youth-charities group visited the halfway house.

Fuzzy: In the middle of the month of July a heat wave was threatening the lives of elderly people who lived in the desert areas.

Clear: In mid-July a heat wave threatened the lives of elderly people living in the desert.

Fuzzy: As far as sexism and sexual harassment are concerned, it seems to me that women can be as guilty as men.

Clear: Women are as guilty of sexual harassment as men.

Fuzzy: Josie is one of those people of whom there are very few in this world like her.

Clear: Few people are like Josie.

All too frequently writers find themselves adding detail to a presentation by using long phrases. The hope is to clarify the meaning. The writers may be impressed by their own pomposity, but the added words steal the reader's time. Here are a number of wordy expressions with their clear equivalents:

Wordy	*Clear*
according to our records	we find
afford an oportunity	let
afford an opportunity to	allow

Wordy	*Clear*
am in receipt of	have
an oral presentation	talk
are in the opinion of	believe
as per our telephone conversation	as we discussed
at the present writing	now
at this juncture	now
attached herewith is	here is
before long	soon
by the same token	similarly
currently prevailing	present
despite the fact that	although
due to the fact that	because
during the time that	while
facts and figures	data
failed to	didn't
firstly	first
for the reason that	because
has the ability to	can
I feel	(omit this phrase)
inasmuch as	because
in accordance with	by
in addition	also
in connection with	concerning
incumbent upon	must
in lieu of	instead
in receipt of	have
in reference to	about
in regard to	about
in spite of the fact that	although
in sufficient number of	enough
in the case of	if
in the event of	if
in the event that	if
in the majority of instances	usually

Wordy	*Clear*
in the near future	soon
in the neighborhood of	about
in view of the fact	because
in view of the foregoing circumstances	therefore
irregardless	regardless
it has come to my attention	(omit this phrase)
it is apparent therefore that	hence
it is interesting to note that	(omit this phrase)
it is requested	please
I think	(omit this phrase)
I would appreciate it if	please
limited number	few
on account of the fact that	because
on the basis of	by
prior to	before
provided that	if
relative to	about
relating to	about
somewhere in the neighborhood of	about
stepped off of	stepped off
subsequent to	after
thanking you in advance	(omit this phrase)
this office	we, us
with reference to	about
with the result that	so
you are in fact quite correct	you are right

Transitions in Sentences

The purpose of a transition is to tie one idea to another. Transitions are words or phrases that carry the reader smoothly from one idea to the next, and therefore they should be placed near the beginning of a sentence. For example:

Joe exercises regularly. However, his legs are weak.

When you see the word *however* at the beginning of the second sentence, you know that a contrasting thought is coming, but without the transition, the second sentence below seems to jump to another idea. The first sentence implies a strong body, while the second does not.

Joe exercises regularly.

His legs are weak.

The physical construction of a sentence or sentences can sometimes cause confusion that could easily be eliminated with a simple transitional phrase, as in this example about some Japanese realizing that the end of the war with the United States must be negotiated:

Though officials were eager for peace, few were willing to sue for it, certainly not the U.S. Military factions were ready to stage assassinations or a coup if bureaucrats tried such a move.

At a first quick reading, this appears to be one sentence through the words *military factions*. Then confusion reigns: who *were ready to stage assassinations*? Going back, the reader finally realizes that the period after U.S. serves two purposes: to indicate an abbreviation of United States and to end a sentence. Only then does the reader realize that *Military* is not part of the first sentence.

To clarify the second sentence, begin it with: "Japanese military factions were ready . . ."

Another example of physical construction causing confusion:

According to the Census Bureau, in 1994 8.7 percent of Americans were born in other countries.

Although a space is left between the *4* and the *8*, the proximity of two numbers with different purposes is confusing. Better: "In 1994, according to the Census Bureau, 8.7 percent . . ."

Here is another illustration of a missing transition:

While writing the final papers for the sale of my condominium, with a selling price of $70,000, my sales agent was commenting on the difficulty she was having getting sellers and potential buyers to agree on actual prices for $350,000 houses.

Then she said, "I'm not getting much commission, but I always say a sale is a sale."

I was puzzled. Six percent of $350,000 is $21,000—and that is "not much commission?"

Finally, I realized that the agent had shifted her thoughts from the expensive houses to my condo sale, on which she had to share half the sales commission with another agent who actually made the sale. She got half the commission for listing the condo. True, three percent of $70,000 is only $2,100, "not much commission" compared to $21,000.

My agent had not made a transition in her comments from the $350,000 houses to my $70,000 condo. She could have said, "I'm not getting a large commission on *this* sale, but then, a sale is a sale, and a little is better than nothing."

The following are a few purposes served by transitional words and the relationship they imply:

To indicate a consequence or result:

accordingly	consequently
as a result	hence
clearly	therefore

Janet invested more time and money; *consequently*, she realized greater rewards.

To indicate sequence:

finally	second
first	then
next	third

We crawled and shot our way to the top of the hill. *Finally*, we routed the enemy.

To present a summary:

briefly	in short
in conclusion	to conclude
in other words	to sum up

This presentation was detailed, I know, but *to sum up*, here are three thoughts to take with you.

To restate an idea:

for exmaple	specifically
for instance	to be exact
more precisely	to illustrate

You should do an honest day's work for an honest day's pay. *Specifically,* arrive a quarter hour early, shorten your lunch period by ten minutes and put away your tools after quitting time.

To express addition or a new idea:

also	in addition
besides	likewise
furthermore	moreover

Jerry normally worked a twelve-hour day five days a week. *Furthermore,* he taught tennis and conducted a Bible class on weekends.

To relate a contrast:

however	on the other hand
in contrast	still
nevertheless	yet

Annette was taking a full load of college studies. *Still* she insisted on working the swing shift at an electronic assembly plant.

To indicate time:

after that	meantime
before	now
later	when

Don changed the oil in his car. *After that* he washed his new "toy."

This subject of transitions will be examined further in Chapter 6, "Sensible Paragraphs." Smooth-reading paragraphs require transitions between words, between sentences and between paragraphs themselves.

Writing Jargon

Jargon is a special, and sometimes highly technical, language used by occupational groups. It is often a shortcut language among those who understand it.

Here is a short example:

You may now use A75C.

This was a memo sent to branch accountants from headquarters. Many branch accountants phoned to ask what an A75C was. They were told it was the new form for reporting monthly sales discounts. Numerous forms were used each month for reporting various accounting data.

Another example: A manufacturer's spokesman said, "We're now a product-focused operation. . . . We will remain one of the industry's leading suppliers with the broadest portfolio in the industry."

Did "broadest portfolio" mean largest variety of products? Probably.

There are reasons for not using jargon when communicating. Readers not familiar with the technical field involved just don't understand what you are talking about. To those readers, jargon often doesn't make you sound professional, but rather insecure in your subject. Also, you may appear condescending to those who don't understand.

The rest of this section gives you some jargon that applies to a variety of fields, and examples of its misuse.

Business:

There is a contribution to corporate prosperity resulting from the interchange of machinery and equipment as an alternative to the purchase of new assets.

This means transferring machinery to another plant is cheaper than buying new machinery.

The company must respond to technological transitions and have inventory underway for a timely response to demand.

This means the company must increase its inventory.

The industry is at a stage of maturity where we should ask customers to pay for commitments. We're past the time for a backlog on the books that gets canceled.

In other words, customers who order goods must pay part of the price even if the order is canceled.

Our computer chips will enhance a broad spectrum of products.

More simply, we will increase our variety of computer chips.

The resident manager of a national corporation responding to a reporter's question of why the manager disliked his plant location said:

We lack vendors in certain *aspects* of our supply needs.

Better: We lack vendors in certain *areas* of our supply needs.

Better: We lack convenient vendors for some of our supply needs.

The closest definition of *aspect* that could relate to this quote is: the appearance or interpretation of an idea, problem or situation as considered from a specific viewpoint.

Thus the word *aspect* seems to be correctly used, but it also seems to be intentionally foggy and showy business jargon.

Academics:

The reviewer of a book on management describes the book as an antibusiness tract passing as academic research. He criticizes the author for making vague statements like:

The most important conceptual requirement for alteration is the availability
of a legitimating appearance for the whole sequence of transformation.

This probably means changes can be made when resources become available. The Aztec school district defines *action plan* in these words:

A detailed description of the specific actions required to achieve specific
results necessary for the implementation of the strategies.

In simpler words, an *action plan* is a plan to arrive at desired results.
The same school district defines *objectives* as:

What the organization must achieve if it is to accomplish its mission and
be true to its beliefs; the commitment to achieve specific, measurable
results.

Why not define *objectives* as specific goals?

Economy:

Three investment firms were accused of deceptive advertising in 1993 by New York City's Department of Consumer Affairs. An article writer stated that mutual fund ads are routinely cleared by the National Association of Security Dealers, but NYC's Department of Consumer Affairs charged that many ads are written in financial jargon that consumers might not understand.

Here is one example of that financial jargon. It is an excerpt from the testimony of an economist at a congressional hearing. No attempt will be made to translate this statement into understandable English:

It is a tricky problem to find the particular calibration and timing that would be appropriate to stem the acceleration in risk premiums created by falling incomes without prematurely absorbing the decline in the inflation-generated risk premiums.

Government:

Here is an example of foggy governmental writing. I have no idea what the writer is trying to say.

The program-year rate of price change is the sales-weighted average of the percentage changes of a company's product price measured from the last calendar or fixed quarter completed prior to October 2, 1978, through the same quarter of 1979.

Another fuzzy statement:

The involved document, though clothed in diplomatic costume, is no more than a transmittal note and is, thus, of no decisional significance.

Perhaps this means your memo is unimportant.

The next example of governmental jargon appears to be translatable into a simple statement.

From the standpoint of regional growth management, the magnitude of this development and the uncertainties inherent in the population growth scenarios pose serious economic problems.

This seems to say that population growth increases economic problems.

The Clinton administration's proposed health care plan covered 1,300 pages. Here is just one sentence from that document:

(B) FAMILY.—In the case of an individual enrolled under a health plan under a family class of enrollment (as defined in section 1011(c)(2)(A)), the family out-of-pocket limit on cost sharing in the cost sharing schedule offered by the plan represents the amount of expense that members of the individual's family, in the aggregate, may be required to incur under the plan in a year because of general deductible, separate deductibles, copayments, and coinsurance before the plan may no longer impose any cost sharing with respect to items or service covered by the comprehensive benefit package that are provided to any member of the individual's family, except as provided in subsections (d)(2)(D) and (e)(2)(D) of section 1115.

The following is a suggested rewrite using four sentences:

(B) FAMILY.—The requirements for an individual enrolled in a health plan that is included under a family enrollment classification are defined in section 1011(c)(2)(A). The total family cost will not exceed the sum of the individual family member's costs. These costs include general and specific deductibles, copayments, and coinsurance required by the insurance plan. Exceptions are provided in subsections (d)(2)(D) and (e)(2)(D) of section 1115.

Insurance:

The St. Paul Fire and Marine Insurance Company of St. Paul, Minnesota, improved the readability of their insurance policies, and provided the following example:

Old policy: Unless otherwise provided in writing added hereto, this company shall not be liable for loss occurring (a) while the hazard is increased by any means within the control of knowledge of the insured; or (b) while a described building, whether intended for occupancy by owner or tenant, is vacant or unoccupied beyond a period of sixty consecutive days; or (c) as a result of explosion or riot, until fire ensue, and in that event, for loss by fire only.

New policy: You must keep your building and property in as safe a condition as possible. If you are aware of a condition under your control that increases the risk of loss, we'll suspend your coverage while the hazard exists. We'll reinstate your coverage as soon as the hazard is removed. You may leave a covered building unoccupied but you must not leave a covered building vacant for more than 60 consecutive days or we won't be liable for your loss.

Legal:

One company's legal department requested that the following revised Equal Opportunity clause be printed on each purchase order:

EQUAL OPPORTUNITY. The provisions of section 202 of Executive Order 11246, as amended, the Affirmative Action Clause for Handicapped 41 CFR-60-741.4 and Affirmative Action Clause for Disabled Veterans of the Vietnam Area, 41 CFR 60-2504 relative to equal employment opportunity and the rules and regulations issued thereunder are hereby incorporated herein. Seller agrees to comply with same unless exempted.

The essence of this statement is that in regard to Equal Opportunity Employment we, the buyers, are law-abiding citizens and we assume that you, the sellers, are also.

The Federal Trade Commission required that the following notice be sent to holders of consumer credit contracts:

> Any holder of this consumer credit contract is subject to all claims and defenses which the debtor could assert against the seller of goods or services obtained pursuant hereto. Recovery hereunder by the debtor shall not exceed amounts paid by the debtor hereunder.

This means the customer may claim that goods or services purchased are defective, but can collect no more than was paid.

At one time I asked an attorney who was preparing a will for me why legal documents were couched in old fashioned and confusing language. He replied that judges rely heavily on precedent, and therefore if certain language was acceptable in the past, it most likely will be acceptable now. Therefore attorneys write in language the courts will approve.

Library:

The serious and staid Library of Congress has joined the ranks of Washington bureaucratese writers (*Arizona Republic*, February 8, 1986). The Library informed journalists that it had begun:

> reconfiguration of the subject authorities product line.

The reporter guessed that meant the Library was making sure it had identified the precise expertise of authorities on various subjects.

The Library also announced:

> Subject headings in our *Microfilm Quarterly*, cumulative microfiche publication, will continue to be issued.

This seems to mean that a quarterly publication will continue to use subject headings.

Military:

The Persian Gulf War of 1991 produced a rash of rich euphemisms according to the National Council of Teachers of English. Its chairman of the Committee on Public Doublespeak, professor William Lutz of Rutgers University, revealed these misleading subtleties:

efforts	bombing attacks
weapon systems	warplanes
force packages	warplanes
visiting a site	bombing mission
hard targets	buildings to be bombed
soft targets	people to be bombed
degraded	killed
neutralized	killed
attrited	killed
suppressed	killed
cleansed	killed
sanitized	killed
servicing the target	killing

The Teachers' Council said war was hell on words, paraphrasing a statement attributed to General Sherman during an address at the Michigan Military Academy of June 19, 1879, when he said, "War is hell."

Space:

In 1986 the National Council of Teachers of English gave their Doublespeak Award to the National Aeronautics and Space Administration (NASA) for this gem:

> The normal process during the countdown is that the countdown proceeds, assuming we are in a go posture, at various points during the countdown, we tag up the operational loops and face-to-face in the firing room to ascertain the facts that project elements that are monitoring the data and that are understanding the situation as we precede are still in the go direction.

No wonder the Russians beat the United States into space.

Political:

At a meeting to provide newspaper reporters with background on the problems of narcotics being sent across the Mexico–U.S. border, a Washington bureaucrat was asked how long the border would be watched. His reply:

> It depends on how long it takes for the effectuality of the effectiveness to become effectuated—effectively.

He probably meant to say, "Until the problem is solved," or, "As long as it takes to do the job."

Sports:

Sportscasters on radio and television are often butchers of the English language. Here is a paraphrase of one episode heard by Nickie McWerter of the Knight-Ridder newspapers:

> Nearly every other play in the football game was a "key" play. How could so frequent an occurance be "key"? A "nickle" formation turned out to be five players lined up like five pennies. Cute? When the sportscaster screamed, "That was an audible!" he twisted an adjective into a noun. Then he went even further and spun that adjective into a verb by noting, "The quarterback audibled that last play." The game ended with the comment that, "Minnesota outphysicaled the Wolverines [Michigan] today."

Perhaps we could call this "fumbling" the English language.

Social Security:

In a pamphlet directed to ordinary citizens becoming eligible for Social Security, one topic is titled, "What Doesn't Count as Earnings." One of the listed items is:

> Income from self-employment received in a year after the year a person becomes entitled to benefits which is not attributable to services performed after the month of entitlement.

My first reaction to this item was, "What say?" Having read it many times since, I now say, "I don't understand."

The rest of this section on jargon consists of words that have special meaning to people involved in the occupations of accounting, retailing, computers and paper manufacturing. Some of the words mean the same in general use as in their technical use.

Accounting	*Retailing*
accrual	book inventory
balance sheet	clearance sale
cash reconciliation	cost basis
check reconciliation	counter stock
check voucher	discount
cost center	display

Accounting

credit

debit

inventory control

journal

journal voucher

ledger

profit and loss statement

profit center

voucher

Retailing

layaway

markdown

markup

overstock

price basis

physical inventory

retail price

Computer Industry

Apple Macintosh

PC

CD-ROM

chip

cyberspace

dot-coms

e-mail

gigabyte

hard drive

hardware

Internet

laser printer

megahertz

software

Windows

Paper Manufacturing

black liquor

calenders

chips

digester

dry end

dry felt

Fourdrinier

groundwood

jordan

king roll

pulp

queen roll

screen

wet end

wet felt

Viewpoint

Viewpoint as explained and illustrated in this section is limited to the need to maintain one, and only one, point of view in each sentence.

Viewpoint is often unintentionally changed in sentences. Review your sentences to correct changes in subject, tense, mood, voice, person, number, perspective, metaphors and formality.

Subject:

Wrong: *Mr. Babbit* is a CPA, but *engineering* is more than a hobby for him.

Subject is shifted from Mr. Babbit to engineering.

Right: *Mr. Babbiit* is a CPA, but *he* also works as an engineer.

Wrong: *Construction* of the stadium was thirty days ahead of schedule, and project director *Evans* should receive the credit.

Subject shifted from construction to Evans.

Right: *Construction* of the stadium was thirty days ahead of schedule, and *it* was due to the management skills of the project manager, Mr. Evans.

Tense:

Wrong: Tim *awoke* to a noise at midnight and *runs* downstairs.

Tense is changed from past, awoke, to present, runs.

Right: Tim *awoke* to a noise at midnight and *ran* downstairs.

Wrong: Johnny *ate* green apples and *gets* a stomachache.

Shifts from past to present tense.

Right: Johnny *ate* green apples and *got* a stomachache.

Mood:

Wrong: *Report* to Mrs. Alieto now, then you *will be assigned* to a post.

Shift from imperative mood, a command or request, to the indicative, a statement of fact or question.

Right: *Report* to Mrs. Alieto now, and *get* a post assignment from her.

Wrong: The sun *is shining*, but I wish it *were* warmer.

Shift from indicative mood, a statement of fact, to subjunctive mood, a wish or supposition or doubt.

Right: The sun *is shining*, and soon it *will warm* the air.

Voice:

Wrong: Bobby *kicked* the football, and the receiver *was tackled* by Ken.

Kicked is in the active voice; the subject performed the action. *Was tackled* is in the passive voice, indicating that the receiver was acted upon.

Right: Bobby *kicked* the football, and Ken *tackled* the receiver.

Wrong: The Westside Opera *was receiving* new stage settings, and Rosalita *signed* a new contract.

The first verb is passive, being acted upon, and the second active, doing the acting.

Right: The Westside Opera *was receiving* new stage settings and *was signing* Rosalita to a new contract.

Person:

Wrong: Before Christmas, *I* "shopped until I dropped"; then *they* sat down to a big dinner.

Shifting from first person, I, to third person, they.

Right: Before Christmas *I* "shopped until I dropped"; then *I* joined Ethel and her friends for a big dinner.

Wrong: Please go home now, and *we* can pick you up later.

The second person, *you*, is implied at the beginning of this sentence, and *we* is first person.

Right: Please go home now, and *you* will be picked up later.

Number:

Wrong: Take an *umbrella* because *they* may be needed tonight.

Shift from singular, umbrella, to plural, they.

Right: Take an *umbrella* because *it* may be needed tonight.

Wrong: Take several golf *balls; it* will be needed if any are lost.

Shift from plural, balls, to singular, it.

Right: Take several *balls; they* will be needed if any are lost.

Perspective:

Wrong: The patio cover was painted a cheerful yellow, and John's Landscaping added some decorative rocks.

An unexpected shift occurs between the colorful patio and John's Landscaping; a transition is needed.

Better: The patio cover was painted a cheerful yellow *and was enhanced by* the addition of decorative rocks.

Wrong: Pedro painted his car a sparkling metalic blue; no striping would be added.

As in the above example, a transition is needed to smooth the reader's thinking from sparkling blue paint to horizontal side striping.

Better: Pedro painted his car a sparkling metalic blue *but thought it didn't need the added decoration* of side striping.

Metaphors and Similes:

Metaphors and similes are figures of speech comparing two things. Similes are usually introduced by *like* or *as*: Her eyes sparkle like blue diamonds. Metaphors are *implied* comparisons: Her eyes are sparkling blue diamonds.

These figures of speech can be colorful additions to informal communications, but do not use them in business or formal writing. In business a machine called a crane is not described as an "awkward giraffe" but as a machine with a long, movable, projecting arm for lifting.

Similes illustrated:

Sightseers flocked around the TV truck like buzzards around a dead animal.

Like zombies, the audience sat motionless.

His voice boomed like a jet plane breaking the sound barrier.

She moved as gracefully as a swan on a mirrored pond.

Metaphors illustrated:

Viewed from outer space, the earth is a round ball covered with loose cotton.

The Pentagon refused comment about security measures.

Knee surgery is no Sunday afternoon tea party.

Janet has joined the track team; she is a real gazelle.

Do not mix metaphors; the comparisons can be out of place.

Wrong: Don rode his high school laurels to the college football team.

Wrong: Thirsty and sunburned, the desert wanderers felt lost at sea.

Wrong: Potielo took the reins of the ship of state.

Wrong: Amelita pirouetted like a bull in a china shop.

Do not mix formal with informal or colloquial styles; it makes the writer's viewpoint inconsistent.

Formal:

Under attack from hard-liners, Yasser Arafat defended a new peace agreement with Israel that gives his people control over one-third of the West Bank and some of the trappings of statehood.

Informal:

Under attack from hard-headed obstructionists, Yassar Arafat stood up for a new peace agreement with Israel that lets his people do things their own way over one-third of the West Bank and have some of the good-ies of owning their own country.

Variety

Variety in sentences improves interest and readability.

Long sentences:

A long, complicated sentence can be difficult for the reader, and even though the words flow smoothly, the meaning can become confusing. For example, here is one sentence containing 207 words:

Regarding husband's assets as separate property, the wife agrees that the property owned or acquired by the husband shall remain the separate property of the husband, and agrees that this property shall include, but not be limited to, proceeds or income of all property whether real or personal, owned by the husband at the effective date of this Agreement, all property acquired by husband out of the proceeds or income from property owned at the effective date of this Agreement or attributable to appreciation in value of such property, whether the enhancement is due to market conditions or to the services, skills, or efforts of the husband, all property acquired by husband by gift, bequest, devise or inheritance or income from such property attributable to appreciation in value of such property whether the enhancement is due to market conditions or the ser-vices, skills or efforts of the husband and all property hereafter acquired by the husband out of earnings or by virtue of the services, skills or efforts of the husband, and the wife, individually and the parties hereto, as mem-bers of the marital community to be formed, do hereby gift to the husband any interest that they might have in and to said property.

Lengthly sentences can cause problems of agreement between subject and verb. Review long sentences to make sure the *main subject* and the *main verb* agree in number: singular or plural. There should be no problem with short sentences.

Correct: The *use is* clear.

Correct: The *oranges are* ripe.

Wrong: The old, bent *farmer* along with several relatives and hired hands *were* going to pick the oranges.

Better: The old, bent *farmer was* going to pick oranges with the help of his relatives and hired hands.

Correct: The safety *concern* caused by too few stoplights, narrow streets, unmarked pedestrian crosswalks and no turn-out lanes at intersections *was* placed on the August city council agenda.

Short sentences:

In contrast, a string of short sentences can become irritating, as in this example:

Communicate thoughts in business letters. Put aside efforts at "perfect" English.

Each business letter should cover only one subject. For two subjects use two letters.

Include topic and summary sentences when writing a paragraph of literature. Keep business-letter paragraphs short. One sentence can be a complete paragraph.

It would be better to write:

In a business letter, the thought communicated is more important than "correct" English.

For the convenience of the reader, cover two separate subjects with two separate letters.

Literary writing often has long paragraphs that include topic and summary sentences, but this is not necessary in business letters. One sentence is often long enough.

In contradiction to what has been said so far, when you become as successful at writing as Ernest Hemingway, you can get by with short sentences in literary works. Here is one paragraph from Hemingway's *The Old Man and the Sea.* It is some of the fisherman's thoughts after he hooked a large fish.

But he seems calm, he thought, and following his plan. But what is his plan, he thought. And what is mine? Mine I must improvise to his because of his great size. If he will jump I can kill him. But he stays down forever. Then I will stay down with him forever.

Length variations:

One way to elicit the interest of the reader is to add variety to the length of sentences. We have mentioned the problem of understanding overly long sentences and of reading short, choppy sentences. A judicious use of long, short and variously structured sentences is required. This is an example:

> A termination of employment letter must be positive. Leave no doubt in the reader's mind that he or she is being fired. The first question that comes to the reader's mind is, "Why me?" This must be explained in order to make the letter complete. The explanation must sound reasonable and plausible, as well as being true, so the employee's goodwill (as much as possible under the circumstances) is retained. Terminating an employee is an integral part of any business, but it is also a painful experience for both parties. Treat the situation as even-handedly as possible. This can be done by including all the following points in the termination letter: 1. state regrets at having to terminate the employee, 2. state the fact of termination, 3. explain why the decision to terminate was made, 4. make a comment that will retain the employee's goodwill, and 5. end on a note of encouragement.

As a general rule a sentence should contain from fifteen to twenty words. This length keeps the reading easy and is long enough for a single thought. But too many sentences of the same length become monotonous. Throw in a short, snappy sentence or a question to wake up the reader. An occasional longer sentence may explain some detail more coherently than a series of short ones. Use a variety of lengths and styles, as in this example:

> Most employees delight in criticizing their supervisors. But wait. Perhaps it's time to stop and think what your supervisor has done right: a helpful hand when you were behind in your work, a suggestion for making a task easier, no complaining when he found you made an error. Should you smile and thank your supervisor? Yes. Say, "Thank you for your help."

One-word sentences:

In special situations a one-word sentence adds punch as well as variety. For example: Stop. Wait. No. Yes. Halt. Why? Here are other uses of one-word sentences:

From a newspaper article:

> The key difference among observers was whether to blame the governor, and some did. Loudly. But even the Attorney General found no link with Governor Symington.

From a book review in *The Atlantic Monthly*, August 1995:

> The first section of the novel concentrates on the futile quest to understand a life that was entirely involuntary, except his will to keep on. Or-

phanage. Farm laborer obliged to marry his wife. Thus his life evolves despite him—and then the war kills him.

Useful techniques:

The rest of this section on variety is devoted to many of the techniques available for making sentence structures varied and interesting to readers.

Periodic sentences:

In a periodic sentence, the main idea is revealed at the end. Usually the familiar subject-verb-object sequence is used, which provides high impact for the point of the sentence. This form allows the use of strong active verbs; it allows a short, crisp sentence to be clear and suspenseful. Some examples:

The boss decided that this week *we will work overtime.*

We worked dilligently.

We completed the *task.*

The *boss congratulated us.*

Only after long hours of trudging over rocks, loose gravel and wet meadows, and swatting a myriad mosquitos *did we stop* for a short snack.

After many hours of difficult breathing because of the altitude, *we stopped for supper.*

The next *day dawned bright and clear.*

Sonja made breakfast.

The coffee *water wouldn't boil.*

The overuse of periodic sentences in one paragraph or article becomes boring. Vary the form.

Parallel structure and repetition:

Parallelism results from the repetition of form or ideas in one sentence.

They ran, they walked, they even crawled to see their idol.

While he studied, she waited tables; while he saw patients, she saw dirty diapers; while he bought stocks, she saved grocery coupons.

More can be learned about parallelism from the section titled "Parallel Word Groups" in Chapter 4.

Subordination:

Because I practiced more than the others, I was assigned first chair in the orchestra.

Jose Gonzales, the fastest runner at our school, came in second in the
regional event.

More on subordination can be found in the section titled "Subordination and
Coordination" in Chapter 3.

Coordination:

I play on the football team and I play on the basketball team.

You will find it in the attic or in the basement.

See the section titled "Subordination and Coordination" in Chapter 3 for more
on this subject.

Add-on sentences:

This is the opposite of periodic sentences in which the main idea is at the
end. In an add-on or cumulative sentence, the main idea is stated at the beginning and is amplified or explained with additional information.

Periodic: *Eppy washed* Ezra's dirty *overalls.*

Add-on: *Eppy washed* Ezra's dirty *overalls* that were splattered with mud
on one side and grease on the other.

Add-on: *Ezra repaired* old *cars*, especially the ones "clean pants" mechanics wouldn't touch.

Add-on: *Ezra didn't mind lying* on his side in the mud under a car because
the mud was soft and Eppy had a washing machine.

Interrupters:

Interrupters can provide interest, information, emphasis—or a reader awak-
ener—to a sentence.

John met Marcia in March of 1985—she was married to Pete Schroeder
at the time—and married her in 1987.

The expanding economy—at least for now according to most economic indicators—will be short lived writes Mr. John Pearson, economist at . . .

Parenthetical inserts can be used to indicate an observation by the author,
which is not essentially a part of the author's commentary or story.

The Board was unanimous in its decision (J. P. Sorbau told me confi-
dentially that he would never vote with the Board on this issue) to close

seven stores next year. Some personnel changes have already been announced.

Almost annual family moves have contributed to the disturbed behavior of the five children. (I know the problem: our family moved regularly every four years while I was growing up.) Two local churches are working together to provide counseling for the family.

Basic types of sentences:

For the sake of interest, vary the types of sentences in a composition.

Rhetorical question:

Why does justice seem blind to the losers in a trial, but an honest system to the winners?

Should professional groups be allowed to strike? school teachers? professional athletes? firemen? doctors?

Exclamations:

It took three years, but Harry finally won!

Congratulations, Harry!

That was the best sales pitch I ever heard!

Imperative:

Take a trip to the museum, and learn something of other cultures.

A college education will give you a good start.

Move up with a postgraduate degree.

A fast walk is good exercise.

Tone:

Tone in writing reveals the emotion in a writer's attitude toward the subject matter and the audience. Attitude toward a subject can vary from formal to casual, from love to hate, from friendly to hostile, from indifferent to enthusiastic. Attitude toward the reader will probably be less volatile than toward the subject, more positive and friendly.

I once wanted to chide a sales manager for submitting reports late month after month. I couldn't outright *demand* action because his rank in the company was one notch higher than mine. I sent him a memo stating that he had won the Sour Apple Award of the Month for being five days late with the salesmen's expense reports. No results. I continued to send him similar memos, each titled Sour Apple Award for April or whatever the month. After four months he got the message. Because he had to approve the reports before sending them to me, he moved up the date he must receive them from the individual salesmen by five days.

Here are examples of the writer's attitude toward his subject matter:

Formal: Discussions with three banks resulted in the selection of the AB-Bank to fund this project because of favorable financing.

Casual: We selected ABBank over two others to fund this project because their lending terms were better.

Love: Nine grandchildren and two daughters celebrated the 80th birthday of Grandma Pepper, a grand old lady cherished by the whole community.

Hate: The whole neighborhood erupted in flames soon after news of the killer and rapist's release became public.

Friendly: Do you suppose, Jack, that by putting in a few more hours each week we could push this project along?

Hostile: Don't you understand, Jack, that what this project needs is a little more effort? Put in a few more hours each week.

Indifferent: If you wish I can get you some help, but if you prefer to go it alone, that's okay.

Enthusiastic: We think this is a great proposal, and I agree you are the right person to carry it forward.

Here are a couple examples of attitudes toward readers:

Friendly: We have had much favorable response to local tours for you shut-ins, and hope you will continue to enjoy the variety of tours we have planned for the fall season.

Formal: Local tours sponsored by the Ladies Help Society for shut-ins at the Retirement Home will continue through November.

Repetition of words:

Repeated words in a sentence can add emphasis. Also, at times the repetition of a word clarifies a statement that becomes awkward while attempting to avoid repeating a word.

Dull: "Big John" was captain of the football team and was also the basketball captain and headed the baseball team and was co-captain of track.

Emphatic: "Big John" was captain of the football, basketball and baseball teams and co-captain of the track team.

Dull: Andre sacrificed his life for Theresa and lost his professional standing and the money he worked so hard to obtain.

Emphatic: For his love of Theresa, Andre sacrificed his profession, his
wealth and his very life.

Awkward: When patients see something like a Medicare overbilling and
the government is able to collect back that money, they should get a
small percentage of that savings they are responsible for.

Clear: When a patient discovers a Medicare overbilling and the government recovers the overbilled amount, the patient should receive a portion of the recovered amount.

Awkward: October is the season for falling leaves and trees turning colorful and the ground being covered with the dead, brown ones.

Clear: In October the maple leaves turn to beautiful yellows and reds
before turning brown and fluttering to the ground.

Alliteration—sound repetition:

Alliteration is the repetition of close consonants: rack and ruin, wild and
wooly, click and clack, willy-nilly. Use alliteration sparingly in formal and business writing. Advertisers, however, have used it with great success: time tested;
livin' it, lovin' it; cash and carry; don't risk it, Whisk it; whiter and brighter.

Bad: The pompous promoter promised better built bungalows for lower
class lovers of leisure.

Better: The home builders promised better constructed small houses for
lower-income families.

Bad: Steve was Carl's closest neighbor, in the same grade in school, and
they shared a liking for hiking through the woods and climbing trees.

Better: Steve was Carl's closest neighbor, in the same grade in school,
and they shared a fondness for hiking through the woods and climbing
trees.

Word order variations:

An occasional change from subject-verb-object order of words can improve
your writing. It can take the monotony out of short or straightforward sentences,
and can put emphasis on the most important word or idea. In the following
groups of sentences, the important word or idea is shown in parentheses:

Love is taught by parents. (parents)

Parents can teach their children love. (love)

To learn love, a child is dependent upon parents and teachers. (parents
and teachers)

Parents and teachers are primarily responsible for what children learn about love. (love)

Learning to love is the responsibility of each child. (child)

Learning to love is a child's responsibility. (responsibility)

Love is a responsibility each child must learn. (learn)

Machine A stopped running. George, the foreman, will report the stoppage to Joe at the maintenance department. The maintenance crew will repair machine A. (repair machine A)

When machine A stopped, George reported it to Joe who will get the machine fixed. (get machine fixed)

Joe will have his crew repair machine A because its stoppage was reported by foreman George. (foreman George)

Machine A is down and it won't be fixed until George reports the incident to the maintenance foreman, Joe. (Joe)

One way to make sentences interesting is to start with a phrase and state the subject later. This technique should be used only occasionally lest it become as monotonous as a series of short subject-verb-object sentences.

Along the river bank the trees leaned out over the river to reach the sun.

To become a writer, a person must have persistence above all else.

Staring at the moon, his thoughts turned to Linda.

Waiting for the train, Waal became impatient.

It's a slow process. *But* patience will be rewarded.

At last he was alone. *And* that made him happy.

A man of many abilities, Kardo excelled in many positions.

Always one to exhibit her happiness, Enid became a professional clown.

Suggests a prominent law professor, "Perhaps society has to suffer more before the court system is changed."

States the president, "Next year you will see an expansion of our sales territory."

Apprehensively sitting on the hard bench, Pam waited for the doctor's report on her child.

Carefully watching for gopher holes, Ted trudged on.

Slowly rising on his injured leg, Alban reached for his two canes.

Victory having been assured, the team relaxed.

The principal having been summoned, the boys could only tremble.

Those swimmers, *the advanced team members*, had practiced all summer.

The crowd, *bored by the slow play*, started to leave before the game was
over.

Must we put up with all this silly talk?

Why do we have to work so much overtime?

Because the ice was thin, we dared not venture out beyond three feet.

Due to an increase in cost, the sales price was raised.

One of the most overused modifiers is the word *very*. Eliminate it in almost
every instance.

It was a *very* long day and we were *very* tired of looking at a *very*
large number of African animals even if the zoo was *very* well known as
a *very* good one.

Other adverbs and adjectives can often be eliminated to add spark and clarity
to sentences.

Fuzzy: The *new, timid* secretary *apparently reluctantly* approached her
experienced co-workers when she *really* needed to ask one an *impor-tant* question, or when she was *specifically* told to *quickly* relay im-*portant* information from her *hard-headed* supervisor.

Better: The *timid* secretary *reluctantly* aproached her co-workers when she
needed to ask a question or was told to relay information from her
supervisor.

CHAPTER 6

Sensible Paragraphs

Definition

A paragraph is a complete thought. This follows from one of the definitions of a sentence: a *single* thought. A complete thought usually consists of a group of sentences all of which are related to a central thought, topic or idea. If part of a topic or idea is to be emphasized, it should be placed in a separate paragraph.

The purpose of a paragraph is to make communication with the reader easily understood. A paragraph keeps segments of the composition unified by helping to prevent digressions from the central idea. A new paragraph gives the reader a breathing and thinking break because the reader knows one topic is concluded and another is to begin.

Conversational statements, replies and exclamations can be one-word paragraphs, but in narrative, descriptive or expository writing, a paragraph is a mini-composition, most often written in the order of occurence or observation. Some magazine articles use long, well-developed paragraphs, complete with one or two topic sentences, a detailed development of the topic and a summary statement or two.

Here is an example using a business letter. Sentence 1 is the topic; it refers to disposal of equipment. Middle sentences provide details about the disposal. Sentence 4 summarizes the subject by suggesting action to be taken.

(1) I agree with your letter of March 25, 19__, except for the part referring to disposal of leased equipment. (2) The lease says that so long as the value of the plant is not materially affected, the lessee may dispose

of minor assets without approval of the leasor: (3) In my opinion, $84,000 is not material. (4) To avoid paying property taxes on equipment we do not have, the disposed asset should be removed from the asset register.

If it does not seem appropriate to start a new paragraph with a well-defined topic statement, the paragraph should be introduced with a transitional word or phrase, such as "therefore," "on the other hand" or "in addition." The transition can be at the end of one paragraph or at the beginning of the new paragraph.

At times it is convenient and logical to combine what could be treated as two ideas in one paragraph. For example, a teacher writing about a subject and his or her students. The teacher would discuss how the students reacted to the subject, perhaps mentioning both together in sentences, perhaps telling about one then the other. Or an accountant working for a division of a corporation is concerned about profits of both the division and the corporation. Sometimes interests of these profit centers conflict. A treatise on the subject of profits would include the relationship between division and corporate profits.

Now a short summary of what a paragraph should and should not be. This quote is from Strunk and White's *The Elements of Style*, following a short discourse on overly long paragraphs.

But remember, too, that firing off many short paragraphs in quick succession can be distracting. Paragraph breaks used only for show read like the writing of commerce or of display advertising. Moderation and a sense of order should be the main consideration in paragraphing.

Topic Statements and Outlines

Paragraphs providing information don't need to be formally constructed with a topic statement, details explaining the topic and a summary. They should, however, be written in an orderly manner, with each sentence logically following the preceding one. Here is an example without a topic sentence; however, this memo was headed Mill Burden Charges, which states the topic of the memo.

Effective March 1, 19__, the mill guard service has been expanded to include a roving patrol twenty-four hours per day. As a result of this added security measure your monthly share will be $324. This is based on a daily cost of $108—your share being 10%. You will benefit from the discontinuance of the check writing charge and a reduction in your Accounts Payable charge. The net reduction is $140. Also the volume of invoices that was paid for your account in February approximated the last quarter of 19__. Until we see a substantial reduction in the number of invoices processed, the charge will remain $400 per month.

This is the outline of the memo:

Guard service
    Changes made
    Cost of changes
Checks and Accounts Payable
    Changes made
    Cost of changes
Invoices paid
    No change
    No cost change

The first sentence of the following paragraph is the topic sentence. It refers to a monthly fleet safety newsletter. The topic is developed, and the paragraph is concluded with a convenient source for obtaining additional information.

Beginning March 19__, the Corporate Fleet Safety Department will publish a monthly fleet safety newsletter for distribution to all drivers of Belleson Company vehicles, leased or owned, automobile or truck. To achieve distribution, we need to know the total number of newsletters required for each operating location and to whom they should be sent. As the first issue will be available March 1, we would appreciate receiving this information as near this date as possible. Should there be any questions, please call me on extension 7152, San Mateo.

This is the outline:

New procedure
    New publication
    Distribution of the publication
Request for information
    What information required
    When information required

The next illustration begins with a topic sentence, but the development shows the result of disorganized thinking.

General availability of railroad freight cars throughout the country improved slightly during the week as the weather moderated in the Northeast. We have shortages of high-roof box cars in the Northwest. In addition, the South Bend mill has been short of box cars throughout the week. We expect to clear up the South Bend shortage by Saturday, and we are using standard box cars in lieu of high-roof cars to avoid delays in customer shipments from the Northwest.

The author organized his paragraph this way:

Problem A, Problem B

Solution B, Solution A

The reader's mind has to jump backward three steps to relate Solution A to Problem A. The paragraph would read much easier if the writer had used a logical outline:

Problem A, Solution A

Problem B, Solution B

Then the paragraph would read this way:

General availability of railroad freight cars throughout the country improved slightly during the week as the weather moderated in the Northeast. We have a shortage of high-roof box cars in the Northwest. We are replacing these with standard box cars to avoid delays in customer shipments. In addition, the South Bend mill has been short of box cars throughout the week. We expect to clear up this shortage by Saturday.

Outlining a paragraph before it is written is preferred to doing it afterward. If, however, you feel intimidated by the chore of noting the topic you want to write about, do the writing first. Then see if you can make a logical outline of the paragraph. Probably rearranging a sentence or two will improve the flow of thoughts.

If a topic sentence is included, every sentence that follows must relate to the topic. A statement that potato farming is more exacting than many people believe should not be followed by a statement that learning to swim is not difficult. Hold that for another paragraph or article.

Organization Methods

Following are fifteen ways to develop and expand the topic sentence of paragraphs:

Chronological:

The topic sentence, written or implied, can be explained in many ways. One of the most common is chronologically. Events or observations are described in the order in which they occur or occurred. Here is an example:

Nicky looked about three but acted more like five. He had a soft rubber ball that came nearly to his knees, and he had just learned how to kick it into the air using a beautiful drop-kick technique. Nicky held the ball at chest level, let it drop, and as the ball started to bounce upward, he whapped it with his right foot. The ball rose another three feet and spun forward about four feet. With an ear-to-ear grin, he toddled over the crackling eucalyptus leaves to his ball, picked it up and ran to the next group of oldsters, performing his delightful act again and again, somehow never tiring either his audience or himself.

General to specific:

Another common arrangement of paragraphs is from a general statement to specific details.

The friendly Anna's hummingbirds look quite different from the tiny, bright yellow hummingbirds Carl had known in the Pacific Northwest. The Anna's hummingbirds are about four inches long, and at first glance they appear to be dark gray. Closer inspection with binoculars reveals bronze-green backs, largely black wings and grayish breasts. The bronze-green of the backs varies from a few specks on dark gray to a solid color. The males have a rose-red crown, while the females sport the same rose-red color on their throats. Females have white-tipped outer feathers and rounded tails, while the males have forked tails and lack the touch of white on their feathers.

Specific to general:

A contrasting order for developing paragraphs is from the specific to the general. The paragraph begins with specific details that support the topic sentence, which in this method of development is usually the last sentence.

Right now, the people best equipped to help runaway kids are pimps. Why? Because a pimp can come off like a father figure to a kid who never had much love at home, particularly when she's scared, lonely, and right off the bus. All he needs is a week to break her in, maybe get her hooked on drugs, and put her out to work on the streets. These kids are castoffs from separated parents, alcoholic parents, drug abusing parents and confusing inconsistencies of a pressuring, loveless society. Well-adjusted children need love, especially parental love.

Definition:

A paragraph can define a word or the special meaning of a word used in the composition.

When accountants speak of *accruals* or of an *accrued* expense item, they are referring to an anticipated or expected expense. A gidget may have been received and used this month, but the bill has not been received or not paid. The cost of the gidget, however, should be accrued as an expense of this month, and this is done by recording the expense in the accounting books for this month.

Description:

A description paragraph seems self-explanatory, but here is an example:

Carlin's mother sat on a wobbly apple box, leaning her frail back against a corner post of the shanty. She spent most of her time just sitting when not making the daily trek to the city dump for scraps of food. Carlin asked her mother for the old kitchen knife to cut three corrugated boxes she had found behind the dime store. She cut the corners down and spread the flattened boxes on the dusty dirt floor. Carlin took the faded blue pillow from on top her rolled up blankets and placed it on the floor. Now she could sit cross-legged without smudging her legs in the dirt. She leaned one elbow on an orange crate with two missisng slats. That was the only other furniture in the shack.

Procedure:

A paragraph can describe a step-by-step precedure. The amount of detail required will depend on the knowledge of the reader and whether you wish to present a complete working procedure or merely an overview. Here is a detailed procedure:

One way to take accurate inventory of items in a store, warehouse or storeroom is to use the three-part ticket method. The three parts are numbered the same. A ticket is attached to each item by the first counter. He records the count on the bottom third and takes that to the record keeper. A second person records his count on the middle third of the ticket and takes that part to the record keeper. If the two parts agree, the count is assumed to be correct. If the two parts disagree, a third member, often with an assistant, makes a third count to determine the true count.

Cause and effect:

Causes and their effects can be described in a paragraph. Either can be stated first and then related to the other.

Summer in the desert had been hot and long. Months without rain. The occasional mild breeze only shifted the hot air, not cooling it at all. The leaves in the citrus groves turned brown, shriveled and fell to the ground. Some of the growing fruit also shriveled and dropped. Then a thunderstorm blew in, rain fell, the nights cooled, the wind tore the remaining dried leaves from the trees. Then new, green leaves began to form. The cycle of Mother Nature continued.

Comparison and contrast:

Comparisons and contrasts can make interesting paragraphs.

Parents frequently remark that two of their children are complete opposites. One was inquisitive, opened every door and drawer available. All contents were pulled out and examined. She even opened windows that were supposed to be childproof. She pulled herself up beside chairs at an early age and walked when she was nine months old. The other observed when a door or drawer was opened by her sister or by an adult but didn't bother to open things herself. She observed her sister crawling and walking but she never crawled, or pulled herself up beside a chair. She went directly from a flat-stomach wiggle to walking—all by herself—with no adult help. Both were honor students.

Order of observation:

One way to devlop a paragraph is to mention things observed in the order seen by the writer, such as glancing back and forth, looking to the right in a circle all the way around or from top to bottom as in this example.

Rhea was hardly over five feet tall and slender. A white rose adorned her shoulder-length hair, framing a sharp-featured but attractive face. A corroding locket hung from a thin, chrome-plated chain around her neck. It just reached to the neckline of her dress. "This old dress seems to turn grayer every time I wash it—no soap, no bluing, no bleach." Each tennis shoe had a hole where the little toe rubbed the side.

Problem to solution:

When discussing a problem in a paragraph, the first sentence or two states and perhaps explains the problem. The rest of the paragraph suggests the solution.

During recent months there has been a substantial increase in the dollar amount of rollers purchased rather than manufactured. The effect of this on profit forecasting has contributed to recent large variances between projected and actual earnings. It appears that in some cases we are actually losing money by purchasing rollers. In the future, before a commitment to purchase rollers is made, I want to review the cost, price and profit relationships. My review will continue until I have satisfied myself that these outside purchases are contributing to our profits.

Narrative or story:

A narrative paragraph should include answers to these questions: who? what? where? when? and why?

Looking down the cliff, Steve imagined Carl splattered there like a broken sack of wheat. He had visions of Carl having broken his ankle or his knee or even his head. He could almost see splintered bones poking out through his skin. "I've got to help him," he muttered. "Is he dying? I've got to get down there now." They had been hiking in one of Arizona's desert mountains when Carl slipped.

Viewpoint:

A paragraph should be written from the point of view of only one person. If you are describing events that occur to Jack, you mention his views of his friend Bill and Bill's girlfriend, his car, his happiness and his thoughts and actions. Do not write that Jack enjoyed the view from Green Point then that Bill thinks Jack should repaint his old jalopy and that Bill's girlfriend says it should be painted blue. Shifts in viewpoint can be made only after the reader is informed that a change is coming.

Bad: Jack always enjoyed the view of Sims Valley from Green Point. He drove there with Bill and Bill's girlfriend. Bill had thought for a long time that Jack should repaint his old jalopy. Bill's girl friend wanted Jack to paint it blue—to match her eyes. Jack kept saying that the only color for a Model T is black, as Henry Ford intended.

The viewpoint has shifted from Jack to Bill to Bill's girlfriend, then returns to Jack.

Better: Jack always enjoyed the view of Sims Valley from Green Point. He drove there with Bill and Bill's girl friend. Jack was told many times by Bill that Jack's old jalopy needed repainting, but the response was always that someday he might give it a coat of black, the only right color for a Model T. Jack always scowled when Bill's girl friend teased that it would look nice painted pale blue to match her eyes.

The viewpoint remains that of Jack when his friends make suggestions about painting his car.

Details:

A series of short paragraphs dealing with the same topic should usually be combined.

>   Collection letters are a standard part of the accounts payable collection process.
>   The first notice to the delinquent is usually a copy of the bill with or without a sticker stating "past due" or "have you forgotten" or "second notice."
>   Following this are short letters, each succesively insistent upon payment. Later letters may be longer and appeal to pride or fairness.
>   The final step is turning the account over to a collection agency or to an attorney for legal action.

Each of the above short paragraphs is a separate thought, but none is complete. The first paragraph is a good topic sentence, which is developed by each of the following paragraphs. Combining the four paragraphs would result in one coherent and complete thought.

Short paragraphs in many instances do not supply enough detail to satisfy the reader.

>   Too brief: Theresa Domingo receives my hearty recommendation as an accounts payable clerk. She did excellent work and I wish I had her back.

>   Detailed: Therea Domingo receives my hearty recommendation as an accounts payable clerk. She did excellent work under my supervision during the last six years. She got the bills paid on time and was cooperative and willing to do other assignments, mostly in the area of accounting reports. Her typing is top quality. She was on time and had a better than average attendance record. I wish I had her back.

Paragraph Length

Planning the length:

A paragraph should be mentally planned or outlined before it is written. The length will be determined by what the reader will expect and whether the paragraph is an exclamation, a straightforward statement of fact, a quick summary or a fully developed idea.

Regardless of its length, a paragraph should be easy for the reader to understand. The purpose of a paragraph is to communicate with the reader. One way to consider length is to write what you want to say then stop. This assumes that you have written a complete thought or idea developed to the extent you intend.

However, always keep the reader in mind by using the "you" attitude: what would you like to know if you were the reader?

A full-page, single-spaced letter with no paragraphing can be an intimidating black mass to the reader. This is a letter that will be put aside until time seems less valuable. White space around typed or printed words is essential to easy reading. It provides a break for the eyes and the mind.

Short paragraphs are great for punch or emphasis. The topic is quickly grasped.

We *will* meet this goal.

The company picnic is scheduled for May 12—all day.

Each of you is to be congratulated on your efforts that enabled us to meet the deadline.

On the other hand, too many short paragraphs in one letter or article can fracture a complete thought. Do not cut an idea in two just to make a paragraph shorter.

The shortest paragraph, of course, consists of one word: Stop! Go! Run! Why? These are exclamations written as separate paragraphs to attract attention and to add emphasis. The emphasis can be created by inserting a one-word paragraph in a composition. Here are two examples from newspaper articles:

Now that the guns are silent, what can two battle-scarred, heavily decorated, four-star generals fight over?

Turf.

What turf? The Caribbean Sea.

Where do you Cardinals [the Arizona professional football team] think you are going? Get back in there while you still have a chance to win another game.

Hmmm.

Ecch.

Amid all the sports turmoil, something may or may not be happening to the Cardinals roster.

From a newspaper article by Keven Willey in the *Arizona Republic*:

If you were asked to rattle off one of the most conservative pockets in Arizona, which would you name?

Sun City?

Mesa?

Prescott?

Mohave County?

Good guesses, but there's another one you would probably overlook. It boasts a quieter kind of conservatism, but the agricultural heritage, racial divisions and voting record make it one of the state's most culturally conservative communities.

Yuma.

A sales manager wanting to compliment a salesman for winning a valuable account, wrote him a letter, which would become part of the salesman's personnel record. The entire letter consisted of one word:

Great!

In business letters, one-sentence paragraphs are common:

Just a reminder that your balance of $205.35 is past due.

Thank you for your interest in our new line of lawn mowers.

Please review the enclosed documents and reply by May 30.

I am just a phone call away.

Please mail your last accounting statement to my attention.

We look forward to meeting you for lunch on Thursday.

Parallel construction:

Parallel construction can make long paragraphs easy to read. A rhythm of thought is created that makes the flow of the message easy to follow.

The occasions for sending a letter of good wishes or goodwill are limitless. Send a goodwill letter to a business friend who did you a favor, to a business friend you may be able to help, to a business friend who is also a personal friend, and to a business that has just opened. Send a goodwill letter to celebrate the holiday season and to celebrate a business friend's birthday. Send a goodwill message to honor the marriage of your friend's daughter, or to an acquaintance in the hospital. And send a goodwill letter when there is no special occasion because being remembered is always appreciated.

Variety:

Variety reduces monotony. An occasional short paragraph among long ones breaks the appearance of the page, giving the reader a psychological respite, an eye-resting pause and a thinking intermission.

Transitions within Paragraphs

Two kinds of transitions can improve the readability of paragraphs by enhancing the smooth flow of thoughts. The first type is directional transitions. These indicate where the reader's thoughts are being sent, and they usually occur at the beginning of the sentence or paragraph. The following are selected transitional words that will direct the reader's thoughts:

Addition:

again	in addition
also	in the first place
and	last
at the same time	likewise
besides	moreover
equally important	next
finally	nor
first, second	then
further	third
furthermore	too

In the first place, Joseph has been a politician for thirty years. *Furthermore*, he has been reelected every time he has run. *Also*, he has a reputation of helping his constituents—*and* I like him.

Result:

accordingly	in short
as a result	in that case
as it is	it follows that
at that rate	otherwise
because of that	since
consequently	so
due to this	then
for that reason	therefore
hence	thus
inevitable	wherefore

My brother and I started a fast-paced morning jog. *As a result*, we tired quickly. *Therefore*, we slowed our pace. *Consequently*, we arrived home later than planned, and *thus* found no breakfast waiting for us. *Because of that*, we walked—not jogged—to McDonald's.

Comparison:

alike	in the same way
by the same token	in turn
correspondingly	like that
equally	like this
in comparison	likewise
in like manner	similarly

The accounting department personnel was cut by 10%. *Similarly*, the customer service staff was downsized 12%. *In turn*, the administrative clerical staff was reduced, but only 5%. All departments were not treated *equally*: production was increased about 5%, and *likewise*, sales was expanded 5%.

Concession:

accept	confess
acknowledge	even though
after all	granted
allow	naturally
at the same time	not oppose
certainly	of course
concede	to be sure

I *concede* that Pepper is a better ball handler, and I *acknowledge* his experience *even though* I have had more training. *Certainly*, he will make the team, and I will *not oppose* his efforts to become captain. But I will *not allow* him to intimidate me.

Contrast:

after all	but
adjacent to	conversely
although true	for all that
and yet	here
at the same time	however
beyond	in contrast

in other words	otherwise
nearby	on the contrary
nevertheless	on the other hand
nonetheless	still
notwithstanding	whereas
opposite to	yet

Jenny enjoyed the concert, *but* her mother thought much of it was too loud. *On the other hand,* her father loved the high volume. Her sister was amazed at the performer's fingering technique, *notwithstanding* a couple wrong notes, *whereas* brother Bob was bored.

Example:

for example	such as
for instance	that is
in other words	thus
namely	to illustrate
specifically	to tell the truth

Here, *for example,* are two essential reference books: a dictionary, *such as Webster's Collegiate,* and a thesaurus, *specifically Roget's International.* *To illustrate* their combined use, find a word you like in the thesaurus then verify its exact meaning in the dictionary.

Explanation:

in fact	the reason for
in other words	the why
simply stated	the why and wherefore
the rationale	to explain

The reason for Greta's starting a new career can be *simply stated*: burnout. That *in fact* means she is tired—overly tired. *In other words,* she is no longer stimulated by her work.

Intensification:

in brief	that is
indeed	the fact is
in fact	to be sure

Indeed, we try hard to please out customers. *The fact is* we meet our goal of less than two complaints each month. *In brief*, we work harder than our competitors.

Place:

adjacent	in the foreground
at the side	in the front
beyond	nearby
here	on this side
in back	on the other side
in the background	opposite
in the distance	there

The roses for the yard were placed *in front*. The dahlias were put *in back*. On the *west side* we planted iris, and on the *other side* we started a low hedge. An orange tree was placed *beyond* the dahlias *in back*. *Nearby* was a dwarf lemon tree.

Purpose:

for this purpose	the object is
is designed to	the point is
the aim is	to this end
the function is	with this object

Alvah declared, "I must win the October foot race." *To this end*, he trotted daily for a month. *The object was* to slowly strengthen his muscles. Then he ran for a month, *the aim being* to build up his endurance. *The point of all this* was to impress his girl friend, Adah.

Repetition:

as has been noted	to be sure
as I have said	to recap
in any event	to repeat
in other words	to wrap up
recapitulate	what I mean to say

To repeat my views of children's special education classes, they require dedicated teachers. *As I have said*, most teachers are not qualified. *In other words*, appointing any available teacher can be harmful to the children.

What I mean to say is that special education classes require teachers with special training.

Summary:

as a result	in short
finally	in summary
hence	on the whole
in brief	to conclude
in closing	to summarize
in conclusion	to sum up

As a result of numerous bank consolidations, customers are confused. *Hence*, they are dissatisfied. *On the whole*, the banks may be better off financially, but *in brief*, it's a bad deal for bank customers. To *summarize*, customers want their small, personalized banks back again.

Time sequence:

after	meanwhile
at last	next
at length	now
before	soon
first	then
immediately	the next day
in turn	subsequently
later	ultimately

Doreen had to catch the midnight plane. *First* she found out the departure time, *then* the distance to the airport, *next* the time it would take to drive there. *Subsequently*, she checked the parking situation *before* looking through her purse for small bills to tip the porters. Parking would be paid for *later*. *Now* she had to comb her hair, *then* put on lipstick. Glancing at her watch, she realized she had to dash off *immediately*.

The second type of transition within a paragraph is words that refer back to the same or similar words. This ties the sentence—and the reader's thoughts—together, and creates a smooth-reading paragraph.

The next two paragraphs were quoted earlier in this chapter for the subtopic, "Follow an Outline." The paragraphs also offer excellent illustrations of transitions within paragraphs: each sentence is related to both the preceding and the succeeding ones.

(1) Effective March 1, 19__, the mill guard service has been expanded to include a roving patrol twenty-four hours per day. (2) As a result of this added security measure your monthly share will be $324. (3) This is based on a daily cost of $108—your share being 10%. (4) You will benefit from the discontinuance of the check writing charge and a reduction in your Accounts Payable charge. (5) The net reduction is $140. (6) Also the volume of invoices that was paid for your account in February approximated the last quarter of 19__. (7) Until we see a substantial reduction in the number of invoices processed, the charge will remain $400 per month.

Here is how the sentences relate to each other with smooth transitions:

Sentence 1—roving patrols

Sentence 2—security measures

> Sentence 2—your monthly share

> Sentence 3—your share

Sentence 3—your share

Sentence 4—the check writing charge

> Sentence 4—reduction

> Sentence 5—reduction

Sentence 5—reduction

Sentence 6—volume of invoices that was paid

> Sentence 6—volume of invoices

> Sentence 7—number of invoices

(1) Beginning March 19__, the Corporate Fleet Safety Department will publish a monthly fleet safety newsletter for distribution to all drivers of Belleson Company vehicles, leased or owned, automobile or truck. (2) To achieve distribution, we need to know the total number of newsletters required for each operating location and to whom they should be sent. (3) As the first issue will be available March 1, we would appreciate receiving this information as near this date as possible. (4) Should there be any questions, please call me on extension 7152, San Mateo.

Here is how the sentences link together to make continuous smooth transitions throughout the paragraph:

Sentence 1—for distribution

Sentence 2—to achieve distribution

Sentence 2—number of newsletters required

Sentence 3—the first issue

Sentence 3—this information

Sentence 4—any questions

The following paragraph is a small part of a letter written to constituents by Congressional Representative Jerome R. Waldie while he was still on the Judiciary Committee that was trying former President Nixon. In the paragraph Waldie refers to two people, himself and Richard Nixon. Notice how smoothly thoughts flow back and forth between the two by using the transitional words *Richard Nixon, person, a President, me, private individual, I, personal sympathy, man, him, his family, his, my, human being, Mr. Nixon.*

Even to pass judgment on Richard Nixon as a private person and not as a President presents some difficulty to me. Confronted with Richard Nixon only as a private individual, I would be deeply involved with a sense of personal sympathy for a man whose career and fortunes have proven ultimately tragic, not only for the country, but for him and his family. The extent of his personal responsibility for his plight only slightly mitigates my sympathy for a human being being reduced to the remnants of reputation that Mr. Nixon now possesses.

It is possible, however, to overdo transitional words by too much repetition.

Awkward: I stood at the top of Lund's Hill watching the sun set behind the Olympic Mountains. I had always enjoyed sunsets. This sunset was beautiful. The clouds appeared to be large, square, copper-colored plates forming the inside of a dome over half the sunset-lit sky.

Better: I stood at the top of Lund's Hill watching the sun set behind the Olympic Mountains. The clouds appeared as massive, copper-colored squares forming the inside of a dome covering half the sky. Numerous times I had paused there to absorb Nature's evening beauty. This, without doubt, was the most spectacular reflection of the sun on evening clouds I had ever seen—or have viewed since.

In the "awkward" illustration, the word *sunset* is found in each sentence. This is a tie-it-together transitional word, but it has a hardness that becomes irritating to the ear, or the mind's ear, when repeated so often.

Transitions Between Paragraphs

To make a composition or article coherent it needs transitions between paragraphs as well as within. A smooth transition between paragraphs can reduce the choppiness you may find upon a review of your writing. One way to eliminate disconnected sounds is to use a key word or phrase in the first sentence that refers back to a previous paragraph. A large selection of transitional words and phrases was introduced in the preceding section, "Transitions within Paragraphs." These same words and phrases can also be used between paragraphs.

The following transitional words and phrases were used between paragraphs in the November 1995 issue of *The Atlantic Monthly*:

a growing proportion	naturally
although	none of this
another	nonetheless
at the beginning	one of
beyond	since
but	so
by relying on	some
despite	still
each of them	that evening
even without	the answer is
finally	the first one
in a good year	the same
kidding aside	unfortunately
later	when
many of them	while
most	yet

Here are three sets of examples of transitions between paragraphs. These are from a letter to voters written by a congressional representative just prior to President Nixon's impeachment hearings. The transitional words in the second paragraphs and the words in the first paragraphs that they refer back to are italicized.

1. ... Among those responsibilities at this moment in history is the solemn, unwelcome duty to determine if the *President* has committed impeachable offenses in violation of the Constitution.

    As a member of Congress, judging a *President* . . .

2. ... And I have generally felt almost *equal awe and respect for* its occupant.

    But perhaps too much *awe and veneration* have been granted . . .

3. *My awe and reverance have disappeared.*

And so, finally, *I find no trepidation, no fear, no uncertainty,* as I approach the responsibility of judging the President of the United States.

Holt Confer, in an article for the Copley News Service, used smooth transitions between his paragraphs. He did this by starting each paragraph with words that gently turned the reader's mind to a new thought. He was writing about interesting parallels between shopping for a computer and a sophisticated camera. He recently purchased a computer. Here are some of the transitional words and phrases that begin his paragraphs:

I know, I know, I've been talking about making this type of move for many months.

I hope you'll forgive me if I digress.

There are a lot of similarities, you know.

First of all,

And when

Now that

Believe it or not,

On the other hand,

Now you have to remember

Here, again

Of course,

Incidently,

The next group of transactions between paragraphs is taken from the introduction to the book, *Lifetime Encyclopedia of Letters* published by Prentice Hall. The reference words in the first paragraph and the transitional words in the second paragraph are italicized.

1. Do you sit down to write a letter and wonder, "Just what is it I'm trying to say and *how should I say it?* . . . When your church asked you to write a fund-raising letter *did you panic?*
    These and many other questions . . .

2. If you *need help* with your writing . . .
    Many writers of business letters and reports *need direction . . .*

3. Just locate your topic, read the lead-in comments and follow the *model letters.*
    All the *model letters . . .*

4. For each type of letter there is a basic outline called *"How to Do It."*
    One special feature of this encyclopedia that helps you organize your thoughts is the *"How to Do It"* section. . . .

5. If you can't find a model letter or a topic outline for the subject of your letter, *this book will help you.*
    The first step is to . . .

6. This book suggests many *beginning and ending sentences.*
    A special feature of the *Lifetime Encyclopedia of Letters* is the 334 suggested *beginning and ending sentences* for letters.

7. Hard hitting sentences like these, while usually productive, *do not appeal to all readers.*
    The *variety of approaches* . . .

8. *Analysis* of appeals . . .
    For most situations, the explanations, suggested outlines and *analyses* will . . .

9. One quick way to locate a model for the letter you want to write is to consult the *Index.*
    In this reference work, . . . information can also be found in the *Index.*

Here are a few more transitions between paragraphs; these are from the November 1995 issue of *The Atlantic Monthly.* The subject matter is New York's Whitney Museum of Modern Art. Again, the reference and transitional words and phrases are italicized.

1. . . . New York's downtown gallery world—by now a fashion-conscious, moneyed, internationally influenced scene that *helps keep the museum controversial.*
    In the 1980s the Whitney *raised critical eyebrows by* . . .

2. *How* had this happened?
    The *answer was* something . . .

3. She has what amounts to a civic mandate to *pay attention.*
    Her genius for *paying attention* . . .

4. When the present moment is considered *in the context of the past,* . . .
    The Whitney, meanwhile, seems to have been refreshed by *the need to rethink its past.* . . .

Transitional Paragraphs

A third type of transition, after those within and between paragraphs, is the transitional paragraph. These are used as a bridge or connecting statement between thoughts. Sometimes they are used to end one topic or to introduce the next topic. For example, as an opening paragraph:

Thank you for the opportunity to add you to our growing list of charge customers.

Your decision to retire as a director from ABC Corporation has been received with deep regret.

We are enclosing another statement of your past due account.

I would like to ask a tremendous favor of you.

Examples of transitions that end a topic:

Please mail your tax-deductible check in the enclosed envelope.

I recommend her highly for a position working with numbers.

Your answer to the above question will be of great help to us.

If we can be of further assistance, please phone us at 000-0000.

Here are four examples of transitional paragraphs connecting one thought to a following thought. The middle paragraphs are the transitional ones.

1. You have received monthly statements and phone calls from us during each of the last three months.
    The result: no response.
    If you have a problem with the merchandise or with your personal finances, please let us know. We will work with you.

2. During the Renaissance, Florence, Italy, was not always the pioneer, but what it did not originate, it refined. Many of the great non-Florentine artists came to participate.
    What made it possible for Florence to set the tone for almost every aspect of Renaissance life?
    Geography came first. Florence had access to an important trade route. It had good communication by river and passes through the mountains.
    (The next two examples are from newspaper articles.)

3. His previous leg problems are well documented. Kevin Johnson has been fortunate enough not to miss any playoff games, but the regular seasons have been nightmares.
    Which is what the Celtics became for the Suns.
    Remember, this is a Boston club whose own owner, Paul Gaston, predicted would "stink" before the season even began. And the less-than-sellout crowd of 17,848 seemed unimpressed by their team until the final minutes when it became apparent the young Celtics were going

to hold off the Suns, who blew a 12-point, second quarter lead, then went on to win 113 to 109.

4. "Virtually all of Dial's consumer operations are domestic and therefore subject to the slow growth associated with this mature, highly competitive environment," she added.

   While Dial logged the largest overall revenues in any Arizona public company in 1994, MicroAge, Inc. posted more impressive numbers.

   The Tempe distributor of computer products (MicroAge) chalked up sales of $2.42 billion for the year. . . .

CHAPTER 7

Topics of Paragraphs

Topic Sentence

Methods of expanding and developing the topic sentence were mentioned in Chapter 6 in the sections titled "Definition" and "Topic Statements and Outlines." More details follow:

A topic sentence is one that states the subject matter and presents subtopics or themes that will support the subject. Mentioning the supporting ideas necessarily limits the range of the paragraph. For example, from the topic sentence: "Sonja was afraid of failure and fearful of the ultimate results of success," the reader would expect a discussion of why she was nervous and upset about both possibilities; the reader would not expect commentary on colds developing into pneumonia.

The topic sentence has many purposes: it helps the writer develop the paragraph, it tells the reader what to expect from that development, it limits the scope of discussion, and, primarily, it summarizes the paragraph for the reader.

Commonly, the topic sentence is the first one in a paragraph.

The Pinyon is a resinous tree, dripping with gum or pitch, as many a hiker or picknicker can testify. The Indians long used the caulking properties of this pitch; The Apaches waterproofed their baskets with it, and the Navajos their water bottles. . . .

Here is an example from the July 1995 issue of *The Atlantic Monthly*:

For more than twenty years the children of the ghetto have witnessed violent death as an almost routine occurrence. They have seen it in the streets, in their schools, in their families and on TV. They have lived with constant fear. Many have come to believe they will not live to see twenty-five. . . . Too many have learned to kill without remorse, . . .

Topic sentences can also be placed in the middle of a paragraph, as in this example from the October 1995 issue of *The Atlantic Monthly*:

By the curious standard of the GDP (Gross Domestic Product), the nation's economic hero is a terminal cancer patient who is going through a costly divorce. The happiest event is an earthquake or a hurricane. The most desirable habitat is a multibillion-dollar Superfund site. *All these add to the GDP, because they cause money to change hands.* It is as if a business kept a balance sheet by merely adding up all "transactions," without distinguishing between assets and liabilities.

Another example of a topic sentence placed in the middle of a paragraph follows:

It is difficult to refuse or say "no." When making a written or oral statement, the goodwill of the reader or listener must be retained. *The key to a successful "no" is tact.* If thoughtfully done, the disappointment of the refusal will be lessened.

Sometimes the topic statement is held until the end of a paragraph. Rather than the paragraph explaining the topic sentence, the paragraph builds up to the topic summary.

Will a sales letter really sell? A need must exist—or be imagined; the customer's interest must be aroused and a choice must be made among competing salespersons and products. *A sales letter won't accomplish all these things, but it can be the final push that wins over the customer.*

The Persian people achieved their short-lived greatness during the Middle Ages because they were a hardworking group making the most of their mix of races. Baghdad became an international trade center for the territory between the Mediterranean Sea and the Indus River, attracting many artists from India and China. *Persia became the center of art for the whole Eastern world and teacher of western Europe,*

Here is an example of a paragraph with topic sentences at the beginning and the end:

Whether you believe you are writing a business or personal letter, keep the reader uppermost in your mind. Write about what will interest the reader, what you want the reader to know and believe, what will appeal to the reader, and foremost, what will get the reader to react. A letter, even a friendly note, is written to accomplish a purpose, and the key to this accomplishment is to think the way the reader does. *Put yourself in his or her place and ask, "How would I react to this letter if I were the reader?"*

Summary Paragraphs

If you have written three or more paragraphs on a subject, it is advisable to follow with a summary paragraph. For example:

To sum up . . .

Of most importance is . . .

The key point is . . .

Here is a concluding paragraph to an article on how to write about lists:

Now that you know what I know about writing and selling list articles, here is what you know:

How to get ideas

Where to get ideas

How to do research

What approaches are best

How to outline the article

How to write the article

How to sell the article.

The next summary paragraph ends an article about surf fishing (standing at the edge of the water—usually with wet shoes and ankles—and casting a line far out into the surf):

Surf fishermen often return home with only their rods. But they are not completely disappointed. Where else can they get such beautiful sunrises and sunsets along with fresh salt air? They will come again and one day bring home the bacon—I mean the fish.

Unity and Coherence

The sections in this and the preceding chapters on the organization of paragraphs, their length, transitions within and between, transitional paragraphs, topic sentences and summary sentences are all techniques for developing unified and coherent paragraphs.

Unity:

A unified paragraph is one that sticks to one idea, one focus, one part of a subject, and one unit that can be summarized in a topic sentence—most often the first sentence of the paragraph. Including thoughts that don't relate directly to the topic sentence destroys the unity.

Here are two examples of non-unified paragraphs:

> Garden books and encyclopedias delight in describing the autumn leaves of the liquidamber, or sweet gum trees. One states, "Its autumn foliage is brilliant." Another says, "The leaves are star-shaped and bright green and make a riotous display of crimson, orange and yellow before dropping in the fall." And to quote a third, "The sweet gum has the most magnificent autumn color of all trees." Paul thought of the old Valley Oak trees that had small green leaves until they turned a dull brown and kept falling all year long.

The last sentence is about trees, but does not fit into the description of highly colored autumn leaves.

> As a tremendous favor to me could you possibly spend part of a day with Jack Herald, who is one of our best customers as well as a personal friend? He mentioned yesterday that he will be spending a week in San Francico starting October 7. I met Jack's son, Tom, last year at their company picnic. Jack is production manager for Ames Company here. He is a camera bug like you, and I am sure he would like to visit such spots as Coit Tower, Harding Park's seventeenth green, and the Cliff House. I seem to visit Los Angeles more than San Francisco. Can I have Jack call you when he arrives in the City?

Two sentences destroy the unity of this paragraph: the one stating that I met Jack's son and the sentence saying that I seem to visit Los Angeles more than San Francisco. It could be argued that these sentences relate to the topic, but they are too disconnected to belong in the same paragraph.

Here are two examples of unified paragraphs. Note that they stick to only one topic, and that each sentence expands upon or explains the topic sentence.

> a. Our new sales representeative, Andy Watson, has a wealth of background in bag-making machinery. This includes manufacturing, assembling and repairing, as well as supervising machine operators and

scheduling orders—and even sales. Not many people have such thoroughgoing experience with a machine they are selling and servicing.

b. It is understandable, Mrs. Miles, that your husband is reluctant to have surgery. Doctors Agnew, Monahan and I feel that surgery is the only treatment if your husband is to recover his good health. Surgery isn't what it was forty years ago, or even ten; and you can be reassured by knowing that the motality rate for this particular operation, when performed in time, is less that 4%. The mortality rate for neglect of this condition is a certain 100%.

The topic sentence in the paragraph immediately above is the second sentence; the first sentence is an introduction. All the sentences refer to surgery, making the paragraph unified.

Coherence:

A paragraph is coherent when all the sentences clearly relate to each other, when they flow smoothly and logically, when the reader never strains to put the separate sentence thoughts together.

This is similar to unity in a paragraph, except that unity places emphasis on each sentence evolving directly from the main paragraph thought: the stated or implied topic sentence.

Following is an example of a coherent paragraph:

(1) If you don't like the food served on your Continental Airlines flight, blame the palates of the airline's top brass. (2) In May, the airline changed its menu to make it more appealing. (3) Continental CEO Gordon Bethune and COO Greg Brenneman had hundreds of entrees carted into their Houston offices for a taste test. (4) What they liked—ice cream sundaes, sliced sirloin and chateaubriand—stayed on the menu. (5) What they didn't like—smoked trout, pepper-sauced swordfish, and French toast—were dropped. (6) "We gave it our own personal taste test," Brennerman says.

The first sentence is the topic sentence and states specifically where to put the blame. In the second sentence, the word *menu* refers back to *palates* in the first sentence. The third sentence names two persons who can be *blamed*, and mentions *taste test*, referring back to *palates* in the first sentence. The fourth sentence tells which food items were retained, and the fifth sentence tells which food items were eliminated. In the sixth sentence the persons to be blamed accept the responsibility. The sequence of sentences is smooth and logical and completely without confusion.

Not coherent: We need more people to work in the Volunteer Office. The hours are easy and flexible, you will receive orientation, and working for the Volunteers is exciting and worthwhile. Call the office and ask for Ms. Waller; she'll get you started. The office number is 000-0000.

Coherent: We need more people to work in the Volunteer Office. You will receive an orientation. The hours are easy and flexible as well as exciting and worthwhile. Call the office, 000-0000, and ask for Ms. Waller who will get you started.

The "non-coherent" paragraph has unity because each sentence relates to the topic of office work. Coherence, however, is lacking because the thoughts jump around. In the "coherent" paragraph, the thoughts are organized to flow smoothly from one to another.

Another example:

Not coherent: This will be the third year members and friends of Riverside Church have been involved in project "Angel Tree." We have agreed to provide two presents each to sixty children of prison inmates, one a toy or "fun" present and the other an article of clothing. The gifts are given "from the inmate" in celebration of the birth of Jesus Christ as a tangible expression of His love. In many cases yours will be the only gifts these children receive.

Coherent: This will be the third year members of Riverside Church have been involved in project "Angel Tree." We have agreed to provide two presents each to sixty children of prison inmates, one a toy or "fun" present and the other an article of clothing. In many cases, yours will be the only gifts these children receive. The gifts are given "from the inmate" in celebration of the birth of Jesus Christ as a tangible expression of His love.

As the "not coherent" paragraph is written, the last sentence is tacked on as an afterthought. The sentence belongs immediately after the description of the gifts. The new last sentence explains why all the foregoing is being done.

Bad News Messages

Saying "no" or refusing is difficult but at times necessary. The key to a successful refusal is tact. Start by agreeing on some point or by thanking your reader. This sets a tone of courtesy, pleasantness and consideration. The second step is to present a reason for the refusal. This step prepares the reader and makes dissent easier to accept. The third step is to state the refusal. End with a pleasant statement, a suggestion, an alternative or good wishes.

Following are random examples of definitely but politely saying "no":

Dinner invitation:

Thank you for your invitation to the alumni dinner on November 20. I regret that only yesterday I accepted an invitation to a meeting with a business group to which I have belonged for many years. Perhaps we can get together next year. Thanks again for the invitation.

Join a group:

I appreciate your asking me to join the Morgan Dell office manager's group. I am new in town, buying a new house, and learning a new job. I don't believe I could do my share as a participating member, but I hope to join you at a later date.

Football game:

Thank you for your invitation to the Cal-Stanford big game this year. Barbara and I have a previous commitment in Los Angeles that weekend. Your thoughtfulness is appreciated.

Information not available:

We are enclosing a tally of the monthly purchases you made during 19__. We are sorry we cannot provide details, but our accounting system does not retain itemized purchases beyond three months. We hope the information we are sending is of some help to you.

Item not available:

We would like to honor your request for fifty copies of *Citrus Tree Diseases*, but we are out of copies and no more will be printed. We suggest you write to the Superintendent of Documents, Washington, D.C., and ask for publications on this topic.

Credit, lack of information:

We would like to grant your request for credit at Tomson's. However, based on the information provided we are unable to do so. Can you send us additional references and current financial statements? Meanwhile cash orders are welcome.

Credit, slow payments:

We appreciate your interest in establishing a credit account with Abbott's. Payments on your other open accounts have been slow and we don't want to add to your burden at this time. At a later date when your accounts are being paid promptly, please apply again.

Charitable donation:

Thank you for your recent request for a donation to the Boys and Girls Club. As a large company we receive numerous such requests and cannot respond favorably to all of them, although we contribute to many worthy causes.

Special assignment:

After careful consideration and the exploration of several possibilities, we have determined that we cannot handle the special assignment mentioned in your letter of November 10, 19—. Please accept our best wishes for success in this endeavor.

Refusing a volunteer:

We appreciate very much your volunteering to lead the Junior Youth Fellowship next year. Looking at the overall program, however, we believe you could serve the church better working with Mrs. Walton and the Senior Youth Fellowship. She is in need of someone with your knowledge and background. We hope you will consider working with Mrs. Walton. The seniors need your helping hands.

Employment termination, cutbacks:

I regret having to inform you that due to company-wide cutbacks in employment, your services will not be required after May 31, 19—. We are sorry to see you leave and will certainly provide you with a good reference when you need it.

Employment termination, poor performance:

We have repeatedly asked you to put more effort and willingness into your work. You have the potential, but your last three reports were late and therefore useless. Perhaps a less demanding position would be more suitable. You will receive two full month's termination pay and your services will not be required after April 30, 19—.

Examples of Good Paragraphs

Here are five examples of short, precise paragraphs from the August 1, 1995 *USA Today*. The first three are from one article; the other two are from separate articles.

   a. Eisner will continue to run the company. Murphy will join the Disney board. The ABC network operation will remain under the control of Cap Cities President Robert Iger.

b. The companies have been talking merger for about three years. They finally agreed to proceed in mid-July after Murphy and Eisner met at a retreat for media executives.

c. Disney also will gain management talent. Last year, it lost its number two executive, Frank Wells, who died in a helicopter crash. Later, studio chief Jeffrey Katzenberg and TV executive Richard Frank left.

d. In Washington, about 200 residents at an apartment building for the elderly were evacuated when firefighters, called to treat heat-exhaustion victims, found the building had been without air conditioning since Saturday. The high Monday in the nation's capital: 93 degrees.

e. Republicans, who have a plan to balance the budget in seven years, said Clinton's plan takes too long and is based on overly optimistic economic forecasts. But private economists say the Clinton administration's budget forecasts are realistic. "Lower interest rates are attainable and efforts by the Republican Congress to cut spending are much more credible than past efforts," says Claudia Furst, MMS International economist.

The following two paragraphs are from a textbook on how to write better letters. In the first example, notice the topic sentence that begins the paragraph and includes two words to arouse interest: *heart tug*. The "how to" is spelled out in four clear steps, and *heart tug* is explained in the last sentence.

a. A written request for a contribution to a charity is a sales letter with a heart tug. Like a sales letter, the fund-raising letter first arouses the interest of the reader, then convinces the reader of the need for buying the product or service (or making the contribution), next tells how the product or service will help the buyer (or giver), and finally makes positive action by the buyer (or contributor) easy. The heart-tugging part is the second step—convincing the reader of the need to give.

This next paragraph presents a problem, clearly discuses the problem and offers a solution.

b. Both employees and employers find matching the person to the job a difficult and frustrating experience. As an applicant, a good letter or resumé won't guarantee you'll get job, but they can help open the door. As an employer, you'll find yourself called upon to write a wide variety of letters ranging from rejections to acceptances, and how you do it reflects not only on you and your company, but may also have legal ramifications. In all these cases, carefully written letters are essential.

Now a personal-description paragraph from James Herriot's *The Lord God Made Them All*. Notice the details: tiny man, bald, smile, unwordly eyes, fussed around, brushing, patting, chatting gaily, and the use of transitions from one facet of description to another: and, that, and then, as, you could see that.

Sitting there in his shop I looked at him as he worked. He was a tiny man in his fifties with a bald head that made a mockery of the rows of hair restorers on his shelves, and on his face rested the gentle smile which never seemed to leave him. That smile and the big, curiously unworldly eyes gave him an unusual attraction. And then there was his obvious love of his fellow man. As his client rose from the chair, patently [clearly] relieved that his ordeal was over, Josh fussed around him, brushing him down, patting his back and chattering gaily. You could see that he hadn't just been cutting this man's hair; he had been enjoying a happy social occasion.

Here is a landscape description from Francis Parkman's *The Oregon Trail*. Parkman describes a sunrise, a hilly desert, a flat desert, vegetation, a scanty stream, wildlife, then a flat and lifeless desert—all these encountered throughout the day. These varied landscapes were unfamiliar and unexpected. Note the smooth transitions from sentence to sentence.

In the morning, as glorious a sun rose upon us as ever animated that wilderness. We advanced, and soon were surrounded by tall bare hills, overspread from tip to bottom with prickly pears and other cacti, that seemed like clinging reptiles. A plain, flat and hard, with scarcely the vestige of grass, lay before us, and a line of tall misshapen trees bounded the onward view. . . . There were copses [thickets of small trees] of some extent beyond, with a scanty stream creeping among them; and as we pressed through the yielding branches, deer sprang up to the right and left. At length we caught a glimpse of the prairie beyond, and emerged upon it, and saw, not a plain covered with encampments and swarming with life, but a vast unbroken desert stretching away before us league upon league, without bush or trees, or anything that had life.

Unusual Paragraphs

This section is a potpourri of unusual paragraphs.

Purplish prose:

Purple prose is often used by reviewers of artistic performances to enhance the reputations—and perhaps the egos—of the performers. The use of this style of writing should be strictly limited and is presented here merely as an item of interest.

a. The *Vienna Express* stated, "he is a perfect violinist with beautiful blossoming tone and noble musicality."

b. After he appeared at Lincoln Center's Alice Tully Hall, *Musical America* hailed his "bright colorful tone, forthright honest musicianship, and above all a welcome acuity of timing."

c. Grand Rapids' *The Press* stated, "Each instrumentalist displays technical mastery and supreme musicianship. Their performance recalls the aristocratic approach of some of the great ensembles of the past."

Exaggeration:

Apparent exaggeration exists in the Bible. The purpose is not to boast, but to impress readers with the absolute importance of the subject. Some examples, using the Revised Standard Version:

Following King Solomon's anointment (*I Kings*, 1:40), "And all the people went up after him, playing on pipes, and rejoicing with great joy, so that the earth was split by their noise."

The earth did not split, but that phrase tells the reader the extent of the boisterous celebration.

The Lord said to Abram (*Genesis* 13:16), "I will make your descendants as the dust of the earth, so that if one can count the dust of the earth, your descendants also can be counted."

Counting the dust of the earth would be an impossible task, but so would estimating the number of one's descendants.

In *II Samuel* 16:22 we are told, "So they pitched a tent for Absalom upon the roof; and Absalom went in to his father's concubines in sight of all Israel."

In reality the statement that Absalom did this "in sight of all Israel" meant that a great deal of publicity surrounded the event, but as written the reader would be impressed if not startled.

Abe Lincoln defines liberty:

Here is a clearly stated paragraph from an address by Abraham Lincoln at Baltimore, Maryland, on April 18, 1864:

The world has never had a good definition of the word liberty, and the American people, just now, are much in want of one. We all declare for liberty; but in using the same word we do not all mean the same thing. With some the word liberty may mean for each man to do as he pleases with himself, and the product of his labor; while with others the same word may mean for some men to do as they please with other men, and the product of other men's labor. Here are two, not different, but incompatible things, called by the same name, liberty. And it follows that each of the things is, by the respective parties, called by two different and incompatible names—liberty and tyranny.

Revising Paragraphs

Good examples of revising paragraphs by combining several too-short paragraphs and by adding details to an undeveloped paragraph are presented in the subsection, "Details," of the section titled, "Organization Methods," Chapter 6. Here is another example of combining short paragraphs:

> When you make telephone calls about your work, have all the information you need or may possibly need at hand.
> Write a report or letter covering what was discussed: what you said and what the other party said. Take notes.
> Put the report in an appropriate file, even if you are not required to send it.
> It is a good idea to mail the report. It can be referred to at a later date. This is often necessary.
> Information you forgot to relate in the phone conversation can be included in the written report. It can reveal any misunderstandings during the conversation.

This message could be better stated if arranged in one unified and coherent paragraph, such as this:

> There is a standard procedure for reporting business telephone conversations when you make the call. First, gather all the data you may possibly need to present facts or ask questions. Take notes or have a secretary listen in to take notes. Afterward write a letter or report of the conversation and mail it to the person you phoned. Items that were omitted in the conversation can be added and any misunderstandings will be revealed. Finally, keep a copy of the letter or report in an appropriate file.

Newspaper writers are supposed to summarize a story in the first paragraph, but when the writer attempts to jam too much into a first sentence that comprises the first paragraph, too much of a good thing becomes confusing. Here is an example from the *Los Angeles Times*:

The jury in the murder trial of O. J. Simpson saw for itself Tuesday the brutal consequences of the June 12 attack that he is accused of committing, grimacing and reeling as autopsy photographs of Nicole Brown Simpson were displayed just a few feet away from the panel.

Clarity could be improved by replacing the comma after the word *committing* with a period, and then starting a new sentence:

Simpson was grimacing and reeling as autopsy photographs of Nicole Brown Simpson were displayed just a few feet from the panel.

The following partial paragraph from Louisa May Alcott's *Little Women*, published in 1868 and describing Jo's despair when her sister Beth died, illustrates what we now think of as "old-fashioned" expressions. For example: *self-abnegation, when self was purified, a sweet example, ceaseless longing,* and *loving service which had been its own reward.*

The suggested revision replaces these expressions with current language. Although this example is taken from classic literature, the same "current language" idea can be applied when you begin a business letter with "enclosed please find" or end the letter with "I faithfully remain yours truly."

Alcott's original:

It was easy to promise self-abnegation when self was purified by sweet example; but when the helpful voice was silent, the daily lesson over, the beloved presence gone, and nothing remained but loneliness and grief, then Jo found her promise hard to keep. How could she "comfort father and mother," when her own heart ached with ceaseless longing for her sister; how could she "make the house cheerful" when all its light and warmth and beauty seemed to have deserted it when Beth left the old home for the new; and where in all the world could she "find some useful, happy work to do," that would take the place of the loving service which had been its own reward?

Suggested revision:

It was easy to promise self-denial when Jo was heartened by the sweet example set by Beth; but when Beth's helpful voice was silent, her presence gone, the daily lessons over, and nothing remained but loneliness and grief, then Jo found her promise hard to keep. How could she comfort her mother and father when her own heart ached with longing for her sister; how could she make the house cheerful when its warmth and beauty seemed to have vanished when Beth left the old home for heaven; and where in the world could she find something useful to do that would take the place of her loving service to Beth? To be of help to a sister in need had been compensation enough.

On the other hand, some paragraphs are improved by cutting out nonessential words. Here are three examples contrasting writings from the *Seattle Post-Intelligencer* and *USA Today*:

Seattle Post Intelligencer:

In their most massive attack yet on Bosnian Serbs, wave after wave of NATO warplanes bombed Serb targets around Sarajevo early today in retaliation for a marketplace massacre that killed 37 people.

USA Today: (A snappier version.)

NATO hit Bosnian Serb targets before dawn with bombs and artillery in retaliation for an attack on Sarajevo that killed 37 people Monday.

Seattle Post Intelligencer:

Judge Lance Ito's courtroom reverberated yesterday with the voice of Mark Fuhrman, the police witness around whom prosecutors have built much of their case against O. J. Simpson, uttering the word "nigger" more than three dozen times. In tape-recorded remarks to an aspiring screenwriter that both riveted and revolted those who heard them, Fuhrman emerges not just as racist and perjurer, but also as a rogue police officer who arrested people without probable cause.

USA Today: (Fewer words, but the same emotions have been aroused.)

A police officer can do almost anything because "you're God," retired detective Mark Fuhrman says in racist and vulgarity-laced tapes played Tuesday in the O. J. Simpson courtroom.

Seattle Post Intelligencer:

Impervious to aces and scorching heat, defending champion Andre Agassi blazzed through the first round of the U.S. Open in 81 minutes yesterday to push his winning streak to 21 matches. Agassi, seeded No. 1, shrugged off 15 aces by Bryan Shelton, drilled all the balls he could reach, and turned a potentially tough opponent into just another patsy, 6-2, 6-2, 6-2, as courtside temperatures soared into the 90s. The women's top seed, Steffi Graf, took nearly an hour longer than Agassi to beat Amanda Coetzer 6-7 (1-7), 6-1, 6-4 and avenge a defeat against her scrappy South African at the Canadian Open two weeks ago. "I don't particularly like losing," said Graf, who succumbed in the first set after fighting off eight set points. "I definitely wanted to play her as soon as I could. I knew it was not going to be easy because I really haven't had a lot of matches," she said.

USA Today: (Although less detail is included, the essence is the same.)

Top seeds Andre Agassi and Steffi Graf earned second-round berths at the U.S. Open Tuesday. Agassi got there in a stroll, but Graf arrived in a wobble. Agassi swept by Bryan Shelton 6-2, 6-2, 6-2. Graf, pushed to the brink, defeated Amanda Coetzer 6-7 (1-7), 6-1, 6-4. Two weeks ago in Toronto, Coetzer ended Graf's 32-match winning streak. "I knew it was not going to be easy," Graf said, "But I was looking forward to it. This is going to help me the next few matches."

CHAPTER 8

Tie It All Together

Now that we have presented ways to make sentences understandable (Chapters 1–5) and how to combine them into sensible paragraphs (Chapters 6 and 7), we will tie these paragraphs together to make a complete composition.

The first step is to write a list of topics, ideas, suggestions, questions or conclusions that will satisfy the goals of your message. The second step is to arrange these ideas in a logical order. The specific order will depend primarily on what you wish to accomplish and how your audience will react to your method of presentation. These two factors are discussed in Chapter 9 in two sections, "Purpose" and "Your Audience." All this suggests the need for an outline—a "road map" showing you how to get there.

Outlining

What outlining can do for the writer:

To be practical, all organized writing requires some type of written outline. Otherwise it is easy to ramble off into vaguely related thoughts or to forget essential ideas. Here is what an outline can do for the writer:

It presets the writer's train of thought, and thus starts the process of organized thinking.

It lets the writer visualize major and minor points.

It keeps the first draft in focus.

It eliminates major revisions.

Types of outlines:

Outlines can be classified in different ways. One way is based on the thought process and includes:

1. Mental outlines—mentally list ideas and then divide them into topics.
2. List or topic outlines—write down ideas then divide them into topics.
3. Random or cluster outlines—write and circle the one basic idea in the center of a sheet of paper, then connect topics and subtopics to it with lines.
4. Formal outlines—write down main ideas or headings and indent topics under them and subtopics under topics.

Another classification is by form:

1. Sentence outlines—follow the formal outline steps. Each heading, sub-heading and topic is a complete sentence that must be a specific, not a general, statement.
2. Paragraph outlines—each paragraph deals with a key topic. This form is not particularly functional because it requires a lot of writing *before* organizing the outline rather than afterward.

We will provide examples of these styles after discussing the order in which topics should be presented to the readers.

Order of presentation:

Base the order of items in an outline on their importance to the reader—the reader, not the writer—and on the purpose of the article or composition. Some purposes follow:

Descriptions are observations through one or more of the five senses—sight, hearing, touch, taste and smell—and are detailed in an order that is logical to the reader.

Comparisons or *contrasts* are similarities or differences stated with the important relationships mentioned first.

Differences in form, style, size, speed and other variables are described, perhaps with examples.

Actions can be described and then compared or contrasted to actions the writer thinks should have occurred.

Cause and effect (or effect and cause) can describe conditions or events and the results.

Under certain conditions a specific effect or result may not be attributable to a specific cause, and vice versa. This provides the writer with the opportunity to offer an opinion of the event.

Orders of items placed in an outline:

Chronological: This is probably the most easily understood order. We learned it early in life: *once upon a time* . . . Tie the sentences and paragraphs together with such words as *first, second, then, later*, and *finally*.

Easy to difficult: This is another easy-to-understand order. Each step prepares the reader for the next step.

Known to unknown: This is similar to easy to difficult. It is useful when background data is necessary for a full understanding.

Listed in no particular order: This is useful when no item is of more importance than the others. Each item is treated as an individual event or idea. Note, however, that when writing the article, transitional words, phrases or sentences must tie each idea to the next one.

Listed with the most important idea at the end: The end is the most emphatic position. You might mention that you will discuss four ways to fry eggs or six reasons for using case-hardened bolts.

From problem to solution: This could be called the "straight line approach." The sequence is usually a short background statement, a discussion of the problem, possible solutions and the recommended solution.

Order of location: Engine parts could be described from front to back; a manufacturing complex could be described from the headquarters building to service buildings, to warehouses, to the manufacturing plant; a residence could be described room by room.

Alphabetically: List personnel, automotive parts, recipe categories, tree descriptions and other appropriate items alphabetically.

Examples of outlines:

List or topic outlines are the simplest and most efficient ones for most writing. List all the topics you want to mention, then number them in an order that will seem logical to your reader. Place the important items first. Indent subtopics under their appropriate topic headings. Here are examples of list outlines with numbers indicating a logical sequence:

Describing outlines:

    2. Style of outlines.

    3. Order of topics in outlines.

    1. What an outline can do for the reader.

    4. Examples of outlines.

Requesting information:

    2. Why you want the information.

    4. Thanks for providing the data.

    3. Help you provided the reader in the past.

    1. What specifically do you want to know?

Requesting favors:

    1. Make request specific and polite.

    2. Explain reason for the request.

    3. Offer something in return.

    4. Show appreciation for the help.

Declining a request:

    1. Agree on some point or offer thanks.

    2. Present reasons for the refusal.

    3. State the refusal.

    4. Offer an alternative.

Selling product or idea or self:

    1. Make an attention-getting opening.

    2. Develop a central selling point.

    3. Be vivid in talking up the point.

    4. Present proofs of your statements.

    5. Close by moving the reader to specific action.

Raising funds:

    1. Start with an interest-arousing first sentence.

    2. Explain persuasively the need for the donation.

    3. Indicate how the giver will benefit.

    4. Make positive action by the giver easy.

Collecting money due:

    1. State the purpose of the letter clearly and politely.

    2. Include data relevant to the situation:

        What the writer is asking for

        How reader can be helped

        Reasons for paying now

    3. Restate the request for payment.

Complaining:

    1. State specifically what is wrong.

    2. Explain your viewpoint in a reasonable manner.

    3. Suggest specific adjustments or corrections.

Sympathizing:

    1. Mention the person about whom the sympathy is being expressed: for example, Harold, Dr. Dobson, your sister or your loss.

    2. State your relationship with the person about whom you are expressing sympathy: for example, our friend at work, my acquaintance of many years or all of us here.

    3. Make a complimentary statement: for example, he was loved by all, he was a warm friend, she was always cheerful, she was helpful or we spent many happy hours together.

    4. If appropriate, and you can do so, offer to help the reader.

Thanking:

    1. State what the thank-you is for.

    2. Mention the appropriateness of what was received.

    3. Be sincere, brief and pleasant.

    4. When appropriate, offer something in return.

Providing instructions:

    1. If there is a change, explain why the change is needed.

    2. List items required to make the change, for example, materials, tools, personnel, report forms.

    3. If this is a construction project, review safety precautions.

    4. List steps in a chronological order.

    5. Do NOT omit any necessary steps.

Here are two examples of ignoring step 5 above:

1. An electronic typewriter *Operator's Instruction Manual* states, "You may change the left and right margins as you would on a traditional typewriter, using the margin release, space, or backspace keys." On a "traditional" typewriter, pressing the margin release key will permit you to type beyond the set margin—but not on this typewriter. This typewriter has three "modes," normal, display and justify. The operator must switch into the "normal" mode before pressing the margin release. That step was omitted in the instructions.

2. Instructions for playing movies on a VCR stated: (1) Turn on VCR, (2) Turn on TV to channel 4, (3) Push play. But when does one insert the tape into the VCR? Between steps 2 and 3. The instructions omitted that essential step.

Listing outline steps:

The letter of encouragement below flows smoothly because the list outline includes all the essential parts of the message, and unnecessary degressions are omitted.

1. Admit that an adverse condition exists.
2. State the condition or problem.
3. Indicate your conviction that the condition can be overcome.
4. Suggest how to overcome the condition.

Teaching at Public School 19 is a difficult assignment for any teacher and even the most seasoned instructors often find that the integration process takes time. Thus, it comes as no surprise that you have spoken of submitting your resignation at the end of the school year.

Discipline remains a problem for many new teachers here, as you have discovered. Students tend to "test" a teacher. However, once the test is passed, teachers often find themselves responding with enthusiasm to the challenge.

Take a little time to reconsider your decision then please see me to discuss the matter at your convenience.

Clustering outlines:

1. Write the core of the subject in a word or two in the center of a sheet of paper. Circle the word (or words).
2. Write any ideas or topics that occur to you, in whatever order, and connect them with lines to the circle.
3. Write any subtopics and connect them with lines to their topics.
4. This gives you a sprawl of items that, when you review them, will fall into a reasonable order. Number the ideas from the most important to the least important.
5. Assume this core subject: Bart owes $10,200.
6. Random topics:

   3. I want my $10,200 now.
   2. He is past due 100 days.
   5. Will give him 10 more days.

1. We have a contract.
0. I could refuse further sales.
0. He was once a good customer.
6. Collection agency might help.
7. Could get a lawyer to sue.
0. He also buys from Zebo Company.
4. No response to phone calls and letters.

The letter from this outline might be as follows:

We have a contract that says you will make payments every calendar quarter. You are 100 days past due, and I think it is only fair that you immediately pay the $10,200 due.

You have not responded to our phone calls and letters, but we are willing to give you ten more days, until July 19, before turning your account over to a collection agency or our attorney.

To avoid this embarrassment and loss of credit standing, please mail your check today.

Formal outlines:

Formal outlines use numbered indentations to indicate a logical order and the degree of subordination of topics.

I. major topic
  A. first subordination
    1. second subordination
      a. third subordination
        1). fourth subordination

In some instances the outline may be headed with a thesis statement. Here is a more detailed formal outline:

Autumn brilliance of tree leaves
  I. Street of beautiful trees
    A. Street name
    B. Location
    C. When first observed
  II. Description of liquidambar tree
    A. Description by first source

      B. Description by second source

      C. Description by third source

III. Range of colors

      A. Green to yellow

      B. Brown to copper

      C. Pink to dark purple

IV. Variations elsewhere

      A. Location

      B. Shape

      C. Effects of soil and sun

 V. Emotional impact

Note that subdivisions of any topic must have at least two subtopics. If particular data can't be divided this way, include it in the undivided topic. Also, each item in a subdivision must be logical and of equal importance.

Make the outline as detailed as required for your purpose. The less familiar you are with the subject, the more details you will need.

When outlining a report or business letter, place the conclusion or main point at the beginning. Supporting details can follow.

Sentence outlines:

Sentence outlines follow the steps of formal outlines, but complete sentences are used rather than words and phrases. This technique requires more thorough thinking by the writer and is an aid to the final writing.

The outline above about colorful autumn tree leaves could be constructed with full sentences.

Thesis: Changing autumn leaves can reveal brilliant colors.

   I. There is a street lined with beautiful trees.

      A. The street is Eschenburg Drive.

      B. It is located in Gilroy, California.

      C. I happened upon this street one October morning.

  II. Garden books and encyclopedias describe the liquidambar trees.

      A. One states that the foliage is brilliant.

      B. A second mentions bright crimson and orange and yellow colors.

      C. A third source says the sweet gum has the most magnificent colors of all trees.

 III. The range of colors is from pale green to an almost black purple.

A. Some leaves change from green to pale yellow to buff or bright yellow.

B. Another series of colors changes from pale brown to deep brown to orange or bronze, and then from orange or bronze to copper.

C. The red series varies from pastel pink to scarlet to crimson to wine to dark purple.

IV. These trees are also seen in other areas.

A. I first saw them in Concord, California.

B. As they grow, the trees develop into a pyramid shape.

C. The trees in adjacent street blocks vary in leaf color because of differences in the ground chemicals and the amount of sunlight.

V. I left Eschenburg Drive filled with a spiritual high from the brilliance of the autumn colors.

Paragraph outlines:

In a paragraph outline, each paragraph covers a major area and uses complete sentences. An example is printed here in the order originally written, but during a review, the writer realized the order of the paragraphs was not the best. The numbers at each paragraph indicate the revised order. This need to revise could have been eliminated by making a brief list outline first. The extra work is one of the disadvantages of a paragraph outline, but, on the other hand, the paragraphing effort has brought out many details helpful in completing the article.

Main topic: How to write a sales letter or flyer.

3. Use POWER words to persuade the reader—such as: absolute, advantage, economical, guarantee, immediate, low cost, quality, successful, today, and you. Also use eye-catchers: CAPITALS, underlines and one-word sentences.

2. Develop a central selling point. This is more appealing than scattering ideas over several items or services.

5. Move the reader to action. Make buying easy by saying: mail the card today, your credit is good, send no money, our supply is limited, return it and owe nothing, or we will be happy to serve you.

1. Learn about your audience. Are you trying to sell yourself to an employer of accountants when your degree is in medieval literature? metric-sized wrenches to a mechanic who refuses to repair foreign cars? the beauty of northern Mexico's cacti to a spouse who longs to visit Paris?

4. Avoid the "come on" appeal of a low price when you plan to push only higher-priced merchandise when the buyer arrives.

Here are two examples of how I make and use outlines. The first is an outline for answering a business letter. This will probably be the style of outline used by most readers of this book. The second is a description of the series of outlines that preceded the writing of the section you are now reading—studying, I hope.

Business letter outlines:

I received a letter from my editor, which I read before reviewing it to decide what parts to comment on.

1. The inside address was wrong because I had recently moved. I put a check mark in the margin by the address.
2. The first paragraph said it had been a long time since we had corresponded, and that a book I had written was still selling well. I did not check that paragraph.
3. The second paragraph mentioned that the publisher was still paying royalties on a computer disk version of the book. I made no check mark there.
4. The third paragraph mentioned the publisher's considering a different electronic version of the book. That paragraph I checked.
5. The fourth paragraph stated she, my editor, would keep me posted on the progress of the new version. No check mark there.
6. The title under the signature was executive editor rather than senior editor. I checked that line.
7. Below, I added the words, "current book" and put a check mark in the margin.

Now I had four of the above items checked, numbers 1, 4, 6 and 7.

That was my outline—four check marks in the margin of the letter I would answer. This is an efficient way to make an outline. My four-paragraph reply follows:

It was nice to hear from you. Your letter of April 28 arrived a little late because, somehow, your secretary hadn't received my current address; the correct address is shown above.

I am always encouraged to hear that additional people are interested in selling my *Lifetime Encyclopedia of Letters* and versions of it. I am anxious to learn what will be done with the new electronic version.

Your title has changed to executive editor. I hope that is a promotion—
if so, congratulations—and not merely an additional workload.

My "messages" book is still progressing, and still slowly. A complete
outline is not ready, but when it is, I'll send you a book proposal.

Outlining this section on outlines:

I began with a list of chapters I might want to include in a book that dealt
with how to write clearly. Here is the list:

Words make a sentence

The chaos and exactness of words

Misplaced modifiers and phrases

Glossary of confusing words

Punctuation

Spelling

Sensible paragraphs

    Coherent

    Coordinated

    Gobbledygook

    Purple prose

Tie it all together

    The complete message

    Outlining

Formal reports

Graphic presentations

Glossary of terms

Some of these topics were later changed or eliminated. The word *Outlining*
is one of the subtopics, but there are many steps yet to go. From nearly 100
textbooks on writing and a vast number of clippings, notes, and comments I
had written from time to time, I listed the items to which I might want to refer
and their page numbers.

When I was ready to start this chapter on tying paragraphs into whole compositions, I went through the listings for each book and folder and wrote down
the book number and page number for each item labeled "tie together" or "planning." That provided me with well over 100 references that I listed under
twenty-four topics, one of which was "Outline."

Under "Outline," I listed twenty-three sources and thirty-eight topics to review. Reviewing these topics resulted in four pages of written notes that I reduced to four topics for this section on outlining:

1. What outlining can do for the writer
2. Styles of outlines
3. Orders of topics in outlines
4. Examples of outlines

Brevity

Brevity is one of the essentials of a good business letter or a nonfiction commentary. Brevity means making the writing as short as possible while still providing the necessary information.

There are times, for a variety of reason, when you have to drastically cut what you have written. This is disheartening, but it can be done. Are there paragraphs or sentences or phrases that don't really relate *directly* to the main point of your composition? Are there adjectives and adverbs that, while seemingly helpful, could be omitted without destroying your meaning? Are there examples or digressions or pet phrases that the reader won't really miss? The chore of cutting a well-written piece can be ego deflating and tough, but it teaches you orderly and precise writing.

Here are four examples of brief letters:

In my absence Tom Jenkins will assume the responsibilities of plant manager.

Your invoice No. 111235 was paid by Shippers Freight Payment Plan on January 15, 19__ as indicated by the "PAID" stamp on the attached copy.

What has taken place on the special pallet-for-sheets project?

What's the status of the baler report?

The following are examples showing how common phraseology can be improved by using fewer and shorter words:

Long: A perusal of the pertinent market data has led to the conclusion that a viable market exists for a new shampoo.

Brief: Market research reveals a good demand for a new shampoo.

Long: Antiquated instrumentality performed during the experimentation.

Brief: Old gauges were used during the test.

Long: Operations for the company during the previous accounting period resulted in a reported deficit situation.

Brief: The company lost money last year.

Even small changes toward brevity can help a writer: consider how many words you can save over the next twenty years.

Long: It was only the factory employees who received a raise in January.

Brief: Factory employees received raises in January.

Long: With respect to next year's production efficiency rating, we expect an improvement.

Brief: We expect next year's production efficiency to improve.

Long: Johnson, who is the new president of Colma Co., is also an attorney.

Brief: Johnson, the new president of Colma Co., is an attorney.

Long: The red book that lies on the far table belongs to Miss Johns.

Brief: The red book on the far table belongs to Miss Johns.

Long: He was born in Kansas City in Missouri on July 1 in 1930.

Brief: He was born in Kansas City, Missouri, on July 1, 1930.

Long: Your wallet is made of leather, and my wallet is made of plastic.

Brief: Your wallet is made of leather and mine of plastic.

Long: On October 20, Mr. Watson, our salesman, questioned the manufacturer to find out who was responsible for the misunderstanding.

Brief: Mr. Watson asked who was responsible for the error.

Two sentences that say essentially the same thing or that are repetitive can sometimes be combined to produce one short, clear sentence.

Long: You asked us how to make a withdrawal from your IRA account. You say you are over the mandatory normal distribution age of 70½. To receive the distribution you must sign the enclosed form No. d2233.

Brief: To withdraw from your IRA account, since you are over 70½, you must sign the enclosed form No. d2233.

Long: There are at least three ways to approach this project. You can do library research to find out what has been done in the past. Second, you can interview project managers who have completed similar projects. And third, you can take a refresher course in concrete construction at the state university.

Brief: You can approach this project by doing library research, interviewing project managers or taking a refresher course.

The following paragraph is taken from a sales letter somewhat disguised as a newsletter. It was sent to homeowners in a limited area. The rewrite cuts the words from seventy-nine to forty. Vague and pompous sentences are replaced with factual statements. The short last sentence of the rewrite adds punch.

This task of selling your home is accomplished through a saturation advertising program designed to highlight the exclusive features of the home and the unique environment and atmosphere of the area. Each home is featured with the widest range of advertising exposure within the framework of successful patterns that will attract the maximum buyer response. The use of attractive brochures, response oriented classified advertising, corporate transferee exposure, and some quite uncommon techniques are employed to generate successful results.

Rewrite:

When selling your home we emphasize its exclusive features along with the beauty of this area and the desireable climate. We advertise with attractive brochures, proven newspaper advertising and direct contact with companies that transfer employees. Our results are successful.

I will end this section on brevity with a little satire:

In a cartoon, a new government employee has just entered the Bureau of Memos office. He hands the boss a memo. The boss reads it and says, "This is too brief, Throckmorton; if you're going to make it in this department, you're going to have to learn to say less with more words."

Clarity

Defining clarity:

A statement is clear when the reader does not become confused, when he or she doesn't say, "I've read this three times and I still don't know what it means."

Correct English may not be essential to an effective composition, but communicating a clear thought *is* essential. The following sentence is perfectly clear, but no one should speak or write this way:

Bad: We ain't got none of them there B boxes here no more.

Better: We are out of style B boxes.

Depending on the writer's purpose, clarity can mean readability or precision. Often precision requires specific details, and the details must be organized in a logical order and stated clearly.

Clarifying words should not be omitted, for example:

Fair: Each branch controller will personally supervise the annual physical inventory at his plant and will report any discrepancies from book inventory to the corporate controller.

This statement would be better understood if a pronoun were inserted to provide a subject for the verb *will report*.

Better: Each branch controller will personally supervise the annual physical inventory at his plant and *he* will report any discrepancies from book inventory to the corporate controller.

Best: After personally supervising the annual inventory, each branch controller will report any discrepancies to the corporate controller.

Reworking a statement is usually the best way to clarify it.

Clarity can include precision as well as brevity. Brevity was discussed in the section immediately above: use only the minimum number of words required to make your writing clear. Precision is accuracy. Cut out the "deadwood" from each sentence, omit paragraphs that don't relate directly to your point, and say your piece as simply as possible.

Use specific words rather than vague or general words:

General: This cake tastes good.

Specific: This moist cake is delicious.

General: Increasingly poor economic conditions have hurt our business.

Specific: Worsening economic conditions have reduced our profit.

General: I banged up my leg.

Specific: I slipped on the ice and shattered my kneecap,

In expository writing, the purpose is to explain.

Vague: I work long and hard every day at my drafting board.

Clear: I work at my drafting board all day, Jannette, until my eyes fail to focus.

Argumentative writing attempts to persuade.

Vague: Practicing an hour a day won't cut it.

Clear: With your ability, if you practice your dribbling and shooting from four to six hours a day, you could become a highly paid professional basketball player.

Inexactness: Here is a cute example of an inexact question. I actually heard this exchange.

First woman: What's Joan's last name?

Second woman: Joan who?

Review your writing:

Writing and music share one truism. My music teacher once told me, "You have to work hard to make music sound easy." Likewise, a writer must work diligently and persistently to make writing clear and easily read.

All writing should be revised before it leaves your desk. You may be surprised to find a missing word or statement, a spelling error, an inaccurate figure or fact, unnecessary words or sentences, vague references or undue criticism.

If you dictate your letters, always read them over before signing them. Secretaries can also make simple or confusing errors.

Ambiguity:

Ambiguity means some words in a composition can have two possible meanings. Examples:

Ambiguous: We must remove all the old chairs from the garage for cleaning.

Clear: Because we need to clean the garage, the old chairs must be taken out.

Clear: The old chairs need cleaning; they will have to be removed from the garage.

Ambiguous: Since the sun was so hot yesterday, we stopped working early and went swimming.

Clear: Because the sun was so hot yesterday, we stopped working early and went swimming.

Ambiguous: Since summer began we usually swam in the afternoon.

Clear: From the time summer began we usually swam in in the afternoon.

Ambiguous: While he had a crippled leg, he kept up with the fastest walkers.

Clear: Although he had a crippled leg, he kept up with the fastest walkers.

Ambiguous: While attending college she spent much study time alone in her room.

Clear: During the time she attended college, she spent much study time alone in her room.

Ambiguous: Tom read the last chapter two days ago.

Clear: The last chapter Tom read was number seven. He read it two days ago.

Better: The latest chapter Tom read was number seven. He read it two days ago.

Ambiguous: Albin hated his boss; he was unsure of his ability to do the job.

Clear: Albin was unsure of his ability to do the job, and he hated his boss.

Clear: Albin's boss was unsure of his own ability to get the job done; and Albin hated his boss.

Ambiguous: Pasco liked his coach, and he was a bright man.

Clear: Pasco liked his coach. The coach was a bright man.

Clear: Pasco was a bright student and liked his coach.

Ambiguous: Stewart didn't quit the swim team because he found it too easy.

Clear: Because the swim team's requirements were too easy for him, Stewart quit the team.

Clear: Stewart stayed with the swim team although its demands were too easy for him.

Ambiguous: The young boy watched his parents scream at each other with fear and insecurity.

Clear: The young boy, filled with fear and insecurity, watched his parents scream at each other.

Clear: As the young boy watched, his parents screamed at each other because of their fears and insecurity.

Ambiguous: John and Marcia often walked together because of love.

Clear: John and Marcia loved each other and often walked together.

Clear: John loved Marcia and often walked with her.

Clear: Marcia loved John and often walked with him.

Ambiguous: With relish Tony ate his hamburger.

Clear: Because he liked the taste, Tony put relish on his hamburger.

Clear: Tony relished the thought of eating a good hamburger.

Here are four longer examples of ambiguity:

1. I once suggested a bulletin board notice of a special credit union meeting during which we would discuss two sides of an issue. To inform the membership, I recommended using a sheet of paper with Group A's arguments on one side and Group B's arguments on the other side.

    After many loud and hurt objections from Group B about which side would show and thus be seen first, I realized Group B's spokesman thought "sides" meant front and back. I thought of "sides" as the left half and right half.

2. The story is told of a company president who wrote to his human resources manager, "What are the steps to obtaining a job with this company?" Six months later he received a thick, bound report detailing the entire operation of the human resources department and changes that had been made in recruiting, testing, hiring and training employees.

    The president exclaimed loudly to his secretary who delivered the report, "What's all this? I just wanted to tell my son how to apply for a summer job."

3. A cartoon conversation written by Dick Cavalli:

Jim: How's your new dog?

Bob: Oh, I don't have him anymore. My father wouldn't let me keep him. He almost wrecked our house.

Jim: Your father?

Bob: No, my dog. He got tired of having his clothes chewed up.

Jim: Your dog?

Bob: No, my father.

4. From one of the *Born Loser* cartoons by Art Sansom:

Angry complainer on the telephone: This is Brutus P. Thornapple! Your paper has me listed on the obituaries again. And dagnabit, I'm not dead!

Voice on the telephone: Oh dear, I'm sorry about that.

Confusing sentences made clear:

Fuzzy: I'm having a hard time getting my handles around that.

Clear: I'm having a hard time getting a handle on that.

Fuzzy: That will be with the exception of the additions which we are adding.

Clear: That will be without the new additions.

Fuzzy: Things are so bad right now that even positions with people are vacant.

Clear: Things are so bad right now that no jobs are available.

Fuzzy: The young men who effectuated a forcible entry into the sheriff's automobile now reside in a correctional institution.

Clear: The young men who broke into the sheriff's car are now in prison.

Double negative: Not wearing a shirt is definitely not allowed.

Positive: Shirts must be worn at all times.

Confusing paragraphs made clear:

Original: One of the things that keeps retirees in retirement communities and which keeps them busy and proud and happily occupied which most people outside don't appreciate and they find very satisfactory.

Volunteers do many things for each other like providing extra beds and cribs and toys for their visiting grandchildren and work for free at libraries and thrift shops and buy groceries for the disabled and help teachers in the nearby schools and donate money to hospitals and community buildings and some work there and for outside charities like the Salvation Army and visit and help those who can't get out of their homes.

Volunteers help themselves and others who need help they can't give themselves.

Revised: People in retirement communities keep themselves busy and happy by volunteering to help with worthwhile causes in nearby communities as well as in their own areas. Many people outside these retirement communities fail to appreciate how much time the retirees donate to helping other people.

Volunteers do many things. To name a few:

Provide beds, cribs and toys for retirees' grandchildren.

Donate time to libraries, thrift shops and hospitals.

Buy groceries for shut-ins.

Work as teachers and teachers' aides in depressed-area schools.

Donate money to hospitals, security guard services and community buildings.

Gather donated items for the Salvation Army.

Make regular visits to the ill and homebound.

Volunteers say it makes them feel good to help others.

Original: Two of the Habitat for Humanity homes were built with donations from ABC Corp. and one with donations from Riverside Church. You will see two more houses being constructed and even an opportunity to see the ladies being carpenters on their own house!

Everyone is invited to the party. There will be open house so you can see the homes of the new owners. There will be fun for all: a program and refreshments, live music and special parking has been arranged. To get there, take Westfield Road to Poppy Street. Go south to Arrowhead Road and you're there.

Revised: Two of the Habitat for Humanity homes were built with donations from ABC Corp. and one with donations from Riverside Church. You will have an opportunity to see these three compeleted houses plus two others now under construction. You will even see ladies working on their own houses.

Everyone is invited to the open house to see the homes and meet the new owners. There will be a program, refreshments and live music. Special parking has been arranged. To get there, take Westfield Road to Poppy Street, then go south to Arrowhead Road and you'll see the homes on the left side of the street.

Examples of clear writing:

Quantities expressed with too many numerals can be confusing.

> Clear: Fifteen percent of our people account for 70% of our profit, while eighty-five percent of our people account for the remaining 30% of profit.

Directions should not wander like a lazy river through a swamp, but like a straight-flying arrow. Add explanations or reasons only if necessary.

> Clear: Your practice of mailing two copies of your invoices to ABC Corporation, Phoenix, one marked "original," and also mailing two copies to ABC Corporation, Los Angeles, one marked "original," is confusing. This has resulted in duplicate payments.

In the future, please mail all four copies, only one marked "original," to:

ABC Corporation

P.O. Box 00000

Phoenix, AZ 00000-0000

The following is a clearly written information letter:

Dear Customer:

As you may know, last summer the government passed a law requiring any institution that pays you interest to withhold 10% of the interest or dividends earned. This system is similar to the payroll tax withholding system, that is, the money withheld will be sent to the IRS for tax payment.

Therefore, beginning July 1, 1983, we will be required by the government to begin withholding 10% of the interest you earn. However, if your account earns less than $150 in interest in a year, we will *not* be required to withhold interest. Also, if you meet certain criteria designated by the

IRS, you can file a certificate of exemption and not have any interest withheld.

We have enclosed an exemption certificate for your convenience. Please read the exemption certificate carefully to see if you qualify. You will need to file an exemption certificate for *each* account at Local Bank that will earn interest. Additional exemption certificates will be available at all Local Bank offices.

For answers to questions about withholding, please contact your local IRS office. If you have any questions about your accounts, contact your Local Bank office.

The following quote is part of a newspaper article written for King Features Syndicate by Dale Dauten of Tempe, Arizona:

After too many memos and too many reports, I have settled upon these attributes of the perfect communique: short, clear, useful and human.

I'll close with an example. What follows is the work of a 17th-century French general, Vicomte de Tureene. After a battlefield victory, he filed this, the perfect report:

The enemy came. He was beaten.

I am tired. Good night.

Completeness

Regardless of its length, a piece of writing fulfills its purose only when it is complete. Before stopping, say *all* that needs to be said. To obtain completeness, the writer must put himself or herself in the place of the reader who will ask: Do all parts of the composition tie together? What else do I need to know? What does the writer assume I know that I don't know?

Say it all in the first letter. The following letter may seem complete to the reader without background in the subject and to the reader not having to use the data provided.

To: Plant Controllers

Following are the current prices for exchange purchases and the effective dates. Please note that prices are not the same for all suppliers.

Prices effective beginning with February 7, 19— shipments:

I. 26# medium $2.47 MSF

    47# liner   4.58 MSF

    90# liner   9.29 MSF

II. For: Alton

    Continental Can

    Owens Illinois

   26# medium $2.37 MSF

   90# liner   9.23 MSF

III. Prices from:

   Inland

   Longview

   Menasha

will be priced as shown on the purchase order.

It is each plant's responsibility to check its invoices for the correct prices. Please forward these new prices to the individual in your plant who would verify them. Advise me of any discrepancies.

                                                         Signed

The first question this letter raised was this: Does the first group of prices apply to all suppliers not mentioned in the second and third groups? The assumed answer is yes, but the question should have been answered in the letter.

The second question was what prices should be paid if the seller does not charge according to this list? This question was anticipated by the writer who sent the following telegram the next day:

To: Plant Controllers

Pay all invoices as priced and send a copy of any invoice that is incorrectly priced to my attention. We will get the credit for you.

To avoid following-day follow-ups, say it all in the first letter.

Completeness over brevity:

At times much that has been said about brevity seemingly must be set aside to accomodate completeness. The following letter gives instructions which apply to a national company with operations in many states, each with its separate tax laws. Please note the following as you read the letter: no excess verbiage, no repetition, logical organization, clear statements and brief paragraphs.

Attention Controllers and Managers:

Subject: Change in Treatment of Sales and Use Tax

Effective January 1, 19__ sales and use tax on the purchase of fixed assets will be charged to expense by all divisions of Alan Corporation except in those states where the law requires that it be capitalized.

Sales tax must be capitalized in the following states:

Arizona
Illinois
Wisconsin
(Other states to which this applies were listed.)

Note 1. In Illinois, retailer's occupation tax must be capitalized, but use tax, service use tax and leasing tax can be expensed.

Sales taxes imposed by counties and cities generally follow the rules of the states in which they are located.

Use tax is generally imposed on the consumer and is, therefore, not to be capitalized, even in the states listed above.

Capital expenditures will fall into two categories for construction during 19__:

1. All equipment purchased or construction started after January 1, 19__ will have all legally deductible taxes charged to expense. Any such taxes capitalized since January 1 must be reversed to conform with these instructions.

2. On all capital expenditures on which construction began prior to December 31, 19__, sales and use tax must be capitalized in accordance with the election in effect for prior years. In accordance with that election, it will be necessary to continue to capitalize sales and use tax until the property is installed or first put into use.

It will not be necessary to submit revised Reports of Construction Costs for Capital Expenditures closed to date in 19__ unless the project falls into category 1 above.

The Monthly Report of Construction Costs must continue to show the amount of sales and use tax capitalized to date on each capital expenditure in progress at December 31, 19__.

The Fixed Property Manual will be revised to reflect these changes.

Signed

To get the best response from the reader, say it all in the first letter.

Make requests specific:

A request for information can be short and direct. For example:

We need quarterly SEC reports, Form C-144, for the year 19__. Submit these by the 20th of the month following each quarter.

A more willing response would be received, however, if the letter were expanded just enough to include a brief explanation of why the request is being made. A word or two such as "please" or "would appreciate" is helpful in eliciting the desired response.

The following letter states why the request is made, what data is required and when it is due. The letter is brief, clear, specific and polite.

> The year-end tax data requirements for the year ended December 31, 19__ unintentionally omitted charitable contributions from the required detailed analysis.
>
> We would appreciate it if you would provide us with a schedule of donations made during the year 19__ showing each donee and the amount donated.
>
> The above information is needed by February 15, 19__.

The next letter states a problem, suggests a solution and requests comments:

> Last year we encountered a number of instances where the specific factory order of a quality problem was difficult or impossible to ascertain. To prevent this in the future, I would like to print factory order numbers of all orders in an inconspicuous place (e.g., inside the flap). By doing so, we can better pinpoint a particular order and be sure it is not a farm-out.
>
> I would appreciate your comments and suggestions.

Long request itemized:

When making a long inquiry, break it down into specific questions. Make the response easier by listing or numbering the questions. In the following letter and its response, note how specific questions resulted in specific answers.

> Dear Mr. Insurer:
>
> Can you help me find the answers to a few questions about my policy No. 5320116 issued March 11, 19__?
>
> I am writing to you directly rather than to a local representative because the local representatives change so often they do not get to learn the various policies with thoroughness. In the past eight years at this location, at least six different local representatives have called on me.
>
> The questions I have are as follows:
>
> 1. What is the present death benefit?
> 2. What is the present cash value?
> 3. What is the present loan against the cash value?
> 4. What will the death benefit be at March 11, 19__7?
> 5. My present procedure for paying premiums is to obtain a loan against the cash value. For the March 11, 19__1 premium, the loan obtainable was less than the premium, requiring a cash payment of $20. Please provide a schedule of approximate annual payments, in addition to the loan, to cover premiums for the years 19__2 through 19__7.
> 6. How much money was provided from policy no. 2501057 as a first

payment on policy no. 5320116? How much of this was cash value and how much was dividend value?

Sincerely,

Dear Mrs. Policy Holder:

I have the answers to the questions you sent to Mr. Insurer on April 25th.

1. The present death benefit is $20,884.00, as of April 30, 19__1.

2. The present cash value is $4,308.00.

3. As of April 30, 19__1, the loan against the policy is $4,116.16.

4. At March 11, 19__7 the death benefit will be $17,626.19, assuming you follow the premium payment plan as described in the schedule of approximate annual cash payments required to pay premiums. Please note that the estimated dividends included in these calculations are not guaranteed. They are determined on the basis we currently hope to maintain.

5. Schedule of estimated annual payments:

Year	Premium Due	Estimated Dividend	Possible Loan Against Cash Value	Cash Payment Required
19__2	$864	$239	$390	$235
19__3	864	252	354	258
19__4	864	265	323	276
19__5	864	278	291	295
19__6	864	290	259	315
19__7	864	303	225	336

6. Cash value of $375.21 and dividends of $488.79 from policy No. 2501057 were used to pay the first premium on policy No. 5320116.

We appreciate the opportunity to communicate with one of our policy holders, Mrs. Policy Holder. It is a pleasure to respond to questions posed with such clarity.

Sincerely,

Read the final sentence of this letter again. A clear question elicits a clear response.

CHAPTER 9

Composition Techniques

Purpose

Stating your purpose:

The purpose of written communication is to accomplish a goal. The goal must be specific: what do you want the reader to do after finishing your memo, letter or proposal? As a guide, write out answers to these two questions:

1. My purpose in writing is to what?
2. Then my reader will do what?

For example:

> My purpose is to remind employees entering the parking lot during shift changes that a head-on collision occurred. Then they will enter and exit the lot using separate driving lanes, and thus avoid further accidents.

Following this basic outline, a memo to all employees might read:

> Last Thursday during the shift change two autos collided head on. The entering car turned left at the front of the parking lot while the exiting car started to turn right.
>
> To avoid such accidents in the future, all entering drivers will use the right lane to the far end of the lot before seeking a parking spot. All drivers leaving will stay to the right until reaching the front driveway.

White directional arrows will be painted on the lanes indicating one-way traffic both entering and leaving. Drive carefully.

A second example:

My purpose is to complain about Bob Boyd's low sales. Then his sales manager will persuade him to work harder.

A letter to Bob Boyd's sales manager might read:

As of your March 31 report to Pete Thompson of Aaron Acres Co., we are running far behind last year's sales to them.

It was my understanding with our salesman, Bob Boyd, that he and Pete agreed on 4 to 5 million units per month this year. At the rate we are going, it looks like we will average only 3 million units per month.

Being Bob's sales manager, find out how he and Pete explain this drop in expected sales.

A third example:

My purpose is to recommend an acquaintance for a job. Then my reader will hire him.

The letter could be as follows:

This is in response to your letter of March 4, 19___ requesting a personal letter of referral on Robert R. Riley.

I have personally known Robert for a number of years. He is a good friend of my son. I also know his family well because his father is my wife's doctor.

Robert is a tenacious young man and seems to be a determined, straightforward individual who knows where he is headed.

If you need further information, please write or phone.

The first letter above was a request—perhaps a demand—that certain actions follow, the second letter asked for an explanation and the third offered a recommendation. Other purposes include convincing, informing, predicting, defining, discussing, agreeing, disagreeing and analyzing.

Always mention the purpose of your memo as well as the topic. It is most discouraging to send a memo to your boss, Peter Perkins, and later see his secretary coming to your desk waving a piece of paper and saying, "Peter wants to know what this is all about."

Your writing represents your organization:

When writing a personal letter to a friend or acquaintance, you reveal yourself by what you write. That is probably your main purpose. In a personal letter you can discuss your love of playing bridge and your dislike of some of the people you play with. When you write as an employee or member of an organization, however, your purpose is to represent the organization and their goals, not their shortcomings.

For example:

Bad: I'm aware that we haven't been paying our bills on time, because we are having internal problems with one of our departments, but I assure you the invoices will be paid very soon.

Better: Yes, I'm aware that we haven't been paying our bills on time, but yours will be paid in short order.

The purpose of your communication should be stated in the first sentence for several reasons:

Readers not concerned with the message will not waste time reading it.

Readers cannot always infer the purpose from the subject even if the subject is stated.

Many writers do their thinking while they write rather than beforehand.

There is a major exception, however, to placing the purpose in the first sentence. That is in a negative message. In that case, put the reason for the "no" first, the "no" itself in the middle and a suggestion or alternative at the end. For example:

We appreciate your interest in Harper's Department Store and your application for a credit card.

Your lack of a permanent work record at this time prevents us from approving your application. Your part-time work references are good, and as soon as you establish a permanent work record, we will be happy to reconsider granting you credit.

However grand and specific your purpose in writing something, your message is wasted if your reader doesn't understand it. The best way to assure understanding is to know your audience. That is our next topic.

Your Audience

The Empire Employment Agency received a letter from Westinghouse making a pitch about affirmative action and the company's policy of "hiring qualified women for positions of responsibility." The letter began, "Dear Sirs:"

Westinghouse ignored the audience. "Dear Employment Recruiters" or "Dear Friends" would have been more appropriate, and would have formed a closer bond with the readers, many of whom were women.

The following is a good beginning of a thank-you letter, but its appeal to the reader could be improved. In the reader-oriented version below, notice that the emphasis has been changed from "I" to "you."

> Good: I really enjoyed meeting with you last Friday and having the opportunity to visit the Alpha production facility. Your operation looked quite good. I find the volume produced in that one location surprisingly high.
>
> Reader oriented: Your personally guided tour of Alpha's well-run production department was both pleasant and informative. The volume you produce in that one plant is amazing.

At one placed I worked, I corresponded frequently by phone and business letter with Rudy Adler at our headquarters office. I learned from his coworkers that he had transferred from a large regional office, had worked many years with the company and was nearing retirement. Not having met him, I imagined he was on the short side of normal height, slightly chubby and graying at the temples. From his conversations and letters, he seemed pleasant and knowledgeable. That is the person I corresponded with. At last I met Rudy. My image was close except that his hair showed no signs of graying. My general impression of him didn't change after our meeting, but Rudy had become a real person, and I was more comfortable when we corresponded.

Learning about your audience:

Ask, and as best you can, answer these questions before writing:

Who is going to read this?

What is the reader's position in the company?

Is the reader a personal friend?

Is this message personal or business or both?

How knowledgeable is the reader about this subject?

How do I expect the reader to react?

What will the reader do with this information or request?

What style of writing will the reader expect: formal, casual, specific facts only? Some corporate managers insist on cold, dry facts with no varied or vivid descriptions.

For example, at one time I was writing monthly cost accounting reports and decided to free my readers from the usual dryness. I wrote, "Water costs were a dramatic 47% lower this month compared with last month because the river water was clear enough to use all month." I was reprimanded lightly and told I should have reported, "Water costs declined 47% from last month."

Does the reader have particular prejudices?

Is the reader expecting this message? Complete surprises are not appreciated, especially if disapproving.

Is the reader a decision maker?

To whom should I send copies?

Which other people will the reader inform?

How to understand your reader:

Learn to understand your reader both as an individual and as a representative of a group. Study the characteristics of the reader's social group. Are you writing to a farmer of seasonal vegetables, a vice president of a multinational corporation, or a young housewife buying furniture on credit for the first time? Each group will respond favorably to different approaches or appeals. A farmer of seasonal vegetables may be tramping a dusty field, but can also be found sitting at a desk studying computer printouts that indicate the amount and type of fertilizer to apply and when to start the next irrigation. This farmer is an astute business person, perhaps a little informal, but completely practical. Write with this in mind. For example:

> This week we are paying $2.15 per bushel for oats, with a 5,000 bushel minimum. All the market forecasts indicate no increase in price through November.
> If you contract this week for 90% of your crop, your income for this season will be assured.
> Please let us know before Saturday.

The vice president of a multinational corporation will want precise facts clearly organized in a brief but complete message or report. Any excess verbiage will leave a bad impression. Here is an example:

> I received a copy of the letter sent to you by the chief accounting officer of the division of corporate finance of the SEC commenting on one of the

financial items on the last 10K report filed by Sara Manufacturing Company. This is not serious and can be clarified by a short amendment to your 10K report.

I am sending a copy of this report to your accountants with a request that they prepare the required amendment.

Here is a suggested rewrite without the excess verbiage:

I received a copy of the letter of May 9, 19__ sent to you by the SEC regarding Sara Manufacturing Company's 10K report.

I am sending a copy of this report to your accountants asking them to make the required amendment.

The approach to a young housewife buying on credit must be one of helpfulness and consideration. She may have little experience buying large items on a limited budget and will appreciate concerned guidance. Also keep in mind that she is a prospect for many future sales. Here is a letter to an inexperienced buyer:

A young couple furnishing a home for the first time can expect to have doubts about what to buy and how much (or how little) to pay for various items. We at Hanford's understand this, and that is why you receive personalized attention to your wishes and needs. We will not let you overextend your ability to pay and will offer you small payments spread over a long time. You will always find us helpful, considerate and pleasant.

When writing a personal note or letter, you have some acquaintance with the reader. But before writing a business letter, learn what you can about the reader, perhaps from your company's sales people who have talked with the reader, from a secretary who has received the reader's phone calls, or from the correspondence file. Even a single letter from the person to whom you are writing will reveal much about his or her personality and character.

Will your reader accept your level of expertise? Abel White tries to convince a group of condominium owners that he knows how to set up and operate a $60,000 annual budget. The members are suspicious, or at least doubtful, of his ability because they hadn't known him until last week. Abel writes:

I have twenty-six years experience making annual and monthly budgets for a manufacturing unit with monthly sales of $800,000 to $1 million. I know how to estimate future expenses based on recent past expenses, trends, inflation and known future changes. My past experience verifies that my budgets are close to actual performance.

When writing an article for a varied audience in which some have highly technical knowledge and some have practically none, two solutions can be effective. First, if feasible, place the technical data in an appendix. Second, place the technical data in a separate section of the article. The nontechnical readers can easily omit the technical portion. This subject is illustrated in a later section on shortening wordy compositions.

Appeal to your readers:

When talking face to face, you get reactions from your listener: a raised eyebrow, a shrug of the shoulders, an outward movement of the hands, a frown, a grin or a smile. Even on the phone, you can get a pause, a questioning reply, a fumbling for the right word, or a tightened-throat sound. When writing you are on your own. You must anticipate questions in the reader's mind and cover them with clear statements. Rewrite until your writing conveys a clear message. For example:

Fuzzy: Could you send us a copy of the recent realty board meeting report, last week I think. It was about land that wasn't developed. Thanks.

Clear: Could you please mail us a copy of the February 7 meeting of the Santo Realty Board Committee? The subject of the report is Undeveloped Land Acquisitions. We will greatly appreciate your mailing us a copy this week.

Many business letters, forms and reports are essentially repeated from time to time. It is all too easy for the writer to go to the files, pick out the last report and copy the first sentence or two, then insert current data. This practice results in writing that long ago was considered outdated, such as: Enclosed please find . . . , Please be advised that . . . , This year's report . . . , Our company is again requesting that . . .

These comments do not mean, however, that you should completely ignore precedents. Some firms have "their own way of doing things," specific forms or arrangements for certain reports, and your job security may depend on your writing following "company procedures."

In any case, be diplomatic and appropriate in your degree of formality, informality and humor. In no case should you use anger, complaint, disparagement, sarcasm or irony in busisness or personal correspondence. Some examples:

Bad: Although it will place a big burden on our department, we will attempt to meet your deadline for the annual telephone report.

Good: Everyone in our department has agreed to do what is necessary to meet your deadline for the annual telephone report.

Bad: I understood that all our buyers in the purchasing department had to have a college degree. I found out that some don't. Why?

Good: A few of our purchasing department buyers are exceptions to our college-graduates-only policy. Could you tell me what special education or training they have received?

Bad: Why haven't you gotten your maintenance people to fix the slippery-sloped entrance to the front door yet?

Bad: We've been too busy trying to repair our snow blowing machines. Then we'll get to the walkway.

Good: For the safety of our employees, the slippery front entrance must be fixed. I would like it done today.

Good: We will lay a carpet over the slush and ice this morning. Permanent repairs will be completed in two days.

Bad: If you want to keep your job here, your department's production had better improve immediately.

Good: I am sure that with a little extra effort you can improve the production rate of your department and retain management's approval of your work.

Formal: The physical messiness of the whole office, the disinterest of employees when asked questions, the lateness of reports requested by the Detroit office, our examination of the physical asset records, the irregularity of bank deposits and the disarray of the petty cash fund suggest the need for a detailed examination by an outside consulting firm.

Colloquial: There's something fishy here!

Goodwill is necessary:

Expressing goodwill is a way of promoting your company, your business or yourself. Goodwill can be thought of as a public relations gesture—something often neglected with good, steady customers or with personal friends. The gesture may be combined with a thank-you, appreciation, request, apology, regrets or just pleasant thoughts. Kindness is not a one-time thing but a continuing relationship.

Here is a business expression of goodwill:

We are sorry to learn of your desire to terminate our sales agreement, which has been in effect for nine years. We can understand your position and appreciate your reasons.

Although nothing was said in your letter, I assume you wish this agreement to end as of October 22, 19— without the ninety-day cancellation notice mentioned in the contract.

It has been a pleasure to work with you, Don, and although our formal arrangement is terminated, I know our paths will continue to cross in the future.

A candidate for elective office made a personal visit and followed with this goodwill note:

I enjoyed meeting with you this past weekend.

A personal expression of goodwill:

Thank you, Tim, and each one of your family for your visits while I was in the hospital. All of you raised my spirits and contributed to my quick recovery.

Topic Statements Developed

The topic statement in a composition tells the reader what to expect from the whole writing. In a manner similar to a topic sentence in a paragraph, it limits the scope of the discussion and helps the writer stay on track.

A newspaper writer for the Santa Rosa, California, *Press Democrat* reported that a communications professional was hired to teach a vice president how to reduce a five-page monthly report, which he spent up to twenty hours writing, to one and a half pages and to get to the point in the first paragraph instead of the third. The vice president's writing time was cut to three hours.

Another author calls those paragraphs preceding the one with the point of the article "warm-up paragraphs." These introductory paragraphs may be useful for overcoming writer's block, but should be eliminated from the final draft. Make your point in the first paragraph so your readers know what you are writing about.

Also, the first paragraph should "hook" the reader. It should grab the reader's interest and convince him or her to read on.

Here are a few short opening paragraphs that get immediately to the point:

a. This memo is a suggestion for changing the procedure for audience participation at our monthly board meetings.

b. The company policy regarding coffee breaks needs to be restated. Here is my suggestion.

c. We should have a clear policy about selecting new members for our twelve-person bridge club. I suggest the following:

d. The report on reducing the accounting staff has been delayed because . . .

   e. Here is a quick summary of the Armstead evaluation of our human resources department.

   f. How do you like this idea for a self-publishing writer's group?

The following three examples were published a few years ago in the *San Jose Mercury News* newspaper:

> How many times have you trudged out to your car during the Lake Tahoe ski season only to find it won't start? Finally, after fiddling with the carburetor and air filter and nearly freezing your fingers off, the motor cooperates.
>
> Wouldn't it be nice if your coupe knew what do do when it got to the mountains?
>
> One little chip may make that possible soon.

Following a discussion of the development and future of this chip, the article ends: "Now, how about a a chip that would help you remember where you left your car keys?"

> You can't really put a dollar value, it seems to me, on human life.
>
> Yet a lot of people try to do it, turning statistics, probabilities and interest rates into a bottom-line figure that's supposed to represent your neighbor's worth.

Then the article continues with a treatise on the use of computers by two enterprising men who settled personal injury claims nationwide between clients and insurance companies. A hypothetical example cited by one of the two men: A female newspaper reporter, age twenty-eight has two children and a husband who is a writer. She was making $19,000 a year before being killed in an auto accident. The value of her life is $500,000. But how do you put a dollar amount on emotions?

> It took ten long years for time to heal Ben Pfister's wounds. But now that it has, Pfister isn't waiting another minute to reconstruct the pieces of his shattered dreams.

As you would expect from this topic paragraph, the story is of Ben's demise and recovery, in this case in the electronics business. He claimed his business was ruined by IBM's giving away free software. He sued. Ten years later he and IBM agreed to work together. It takes a strong man to forgive and forget.

Closing a piece of writing:

In the last three examples of topic sentences, a closing thought, comment or question was made. These tie back directly to the topic paragraphs, giving the message a feeling of completeness.

Closing comments for the previous lettered group of short opening paragraphs could include these:

a. If you agree with my suggested changes, let me know and I will work out the details.

b. To keep this policy in force, we may have to do some close monitoring for a while.

c. Please let me know your thoughts about my suggestions.

d. We will let you know when the evaluation will be continued.

e. A detailed report will be ready by June 30.

f. Please let me know what you think of my idea.

Emphasis

Arrange sentences, paragraphs and compositions so that the emphasis is placed on the words and thoughts you, the writer, want to make important. The ending is the best place for emphasis, with the beginning second best. If, however, you start a sentence with The King, The Emperor, The Dictator, The Pope or The President, you are starting with a high impact thought.

A couple of examples applying to sentences:

Weak: A delicious almond sauce made the pudding taste good.

Emphatic: The pudding was improved by adding a delicious almond sauce.

Weak: The ability of our house to withstand all the hotest and coldest weather is made possible by plastic siding.

Emphatic: Plastic siding makes our house capable of withstanding the hottest to the coldest weather.

Illustrations of emphasis in paragraphs:

Weak: An employer may wish to hedge his bets by writing a letter that accepts an applicant thus putting him or her on hold while the employer searches for another candidate. If that is unsuccessful the present candidate may be hired.

Emphatic: An employer may wish to write a letter tentatively accepting an applicant. The applicant is not an ideal choice but may be acceptable if the first or second person hired doesn't work out. The interest of the applicant is retained while the employer searches for a better employee.

Weak: A letter of good wishes is appropriate for a business friend who is also a personal friend, one to whom you can express your feelings in a friendly and natural way. Whatever the occasion—even if there is no occasion—being remembered is always appreciated. The year-end holiday season is a special occasion for sending good wishes and wishing your customer friend a prosperous new year.

Emphatic: A letter of good wishes is appropriate for a business friend who is also a personal friend, one to whom you can express your feelings in a friendly and natural way. The year-end holiday season is a special occasion for sending good wishes and thanking your customer for being *your* customer. Whatever the occasion—even when there is no occasion—being remembered is always appreciated.

Here are three longer examples of strong endings. Note that the dominant emphasis—punch line if you wish—is at the end:

1. Many people find it difficult to make a request that seems to impose upon others. Often, the person asked feels complimented that he or she is capable of helping you solve a problem, thus, assuming the request is reasonable, you should not be reluctant to ask. Let your acquaintance know how that help will be used.

The key to getting results from a sensitive request is having a persuasive and convincing explanation of the reason for the request. Think before you ask: What will appeal to your friend? How are your wants tied to your friend's wants? A request is more willingly granted if give-and-take is recognized. Your friend may ask, "What's in it for me?" Whenever possible offer something in return.

Close your request with confidence. Make no apologies. If you suggest that your friend is too busy to help, the response may be, "You're right. I don't have time." End on a polite note of confidence that the request will be granted.

2. I had to be four or five while we lived in the brown house in Edmonds, Washington. The outside was covered with shingles or clapboards. In either case, it was a deep, dark brown.

The wide front door was also dark brown, but its three, narrow stained-glass windows added sparkle, especially when the afternoon sun shown through.

The entry door led directly into the living room, and what always caught my eye was the divider immediately to the left, between the living and dining rooms. Two walls about three feet high did not meet, leaving a walkway in the middle. The walls were topped with dark brown boards, and two dark pillars at the opening supported a brown ceiling beam.

Both rooms had window trim, baseboards and wide picture moldings in the same monotonous brown. The walls, in pleasing contrast, were a creamy white. Thankfully, there was no wainscoting, but the wood-paneled stairwell was as dark as the well-worn steps. The upstairs bedroom, shared by me and two brothers, repeated the same dark brown in the door, window trim and baseboards.

Fifty years later while working in the office of a mill in Antioch, California, a co-worker suggested we have lunch at This Old House, an old house converted to a restaurant. I was startled as we approached the restaurant to find that it was designed exactly like our old, brown house in Edmonds.

The outside had been painted white, but the front door was the same. Inside, I paused as old memories became as heavy as that familiar dark brown trim. After a few moments in a nostalgic trance, I awakened to the realization that whatever the sentimental value, being immersed in nostalgia does not necessarily mean that what one recalls is appreciated forever. Since childhood, I have avoided living in a house decorated with dark brown trim.

This third example consists of excerpts from an article published in the *San Jose Mercury News* in 1982. This essay seems to belie the advantages of what we call "advancing civilization."

3. Church was over, and I walked to the dressing room, shed my altar boy cape and quickly dressed. With my friend, Sam Maggiore, I walked to the end of the bridge on San Fernando Street. We jumped the railing and quickly slid down the long embankment.

The creek and its banks were teeming. We were in the midst of a jungle of trees and shrubs—sycamores, willows, laurel, locust, poplar, buckeye, maples, oak—and a myriad of wild bushes and weeds. There were fish, frogs, snakes, squirrels, rabbits, quail, robins and woodpeckers.

The year was 1923 and I was twelve. A day spent exploring was like a trip down Mark Twain's Mississippi. We kept walking along the bank until we reached a pool of cool, clear water. In the shade of sycamores and willows we spent an hour fishing and eating our lunch.

I look back and wonder why this doesn't happen to kids today. It's because they spend all day glued to the television, the stereo and a blaring Walkman.

Santa Clara Valley was once filled with orchards and truck farms, deer and coyotes, mustard and wild poppies, country lanes and dairy farms. Where has it all gone?

We have become afflicted with urban psoriasis and acne, a disease that has given us enormous growth but no identity. "Progress" has become a cancer that grows nothing but dissatisfaction and violence. For every 1000 cars on the freeway, in 900 the driver is the only occupant. Does everyone want to live in California?

In 1909, James Brice, in a speech at the University of California at Berkeley, said, "When California is filled by 50 million people [1909 population 2.4 million, 2000 population 33.9 million] and its valuation is five times what it is now, the wealth will be so great that you will find it difficult to know what to do with it. The day will still have only twenty-four hours and each person will still have only one mouth. There will be as many people as the country can support—and the real question will not be about making more wealth or having more people, but whether the people will be happier or better."

Rewrite All Your Writing

The fact that all your writing should be revised and rewritten as necessary has been stated and illustrated numerous times in the chapters on sentences and paragraphs. This is one more reminder of the importance of revising everything you write before passing it on.

Whether writing a literary work or a business memo the only good writing is really good rewriting.

William Faulkner reportedly said that he rewrote *The Sound and the Fury* five times. The writer Alberto Moravia said he worked each book over several times. Humorist Dorthy Parker said that French novelist Gustave Flaubert (1821–1880) "rolled around on the floor for days, trying to think of the right word." An encyclopedic account is less dramatic: His obsession with the writer's craft is legendary. Hour after hour, he would labor over the rhythm or the music of a particular sentence, seeking just the right word.

The following examples are excerpts taken from *Writers at Work*, a group of interviews edited by George Plimpton:

> Mary Sarton is a writer of over forty books of poetry, novels and memoirs. She was asked if she had written poems in free verse. She said, "Oh, yes, a lot. I find it exhilarating." "How do you know when you are finished?" She replied, "That's the problem. I can go on revising almost forever."
>
> Elizabeth Hardwick from Kentucky has received many literary rewards for her novels and essays. She was asked, "What is it about the writing process that gives you the most plesure?" Her answer, "The revision. That's what I like, working on a page or scene."
>
> Raymond Carter was born in Oregon and has written several books of poetry and collections of short stories. He stated, "When I'm writing, I put in a lot of hours at the desk, ten or fifteen hours at a stretch, day after

day. . . . Much of this time, understand, is given over to revising and re-writing. . . . I've done as many as twenty or thirty drafts of a story. . . . Tolstoy did a great deal of writing; he rewrote *War and Peace* eight times."

John Asbery of New York learned how to bypass the chore or rewriting. He is a Pulitzer Prize winner for his poetry. He was asked, "Do you revise your poems heavily?" "Not anymore. I used to labor over them a great deal, but because of my strong desire to avoid all unnecessary work, I have somehow trained myself not to write something that I will either have to discard or be forced to work a great deal over."

Experience does help. Shortly after college, I applied for a job with Boeing, the airplane manufacturer. As part of the interview I was given a problem about an item received by the stockroom that didn't meet the specifications of the order. I was told in vague terms how to respond to the supplier, then given one sheet of paper and a pencil. "Write a letter to the supplier," I was told. Immediately I started writing, crossed out a few words, changed more words and a couple sentences, and turned in my letter. I did not get the job. Later I wrote a highly successful book on how to write letters—thirty years later.

Here are three ways to revise: adding, eliminating and substituting. The latter includes transposing and repositioning words and phrases.

Adding explanations:

Skimpy: When you come to Seattle for your sales meeting, you could stay at our company hotel room.

Better: When you come to Seattle for your March sales meeting, perhaps you would enjoy staying at our company hotel room; we can reserve March 15, 16 and 17 for you.

Skimpy: When you come to Seattle for your sales meeting, you could stay at our company hotel room. It's a good location. I'll be pleased to reserve the room for you. Let me know.

Complete: When you come to Seattle for your March sales meeting, per-haps you would enjoy staying at our company hotel room. We can reserve March 15, 16 and 17 for you. I think you would enjoy the location, as well as the room, because the hotel is only three blocks from your meeting place. It will be a pleasure to reserve the room for you, but I must have your decision by March 10. Please let me hear from you.

Skimpy: The union is on strike.

Better: Because of a failure to agree on terms, the union has called a strike that may affect our operations.

Skimpy: The union is on strike. But we plan to continue shipping from our warehouses. We will try to keep you supplied and hope you can put up with the possible inconvenience.

Complete: Because of a failure to agree on terms, the union has called a strike that may affect our operations. Despite this, our company intends to do everything possible to maintain normal shipping operations from our warehouses. Our priority will be to minimize disruptions that might inconvenience our customers. Your cooperation during this period is appreciated.

Eliminating excess thoughts:

Excessive: The San Antonio Fiesta tour is open to all members and their friends. Please join us for this fun tour to the beautiful San Antonio Fiesta.

San Antonio, a city of historical importance and unique charm, offers visitors a sumptuous smorgasbord of cultural diversity. Its wealth of cultural diversity matches the Texas-size hospitality. Join the Better Business Board on their July 24–28 tour during the time of the Fiesta, a dazzling San Antonio party. The Fiesta, filled with pomp and circumstance, consists of art exhibits, concerts, parades, band festivals and much, much more centered around the famous River Walk. Call Ella Elison for information at 000-0000.

Concise: The San Antonio Fiesta tour is open to all members and friends of the Better Business Board. Please join us for this fun tour of the beautiful and exiting San Antonio Fiesta.

Come with us on July 24–28 for this dazzling Fiesta party. Call Ella Elison for information, 000-0000.

Excessive: The daily Milk and Meal Sheets must be turned in to John Barber on the first working day of each month. We know keeping the details of milk usage and the number of meals served each day is a time-consuming task. But it is a part of your job and all house supervisors have to do it. We appreciate your full cooperation.

These sheets are part of a long report that the state requires by the seventh of each month, which is one of the sources for setting our monthly reimbursement. A timely turn-in of the Meal Sheets is money in our pockets.

Concise: The daily Milk and Meal Sheets must be turned in to John Barber on the first working day of each month.

These sheets are part of a report the state requires each month, which is one of the sources for setting our monthly reimbursement. A timely turn-in of the Meal Sheets is money in our pockets.

Substituting words, phrases and thoughts:

Straggly: The club completed its holiday project, helping a family which was given us by the Salvation Army. We raised $750.00 which was given for a single-parent family—a man with three sons—two years, seven and eleven. Alonso Serra, Jo Wise and Sue Devon did a super job. They gave fifteen gift packages, food, and a turkey from the Seniors. With discounts and coupons there was $140.00 left and the Army asked us to purchase gift packages from a grocery store. I learned that they had received their gifts and were overjoyed.

Concise: Members of the club completed their holiday project, helping a family that was given to us by the Salvation Army. We raised $750, which we donated to a single-parent family—a man with three sons of two, seven and eleven years. Alonso Serra, Jo Wise and Sue Devon did a super job! They gave fifteen gift packages, food and a turkey from the Seniors. I learned that the family had received their gifts and were overjoyed!

Fuzzy: Club Information Dinner.

Date: September 3 or 4—Reason for two dinners is to have smaller groups and get quicker service.

Time: 6:00 P.M.

Cost: $5.00 per person—Reason for increase: increased cost by the caterer.

Tickets go on sale two weeks before the dinner. Information will be given by all club committees and time will be available for questions. There will be music and entertainment during the evening. We want this to be a time for getting together for a social event as well as being informative about our club activities in order to learn the financial needs of our club.

Concise: Club Information Dinner

Date: September 3 and 4—two dates will accomodate smaller groups and provide faster food service.

The cost is $5 per person. Tickets will go on sale two weeks before the dinner.

The dinner of spaghetti, salad, bread sticks and spumoni will be served at 6:00 P.M. by a caterer.

Information will be given by all club committees, and time will be available for questions. There will be music and entertainment during the evening. This will be a social event and will also provide information about the club's financial needs.

Substituting with subordination and coordination:

Wandering: The winter was cold, exceptionally cold, and the snow piled up every day for a week, and it came up past our kitchen window, and the snow plows didn't arrive.

Better: The snow that piled up past our kitchen window that cold week stayed on the streets because the snow plows were behind schedule.

Better: Even though the snow piled up beyond our kitchen window that exceptionally cold week, the snow plows did not arrive to clear the streets.

Better: The snow piled up beyond our kitchen window that cold, cold week, and the snow plows couldn't clear the streets.

Better: The winter was exceptionally cold, the snow piled up for a week, our kitchen window was covered and the roads remained unplowed.

Better: During that cold, cold week when the snow piled up beyond our kitchen window, the snow plows were unable to clear the streets.

Better: Snow, that cold favorite of Midwest winters, covered our windows and blocked our streets for a whole week.

Tactics for revising:

The first step in revising is to wait—wait for a couple days if possible, or at least one day. This permits you to look at your writing objectively; you can see it from an outsider's viewpoint. You can ask, "Did this writer (you) do his or her best?" If this waiting period is not possible under the circumstances, putting the piece aside for an hour will be helpful.

Do *not* try to cover the following steps during one reading. Go through the composition several times:

to review the general idea

to review the organization and order of ideas

to check spelling

to check proper English

to review completeness

to review wordiness

to review accuracy

to review clarity of statements

Cut Out the "Deadwood"

The section, "Revising Paragraphs," at the end of Chapter 7, "Topics of Paragraphs," presented examples of paragraphs shortened to improve clarity. In this section, the emphasis is on eliminating excess words that make readers feel they are becoming lost in a fog of verbiage.

The first example is taken from the *Member's Handbook* of SPELL (Society for the Preservation of English Language and Literature). The original is 201 words, the revision is 105 words.

Verbose:

Customer perceptions are the cognitive events that precede buying behavior. Vendor organizations that stay attuned to customer perceptions can deal more successfully and effectively with their customers' needs and concerns. This article provides specific viable suggestions and implementation procedures for developing specific ways to improve customer perceptions.

Specific actions by the vendor organizations can have a very immediate, positive impact on the customer. They may in addition provide the customer with bona fide, quite positive consequences that may serve to distinguish a particualar vendor entity from competing vendors. Some of these suggestions for reinforcing activities are as follows:

1. Install toll-free 800 numbers and make absolutely certain it is physically present on all your sales and marketing brochures, advertising, and other printed matter.

2. Assign key managers the task of contacting every one of your new customers and every one of your lost customers.

3. Develop and conduct a comprehensive survey covering all present and past customers and share with these customers the information from the survey data.

4. Once the survey has been completed, respond personally to any questions that may have arisen during the taking of the survey and make a firm commitment to correcting any problems that may have been pinpointed.

Revision:

Perceptions affect buying habits, and a vendor attuned to customers' perceptions can deal more effectively with their needs. This article suggests ways to improve customer perceptions.

Actions by the vendor can have an immediate, positive effect on the customer. They may also help to distinguish a vendor from competitors.

Some suggested actions are:

1. Install a toll-free number and publish it in advertising and sales literature.

2. Have managers contact all present and former customers.

3. Survey present and former customers and share with them the information from the survey.

4. After the survey, respond to questions that may have arisen and commit to correcting problems it uncovered.

Here is an example of "complete deadwood." A business executive is reported to have written:

Expansion communication is fundamental to successful resolution of these intrinsic conflicts and to the optimization of resource allocation for the emerging department in an increasing competitive environment.

This seems to mean: Communication is essential if this department is to withstand competition. Or, perhaps: Communication is necessary in this department.

Even headlines can contain lots of "deadwood":

Senate fails to override veto of late abortion ban

The four negatives in this headline, fails, override, veto and ban, add to the reader's confusion. I suspect all that was intended is:

Late-term abortion is still legal

Much of the "deadwood" in "teen-talk" is probably due to immaturity. For example:

Some of these, you know, college profs, and them, think we teens, like, talk mall speak—like we don't, you know, know how to talk like English majors. Why, you know, can't we talk like they say we always do?

This probably means: We teenagers like the way we talk.

The following letter is a well-organized request, a model of good composition and clear, but as a business letter, 78% of the words should be eliminated.

All Plant Accountants

Subject: Form 200—Reports of construction cost

The Fixed Property Department has requested the Form 200 be executed at the completion of each capital project involving a capital addition. This form is used in determining the total cost of a project and the amount to be added to the asset records. It thereby determines the depreciation that the plant will be charged.

Instances have been found where major pieces of equipment have been removed, sold, or otherwise disposed of, and only the book value of the basic machine was removed from the asset records. Attachments and major additions made after the basic machine had been in service for several years frequently are not removed from the records since they are listed on a different page and are not recognized as a part of the basic machine.

To avoid this problem we would like each Form 200 to have the cost tie in with the IDN number of the basic machine. For example, a hand-held cutting attachment for a press purchased on a separate capital project and its cost reported to the Asset Record Department on a separate Form 200 should have the press IDN number shown on the Form 200 so that when the press is sold, every entry tied into the basic IDN number would be removed from the records.

Should an attachment be of such a nature as to carry its own IDN number, the Form 200 would still show that this attachment is used on, or is a part of, a basic machine having IDN number so and so.

Your cooperation in showing the IDN number of the basic machine, as well as the various attachments, on Form 200 will be greatly appreciated.

The "live wood" in this letter is as follows:

Revision: The Fixed Property Department has requested that Form 200 be filled in at the completion of each capital project involving a capital addition. Each Form 200 should show the IDN number of the machine to which it applies. If an attachment has its own IDN number, also list the IDN number of the basic machine.

We would appreciate your starting this procedure immediately.

If this next letter seems unduly long, it is because an unusual problem requires an unusual solution. The problem was a three-year (1976–78) drought in California, which was serious enough to receive two mentions in the *1978 Annual* of the *Americana Encyclopedia* (pages 56 and 134).

The writer had two problems to meet: first the drought was adversely affecting the operation of a paper mill, and second, the audience to be addressed consisted of people whose education varied from eighth grade through master's degrees in chemistry.

There were three possible ways to have made the letter more readable—and shorter.

1. Rewrite to the least educated persons.
2. Send a second letter to the technical personnel, detailing the technical aspects.

3. Place the technical information at the end and preface it with a statement that it is technical information.

The revision of this letter will illustrate the third method, and eliminate some of the repetition. The writer assumed, incorrectly, that a long explanation was better than a short one. Some names have been changed.

March 22, 1977
Dear Fellow Employees:

There has been considerable press coverage, TV coverage, and comments in reference to the drought in California and the impact of this drought on the Langley Mill. We would like to take this opportunity to clarify the situation at the Langley Mill.

We receive water from three sources normally: 1) the river, 2) the South Coastal Canal Water District, commonly referred to as "the canal," and 3) the City of Langley.

Our requirements for water are the cooling water for the turbine, the process water, and the potable water to be used for drinking water, showers, etc. The river supplies the cooling water for the turbine, and, dependent upon the salinity, the process water. However, now that the salinity level of the river is so high, we are dependent upon the South Coastal Canal to obtain the approximate 4,200,000 gallons/day of process water.

In respect to the South Costal Canal Water there are two aspects to this situation: 1) quality of the water, 2) quantity of water. If the chloride ions of the process water exceed a certain level we are not able to produce linerboard off the No. 1 Paper Machine which meets "can" linerboard quality. The salt content of the linerboard is too high. Through hard work and close attention by the personnel in the Maintenance Department, Steam Plant, and No. 1 Paper Machine, we have been able to produce quality "can" linerboard with process water in the range of 260–280 ppm chloride ion content. This is the quality of water we can expect to receive from the "canal" and if we do, we should not experience any curtailment due to quality.

In respect to the quantity of water we are to receive from the canal, we are facing a very serious situation. On March 11, 1977, we were advised by the South Coastal Canal Water District that we have been allocated 3,661 acre feet of water for the entire 1977 calendar year. What does this mean? Based on water usage in January and February and our estimated March usage, commencing April 1, 1977, we will have to average approximately 3,164,000 gallons/day. Based on our normal requirement of approximately 4,200,000 gallons/day, we have to reduce our usage by 1,000,000 gallons/day effective April 1 or face the possibility of curtailment if we exceed our alloted quantity.

We have numerous programs under way and in mind, and we are confident that we can reduce our usage sufficiently to stay within our allocated amount. It should be noted that we cannot have all these programs in effect by April 1, and thus to meet the average for the balance of the year of 3,146,000 gallons/day we will have to reduce our usage by more than 1,000,000 gallons/day. This can only be done by your cooperation, assistance and ideas on how to reduce water usage. We all have a piece of the action.

In respect to the potable water from the City of Langley we will be rationed the same as the citizens within the city. We have installed restrictions in the shower heads and toilet dams in the restrooms. We are exploring the use of the wells in the orchard, but naturally this is dependent upon meeting the health codes.

Let me assure you this drought is a very serious situation. However, I am confident with everyone's cooperation and attention we will work our way through it with minimum impact. It will require some changes in our actions and methods of working, but we can do it.

Thank you for your cooperation.

Revision:

March 22, 1977

Dear Fellow Employees:

There has been considerable press and TV coverage about the drought in California and its impact on the Langley Mill. We would like to clarify the situation for you.

We receive water from three sources: 1) the river, 2) the South Coastal Canal Water District canal and 3) the City of Langley. When the rainfall drops, the water level of the river drops and salt water from the Bay enters the river to the point where we withdraw water for our processing operation. We then have to purchase canal water, which is more expensive and, since the drought, has become limited.

On March 11, 1977, the South Coastal Canal Water District alloted us 3,661 acre feet of water for the 1977 calendar year. This means we must reduce our usage by more than 1,000,000 gallons each day effective April 1 or we will face possible curtailment because of exceeding our allotment.

We have numerous programs both planned and now underway to reduce our water usage. We are exploring the use of the wells in the orchard at the south end of our property. We can reduce our water usage with the cooperation of each of you. If you have any ideas you think might help, please let your supervisor know.

Our usage of city water has been rationed the same as citizens within the city. We have installed shower head restrictors and toilet dams in the rest rooms.

Let me assure you this drought is a serious situation. I am confident, however, that you will cooperate to help us all get through this problem with a minimum of inconvenience.

Your full cooperation will be truly appreciated.

For those concerned with technical details, here are further data:

The river supplies cooling water for the turbine and, depending upon the salinity, the process water. With the salinity level so high now, we are dependent upon the canal to supply 4.2 million gallons daily of process water.

In addition to reducing the quantity of canal water, quality is a problem. If the chloride ions of the process water exceed a certain level, we are not able to produce linerboard off the No. 1 Paper Machine that meets "can" quality.

Through hard work and close attention by personnel of the Maintenance Department, Steam Plant and No. 1 Paper Machine, we have been able to produce "can" linerboard with process water in the range of 260–280 ppm chloride ion content. This is the quality we can expect from the canal.

We must continue to operate with some changes in our methods, some risks, some inefficiencies and some discomforts, but we can do it.

Checklist—The Final Review

Reading this checklist *before* you start writing alerts you to possible errors and fuzziness during the writing process. Reading it afterward provides one of the advantages of hindsight: this is your second chance to make that first impression on your readers.

Could your choice of words be improved?

Could your arrangement of words be improved?

Are most sentences active rather than passive?

Is each sentence clear, concise and easily understood?

Are sentences varied in length?

Are short series of items listed in parallel structure?

Will the first paragraph get the reader's attention?

Are important points emphasized?

Paragraphs of more than three sentences should have a topic sentence.

Compositions of more than three paragraphs should have a topic or introductory paragraph.

Could the order of paragraphs be improved?

Will the composition appeal to or inform your reader?

Is the central point of the writing clear?

Is the writing clear to the intended reader?

Should material be added?

Should material be eliminated?

Is the topic limited in scope: distantly related ideas omitted?

Is the arrangement of data logical?

Are general statements supported by facts?

Are facts and figures correct?

Have redundancies, deadwood, dullness and affectations been removed?

Have you used a positive approach?

Is proper English used?

Are clear transitions used—between words, sentences and paragraphs?

Are series of facts presented in list form?

Is the tone appropriate for the situation and the audience?

Is the correct degree of formality used?

Is the writing tactful?

If one item is changed during the revision, does that change its relationship to other items?

Are the conclusions supported by the arguments?

Does the ending read like the topic's conclusion?

If possible, read your composition out loud: parts needing change often pop out.

CHAPTER 10

Why Spelling?

Why Learn to Spell Correctly?

The point of spelling correctly is clear understanding by your reader. You can't substitute *plain* for *plane* or *rite* for *right* or *bad* for *bid*. If your word processor has a spell check program, by all means use it, but be aware that it will not distinguish between *too* and *two* or *there* and *their*. If your communication leaves the office with spelling errors, you can't blame your typist because you should have reviewed the document before you signed or approved it.

We are all human and make occasional mistakes, but spelling errors are not readily forgiven. All your readers, from your boss to your spouse to your brother to your sister to your father or even to your mother, judge you by your spelling. Why? Because, with few exceptions, words have only one correct spelling.

A sampling of the exceptions follows. The first spelling is the preferred one:

acknowledgment or acknowledgement	fulfil or fulfill
	taboo or tabu
adviser or advisor	tradable or tradeable
ax or axe	tunneling or tunnelling
bluing or blueing	tying or tieing
cacti or cactuses	wedded or wed

Learning that a word has more than one correct spelling can be an interesting experience as the next paragraph illustrates.

When I arrived in San Francisco from the Seattle area, I was surprised to see that *theater* was spelled *theatre*, in advertisements, in the newspapers and even in the telephone book. I thought that was being a little high-hatted by the people of San Francisco. But then I learned that in the 1850s while the Wild West was being settled by cowboys, ranchers and gunslingers, the people of San Francisco were enjoying opera. According to Doris Muscatine in her book *Old San Francisco*, "As early as February 1851, San Franciscans were enthusiastically attending the Pelligrini Italian Opera Troop's chorusless performances of *La Sonnambala, Norma* and *Erani*." I therefore concede that San Franciscans are entitled to use the highbrow, British spelling of *theatre*.

Correct spelling is imperative on job applications. Personnel—human relations—managers will quickly spot a misspelled word, especially if you address your application to the "personell" manager. If you apply for a position as a psychiatric nurse, your four or six years of training will not get you the job if you misspell *psychiatric*.

Why Is Spelling So Difficult?

Spelling is difficult because English is a conglomeration of the words of many other languages. English has twenty-six letters in its alphabet, and although language experts don't agree exactly, there are forty to fifty distinct sounds and from 300 to 600 spelling combinations of these sounds. For example, the sound of *er* as in *her*: blur, err, fir, myrrh, shirr, were and chauffeur; or the sound of *air* in bare, bear, prayer, their, there and millionaire.

In contrast, some of the same spellings have quite different sounds, for example, *ough*, as in bough, cough, slough, rough, ought and dough.

How Do We Learn to Spell?

In spite of these difficulties, you can learn to spell—although it may take a little bit of effort. The three basic methods of learning are visual, auditory and motor—seeing, hearing and writing the words.

Visual Learning

For the majority of people the most helpful approach is the visual. But a person has to look carefully to see what the letters are.

At one time I lived in a community near Phoenix, Arizona. Traveling from Phoenix to my home along the main roadway, I passed a few towns, each of which was pointed out by a sign. One day I was astounded after looking at one sign to realize that it spelled *Youngtown*. For three years I had passed that sign and assumed it spelled *Youngstown*—like the city in Ohio, noted for its heavy industry and steel making. Assuming is not a proper technique for learning to spell.

Another visual device is making a list of all the words you misspell. Look carefully at each letter. Imprint it on your mind. Your task here is to review this list tomorrow and next week.

Proofread your written material to catch mistakes. This should be done before you release any writing at any time. If you are fortunate enough to have the time and a helpful friend, ask your friend to read over your message. An outsider viewer will often catch little mistakes you glanced over too quickly because you know what you *meant* to write. Proofread for spelling as a separate step from checking rules of writing, punctuation, flow of thought and overall impression.

Auditory Learning

Pronouncing words correctly will help in many instances. Some examples:

casualty/causality	finally/finely
elicit/illicit	pastor/pasture

athletic, not athaletic

February, not Febuary

garage, not gararge

government, not goverment

poem, not pome

recognize, not reconize

sandwich, not sanwich or samwich

tragedy, not tradegy

umbrella, not umberella

As mentioned earlier, however, correct pronunciation will not help your spelling of such words as *bough, cough*, and *dough*.

Some words are confusing because they sound the same as or similar to quite different words. For example:

accept/except	heard/herd
altar/alter	holy/wholly
bare/bear	its/it's
dairy/diary	moral/morale
dual/duel	pray/prey
fair/fare	sense/since
hare/hair	weather/whether

Motor Learning

Motor learning is writing a word over and over until the motions of your hands automatically follow the proper sequence when you think of a word. Here is an example:

When in the third grade, I proudly spelled *dimond* on the blackboard. After a few pupils in the class pointed out that the correct spelling is *diamond*, Miss Casper, whose brother owned and operated the popular gas station on Casper's Corner, said, "Perhaps if you sit down now and write the word correctly fifty times, and turn the paper in to me, you won't have any more trouble with *diamond*." I did her bidding, but I still struggle to put in that unpronounced *a*—although I always remember to do it.

This technique does help some people.

Using Memory Devices

Various devices can be used to tune your memory to the correct spelling of words, for example: *stationary* and *stationery*. *Stationery* is writing paper and includes envelopes—an *e* in both words. *Stationary* means not moving.

I had trouble with those words until I heard the relationship between *stationery* and *envelope*. I also had trouble with *calender*, a word I wrote often when working for a company that used *calenders* (rollers) in their paper-making machinery. I wrote the word *calendar* frequently. I associated *stationery* with office-work paper, and I also wanted to associate *calender* with my office work. But the use of *a* and *e* are opposite when both *stationery* and *calendar* are related to office paper work. To make this memory device work, I have to go back to *stationery* and *envelope* and office paper work and then remember that *calendar* includes the *a* opposite the the way it us used in *stationery*. No wonder people with non-photographic memories have difficulty spelling. But I think I now have *stationery* and *calendar* properly related to paper.

Use Your Dictionary

"Use your dictionary," is often the quoted advice when you ask how to spell a certain word. If you have a fair idea of the correct spelling, or wish to know if *diamond* includes an unpronounced *a*, a dictionary can be helpful.

But suppose you can't find the correct spelling in your dictionary because you don't know how to spell the word. For example: you think *agast* doesn't look quite right and look for it in the dictionary. It should be between *agarose* and *agate*, but it isn't and now you are lost. Turn to your thesaurus. If you should think of *terrified* as a synonym, you will find that the suggested synonyms are a group of words beginning with *terrified*. Among those words you find *aghast*. There is an unpronounced *h* in the word.

If you should think of the synonym *shocking*, that would lead you to *terri-*

fying, which doesn't help directly, but you look about and nearby see the word group starting with *terrified*. By this different route you have again found the correct spelling of *aghast*.

Another example: How do you spell *essence*? One or two *s*'s? Does it end in *se* or *ce*? Look for the word *odor* in your thesaurus. One base word is *fragrance*, another is *smell*. Under *fragrance* we find *essence*. Also under *smell* we find *essence*.

One last example: You are writing the phrase, "nooks and crannies." You aren't sure how to spell *crannies*. You think it might be *cranies* and check in the dictionary. It's not there. You know a nook is a corner and think a cranny is a small slit or crack. You look in your thesaurus under *crack* and find a subheading of *cleft*. That sounds close, and under *cleft* you find the word *cranny*. Back to the dictionary, which shows the plural as *crannies*.

Simplified Rules

Rules are appreciated by those who need a strong leader and those who need a firm base upon which to stand. The rest of us try to learn the rules while ignoring them. But rules provide a standard by which our literacy is judged. We therefore should learn some of the basic rules of spelling. We might also note that spelling rules have exceptions.

The rules stated here are ones I found most often violated during my years in the worlds of business and writing. You will find this section a reference for the most common spelling errors.

Hyphens

A hyphen is a link, tying two parts of a word together or connecting two or more words.

Words with the prefixes *self* and *ex*:

self-centered	self-defense
self-image	self-respect
ex-governor	ex-partner
ex-president	ex-wife

Selfish and selfless are not hyphenated.

Words with the prefix *co*:

co-op, but cooperation

Hyphenate two or more words when they are used as one to modify a noun and are placed in front of the noun:

long-haul trailer

not-to-be-forgotten event

seventy-five-voice choir

three-room house

well-known citizen

Use a hyphen to connect compound nouns and single capital letters:

half-awake	T-shirt
quarter-hour	Y-formation

Use hyphens to tie together words with numbers:

four-fifths	twenty-one
pages 42-56	50-cent stamp

Suffixes

A suffix is a letter or letters added to the end of a base word. For example:

accept—able	combust—ible
actual—ly	immediate—ly
attend—ance	prefer—ence
automatic—ally	solid—ify

A few rules will help you add the suffixes correctly.

1. *Drop the final e:*

Usually drop the final *e* if the suffix begins with a vowel:

age, aging	scarce, scarcity
arrive, arrival	write, writing

Usually retain the final *e* if the suffix begins with a consonant:

arrange, arrangement	force, forceful
care, careful	like, likeness

Note that these last two rules begin with the word *usually*. Practically all rules applied to the English language are plagued with exceptions.

Some exceptions when the final *e* is retained:

acreage	noticeable
advantageous	outrageous
mileage	serviceable

Some exceptions when the final *e* is dropped:

argument	possibly
judgment	truly
ninth	wholly

Other exceptions intended to avoid confusion:

die, dying	shoe, shoeing
dye, dyeing	sing, singing
hinge, hingeing	singe, singeing

2. *Double the final consonant before the suffix:*

This rule applies to more words than any other rule, and therefore is quite useful, although it may seem as complicated as memorizing the words by the visual learning method.

a. Double the final single consonant except *h* or *x* before a suffix beginning with a vowel if (1) the base word is one syllable or (2) the accent is on the last syllable and (3) the final *single* consonant is preceded by a *single* vowel. For example:

abhor, abhorred, abhorring, abhorrence, abhorrent

acquit, acquitted, acquitting

admit, admitted, admitting

blacktop, blacktopped, blacktopping

can, canned, canning

clip, clipped, clipping

concur, concurred, concurring

control, controlled, controlling

dim, dimmer, dimmest, dimmed, dimming

drug, drugged, drugging, druggist

fit, fitted, fitting, fitter, fittest

forget, forgetting, forgetter, forgettable, but forgetful

get, getting

grip, gripped, gripping

incur, incurred, incurring

jet, jetted, jetting

knit, knitted, knitting

mad, madder, maddest

nap, napped, napping

occur, occurred, occurring, occurrence

prefer, preferred, preferring

rebel, rebelled, rebelling

refer, referred, referring

rim, rimmed, rimming

scrap, scrapped, scrapping

ship, shipped, shipping

sit, sitting

slim, slimmer, slimmest, slimmed, slimming

snag, snagged, snagging

stun, stunned, stunning

tan, tanner, tannest, tanned, tanning

whet, whetted, whetting

b. If the accent is *not* on the last syllable of the base word when the ending is added, usually do *not* double the final consonant. For example:

benefit (accent on ben) benefited

happen (accent on hap) happened, happening

confer (accent on fer) conferred, conferring, but conference (accent on con)

refer (accent on fer) referred, referring, but reference (accent on ref)

c. A partial exception to section b above is that many words that are accented before the last syllable can be spelled with or without doubling the final consonant before adding the suffix. These are a few examples:

bedevil, bedeviled or bedevilled

carol, caroled or carolled

diagram, diagramed or diagrammed

funnel, funneled or funnelled

panel, paneled or panelled

pencil, penciled or pencilled

program, programed or programmed

shovel, shoveled or shovelled

shrivel, shriveled or shrivelled

signal, signaled or signalled

tassel, tasseled or tasselled

The following are a few words that follow no regular rules for doubling or not doubling consonants:

cancellation	personnel
excellent	questionnaire
handicapped	transferable
metallurgy	

3. *Change y to i before adding a suffix:*

This rule has two parts: words ending in *y* preceded by a *consonant* and preceded by a *vowel*.
a. When a word ends in *y* preceded by a *consonant*, change the *y* to *i* before adding the suffix, except a suffix beginning with *i*, as in *ing*. Some examples:

angry, angrily

apply, applies, applied, but applying

city, cities

defy, defied, but defying

easy, easier, easiest, easily

shy, shied, shier, shies, but shying

try, tried, tries, but trying

b. When a word ends in *y* preceded by a *vowel*, do *not* change the *y* to *i*. For example:

annoy, annoyed, annoyance

boy, boyish

play, played, playing
stay, stayed, staying

These rules, 3.a and 3.b, also have exceptions. Here are a few:

baby, babyhood	pays, paid
day, daily	say, said
lay, laid	shy, shyly, shyness

4. *Retain the final 1 when adding ly:*

accidental—ly	general—ly
annual—ly	natural—ly
cool—ly	real—ly
final—ly	successful—ly
formal—ly	usual—ly

Also, add *ally* if the adjective ends in *ic*. Examples:

automatic—ally	fantastic—ally
basic—ally	systematic—ally

Exceptions to rule 4 include:

duly	publicly
only	truly
possibly	wholly

Prefixes

A prefix is a letter or letters placed in front of a base word to change its meaning.

The rule for prefixes is simply to add the prefix to the base word, without adding or subtracting any letters. (That accounts for the two *s*'s in the word misspell, which is often misspelled.)

Common prefixes are: de, dis, il, im, in, ir, mis, re, un. Some examples:

de—activate	de—value
de—emphasize	dis—affection

dis—agree	ir—reducible
dis—establish	ir—relevant
il—legal	mis—judge
il—literate	mis—spell
il—logical	mis—trust
im—balance	re—call
im—moral	re—elect
im—practical	re—grind
in—accurate	un—dress
in—action	un—necessary
in—conclusive	un—noticed
ir—rational	un—realistic

i before e except after c:

This rule starts with an exception: *i* before *e* except after *c, except* when the sound is a long *a* as in *bale* or *bay* or *vein* or *weigh*.

The words below follow this basic exception to the rule: the *ei* part of the word has the long *a* sound:

beige	rein
eight	sleigh
freight	vein
neighbor	weigh

Even this exception has its own exceptions—*e* before *i* but not with a long *a* sound:

caffeine (or caffein)	protein
either	seizure
foreign	sleight
leisure	weird

The word *financier* fits none of the above rules or their exceptions. The *i* comes before the *e* after a *c*.

Endings of Words

The endings of some words cause great confusion in the minds of spellers without photographic memories. Among the most common doubtful endings are *able* or *ible*, *ance* or *ence*, *ar* or *er*, and *cede* or *ceed* or *sede*.

Let's try to dispel at least some of this confusion.

1. *Able or ible?*

Two basic rules cover most words ending in *able* or *ible*. Please note that each rule includes the word *usually*.

a. If the base word is a complete word, the ending is usually *able*.

accept—able	favor—able
break—able	notice—able
consider—able	read—able

b. If the base word is not a complete word, the ending is usually *ible*.

aud—ible	horr—ible
ed—ible	infall—ible
feas—ible	vis—ible

Here are some words that do not follow the rules. When in doubt, the standard answer is, "Use your dictionary."

affable	memorable
contemptible	perceptible
equitable	portable
flexible	probable
gullible	resistible
inevitable	vulnerable

2. *Ance or ence?*

Only one rule exists to help you determine if a word ends with *ance* or *ence*.

The rule: If a verb ends in an *r* that is preceded by a vowel, and is accented on the last syllable, the noun form ends with *ence*. Examples:

coher—ence	prefer—ence
confer—ence	refer—ence
infer—ence	

Three words that double the *r* before the *ence* ending are:

abhorrence	occurrence	recurrence

The remainder are exceptions and must be memorized or checked in a dictionary. Here are a few commonly misspelled words:

ance endings:	*ence* endings:
allowance	absence
appearance	audience
assurance	circumference
attendance	magnificence
balance	patience
dissonance	permanence
distance	persistence
grievance	pertinence
malfeasance	preference
perseverance	reverence

3. *Ar or er or or?*

If rules seem to be adding to your confusion rather than lessening it, relax: there are no rules for the *ar*, *er*, and *or* endings. Here are short lists of words many people have difficulty spelling correctly:

ar endings:	*er* endings:	*or* endings:
burglar	adviser	author
calendar	diameter	commentator
familiar	laborer	debtor
grammar	manufacturer	governor
pillar	prisoner	legislator
scholar	writer	supervisor

4. *Ary or ery or ory?*

These endings seem confusing because they are often pronounced the same. Words ending in *ary* include:

actuary	alimentary	aviary
adversary	apothecary	beneficiary

boundary	January	probationary
breviary	judiciary	secretary
budgetary	legendary	sedimentary
deflationary	monetary	seminary
depositary	mortuary	stipendiary
(also depository)	necessary	subsidiary
dignitary	obituary	supplementary
disciplinary	ordinary	tutelary
discretionary	pecuniary	unnecessary
elementary	penitentiary	veterinary
emissary	pensionary	visionary
fiduciary	pituitary	vocabulary
fragmentary	precautionary	voluptuary
hereditary	preliminary	

The most familiar words ending in *ery* are:

bakery	discovery	misery
battery	drapery	nursery
blustery	drudgery	recovery
bravery	flattery	rubbery
brewery	grocery	scenery
confectionery	machinery	shrubbery
creamery	mastery	stationery

The following list contains less familiar words ending in *ery*:

baptistery	drollery	nunnery
bufoonery	dysentery	philandery
butchery	effrontery	quackery
chancellery	embroidery	raillery
chandlery	hatchery	rookery
deanery	leathery	shimmery
debauchery	monastery	skulduggery
distillery	mummery	snobbery

sorcery	trumpery	watery
tomfoolery	vinery	winery
treachery	waggery	witchery

The *ory* ending of words is usually more clearly pronounced than the *ary* and *ery* endings, but if not vocalized, the correct ending is often in doubt. Here is a selection of words ending in *ory*:

accusatory	explanatory	prohibitory
admonitory	exploratory	promontory
allegory	expository	purgatory
anticipatory	interlocutory	rectory
auditory	introductory	reformatory
circulatory	inventory	refractory
clerestory	judicatory	retaliatory
compensatory	laboratory	reverberatory
conciliatory	lavatory	salutatory
depository	observatory	statutory
(also depositary)	offertory	supervisory
deprecatory	olfactory	suppository
derogatory	precursory	suspensory
directory	predatory	trajectory
dormitory	prefatory	vibratory

5. *Cede, ceed, sede*

Finally there is a straightforward, simple rule. Although it has three parts, you need memorize only four words.

a. Only one word ends in *sede*:

   supersede

b. Only three words end in *ceed*:

   exceed   proceed   succeed

c. All the rest end in *cede*. Some examples:

   accede   cede   concede
   precede   recede   secede

Silent Letters

Although correct pronunciation of words is one method of learning to spell, it is not nearly as good as attentive sight. Look closely at words as you read them. That is when you discover that many words contain letters that are not sounded.

To illustrate, below are some of the numerous words with silent letters:

aisle	fourth	numb
almond	ghastly	often
alms	ghost	plumber
balm	gnat	pneumatic
bomb	gnaw	psychology
bulk	honest	raspberry
calm	indebted	salmon
comb	island	thumb
condemn	isle	tomb
crumb	knack	wrap
dead	knee	wrench
depot	knife	wrestle
doubt	knot	wring
dumb	lamb	write
eight	mnemonics	wrought

Its or It's

The difference between *its* and *it's* should be simple, but for some reason many people are confused. Simply put, *it's* is a contraction of *it is* or *it has*. The apostrophe takes the place of a letter, in this case the *i* in *is*. The exclamation, "It's mine!" was shouted by my two children when they matured past the stage when their cry was a simple, "Mine, mine!" *Its* is one word and indicates possession. In the sentence, *The dog chased its tail*, the use of *its* means the dog owns the tail. You would never say, the dog chased it's—meaning it is—tail.

Plurals

A few rules will take the worry out of forming plurals.

1. Most nouns and proper nouns form the plural by adding *s*.

airport—s	cat—s	the Elby—s
book—s	chair—s	nail—s
the Carlson—s	dog—s	pan—s

2. Words ending in *ch, sh, s, x* or *z* add *es* to form the plural.

ash—es	fez—es	nexus—es
box—es	(also fezzes)	octopus—es
church—es	loss—es	rich—es
fax—es	marquis—es	six—es

3. Many nouns ending in *f* or *fe* change the ending to *ve*, then add the *s* to form the plural. Others add only the *s*.

chief, chiefs	sheriff, sheriffs
elf, elves	staff, staffs
life, lives	thief, thieves
roof, roofs	wife, wives

4. A noun ending in *y* preceded by a consonant changes the *y* to *i* then adds *es* to form the plural.

baby, babies	fairy, fairies
company, companies	industry, industries
eighty, eighties	

5. To make hyphenated words plural, add *s* to the principal word. For example:

attorney-at-law	father-in-law
attorneys-at-law	fathers-in-law
court-martial	maid-of-honor
courts-martial	maids-of-honor
daughter-in-law	mother-in-law
daughters-in-law	mothers-in-law

6. Use your dictionary to make sure you use the correct spelling of the many irregular plurals. A sampling:

analysis, analyses

axis, axes

basis, bases

brother, brothers, brethren

child, children

datum, data (original usage)

data, data (common usage)

deer, deer

echo, echoes

foot, feet

formula, formulas, formulae

goose, geese

hero, heroes

man, men

motto, mottoes, mottos

mouse, mice

nautilus, nautiluses, nautili

nucleus, nucleuses, nuclei

ox, oxen

perch, perch, perches

potato, potatoes

quiz, quizzes

radius, radii, radiuses

series, series

sheep, sheep

stimulus, stimuli

swine, swine

thesis, theses

tomato, tomatoes

tooth, teeth

vertebra, vertebrae, vertebras

woman, women

For those of you who are not so sure my thesis is sound—that is, that correct spelling is always important—here is an illustration you can throw back at me. The spelling is pathetic, but the message is clear.

Sign in the window of a local business:

JAYNES HAIR SOLON
HOURS
MON–SAT 7:30–5:00
EVINNGS BY APPOITMENT

A couple of months later, I walked by the beauty solon again and noticed that the sign had been changed. Perhaps someone had suggested there was a spelling error. The line now reads:

EVNININGS BY APITMENT

CHAPTER 11

Punctuate It This Way

What Is Punctuation?

Punctuation in writing is an attempt to replace physical movements that accompany conversation with symbols. In conversation we wave our arms to accent a statement, we raise four fingers to add visual emphasis to four points of our comments, we stand up straight to stress the truth of a statement, we lean forward to take the audience into our confidence, we shift from foot to foot to unintentionally reveal our nervousness, we raise our eyebrows to express astonishment, we frown to reveal a disturbing thought, we raise our voice to demonstrate our belief in what we are saying, we soften our voice to get closer attention, we raise the pitch of our voice to reveal concern, we lower the pitch to indicate positiveness, we increase our rate of speech to indicate intensity, we slow our rate to be clearly understood, and we stop occasionally to let a point sink in.

It is difficult to imagine a few small marks between printed words—the period, comma, semicolon, colon, exclamation point, hyphen, capital letter, dash, quotation mark, apostrophe, parenthesis, bracket, italic and virgule (slash)—conveying the effects of all these physical movements, but that is what the writer is up against. And that is why punctuation is important.

Why Use Punctuation?

Here are two illustrations, one of missing and one of misplaced punctuation:

At one time I worked as a billing clerk in a branch of a multinational truck trailer manufacturer. The billing policy was that the longer the description of repair work, the easier it would be to explain our high charges to our customers.

The shop foreman, George, wrote the repair work descriptions. This is what he gave me after repairing a gasoline motor that powered the refrigeration unit in one customer's trailer:

Disconnect fuel line and battery cables removed motor from its mounting removed grease from outside of motor steam sprayed removed and took apart carburetor cleaned all parts with sovent gaskets removed two checked and replaced spark plugs all belts tightened and replaced one belt removed valve cover and inspected valves timing adjusted replaced oil and oil filter removed engine replaced battery cables fuel line connected and gave engine trial run.

You read that correctly. In all his repair outlines, George used only two punctuation marks: one capital and one period. My job was to rewrite his descriptions and type them on the customer's invoices.

My rewrite went like this:

Disconnected fuel line and battery cables.

Removed motor from its housing.

Steam cleaned outside of motor to remove grease.

Disassembled carburetor and cleaned with solvent, and replaced two worn gaskets.

Removed and inspected spark plugs. Installed two new ones.

Inspected and tightened belts. Replaced one.

Inspected valves.

Adjusted timing.

Drained and replaced oil. Installed new filter.

Reinstalled motor; reconnected battery cables and fuel lines.

Test-ran the engine.

The reason for listing the steps in the repair operation is that a list is easier to read than a solid paragraph. Compare the readability of the above list with the following description of servicing my automobile:

LUBRICATION SERVICE AND INSPECTION: This service includes: Change oil and filter, lubricate chassis, hood latch, hinges, door locks, hinges, check tire pressure, inspect all tires and spare tire. Inspect hoses, belts, check and top up all fluid levels, check wiper/washer and under-car inspection.

ENVIRONMENTAL FEE: Waste disposal compliance charge. This

charge insures that all waste products removed from your vehicle have been collected for legal disposal and recycling. No wastes go to the landfills. We thank you for your voluntary contribution to a cleaner environment.

This description of work performed needs several changes in punctuation to improve the flow of thoughts. In the first sentence, the lists of services do not follow from the verbs introducing the lists.

The following rewrite of the first paragraph would be an improvement:

This service includes: change oil and oil filter; lubricate chassis, hood latch, hood hinges, door locks and door hinges; check tire pressure; inspect hoses, belts, underside of car, and tires including the spare; check and top up all fluid levels; check windshield wiper operation.

From these illustrations it should be obvious that correct punctuation enhances the readability and understanding of written messages.

The punctuation marks discussed in the remainder of this chapter highlight ways a writer attempts to replace vocal and physical expressions when communicating on paper.

Comma:

Commas are the most frequently used punctuation mark because they serve many purposes. Primarily commas clarify the meaning of a sentence, but they are also used to slow the reader, to replace intentionally omitted words (thus helping the reader to hurry along), to introduce, to enclose and to separate.

Reluctantly, it must be admitted that commas are the most confusing of all punctuation marks. Because of this, usage varies with writers, publishers and news associations. With our ever-changing language, some rules for comma usage are subject to variations.

A few illustrations will show how commas can clarify (or completely muddle) a sentence. A merchant marine officer testified that, "The helmsman made a change of course." The court reporter, not familiar with marine terminology, wrote, "The helmsman made a change, of course." The officer meant the helmsman made a change of direction. The court reporter implied that the helmsman made a change in procedure.

For you as a writer, it is important to note that the misunderstanding could have been avoided if the officer had testified that the helmsman changed the ship's direction. Try to write sentences that avoid the possibility of misinterpretation.

The placement of a comma in a sentence can change its emphasis. In the sentence, "Due to the work of Simpson three years ago, the system was changed," the emphasis is that the system was changed. However, in the sentence, "Due to the work of Simpson, three years ago the system was changed," the emphasis is that the system was changed three years ago.

You dictate a memo to an employee who has been a little difficult lately, "It's time for us to talk turkey. We need to clear the air. Please meet me in my office at 9:00 A.M. tomorrow, Wednesday." The clerk types, "It's time for us to talk, turkey. We need to clear the air . . ." The employee must have felt he was already fired.

A gardener left his helper a note reading, "I need bean poles and fertilizer." The next day the helper brought beans, poles and fertilizer. He had mentally inserted a comma between the words *bean* and *poles*.

The next example shows how excess commas can slow the reader to near numbness:

> Tom's viewpoint is, obviously, that the assistant, rather than the supervisor, has full responsibility, and admittedly, he is correct, according to the manual of operations.

A complete rewrite would eliminate a batch of commas, speed the reader along and clarify the meaning:

> Tom believes the assistant has full responsibility as stated in the operations manual.

To avoid confusion, reconstruct a sentence that could have more than one meaning, or use two sentences.

The next three paragraphs illustrate the most common uses of commas.

A comma is used to set off an introductory word or phrase. For example:

Yes, you must go now.

Bill, the book is on the upper shelf.

"I'll go now," the girl said.

In the ancient lands of Moses and Jesus and Mohammed, Rabin and Arafat were making history.

Commas are used to set off or enclose parenthetical words in a sentence:

We will, however, reconsider at a later date.

At midnight, when Bob hadn't returned, Rachel became concerned.

Critics have long charged that John Balder, head of the Pipe Fitter's Association since 1987, no longer held real power.

Commas are also used to separate many of the parts of sentences. The above are two examples. Some others:

When all is said and done, Mary was our best candidate.

She tried returning to school, but she could not manage it with two children to care for.

The sun was hot, and the crew grew thirsty.

From the garden he picked tomatoes, beans, strawberries and peas.

Pete picked up the old, rotted board.

It was his voice she hated, not his words.

After eating, we began our game of bridge.

It was a cold, windy morning.

The Senior Picnic will be held on July 4, 1977, at the Civic Park, Area B, at 2:00 P.M.

September 1970 will mark our fortieth year in business. (No commas.)

Mr. Albers lives in Glendale, California.

More is less, less is more was the philosophy and practice of Jerry Brown while governor of California.

With all the tentativeness among writers and language experts about the use of commas, a few rules will point out specific instances not already illustrated when commas must be used:

1. To introduce direct quotes:

    Mary replied, "Perhaps tomorrow."

    "I must go," Bert said, "even if I'm wanted here."

2. To separate thoughts at the end of a sentence:

    It's windy today, isn't it?

    We can go today, can't we?

    Betty went yesterday, I'm sure.

3. To indicate the omission of words:

    There are nine here, twelve over there.

    To others he seems carefree, to himself frustrated.

4. To separate first and last names listed in reverse order:

    Diaz, John B.

    Wallace, Billie Jo

5. To separate a name from a title:

    Jonathan Sparks, President

    William Sexton, M.D.

6. To set off a direct address:

> You know, Jerry, that this is important.

> As we have said before, ladies, you are always welcome.

Period:

Basically, a period is used to mark the end of a sentence. It means stop this thought; take a breath before going on—at least figuratively. Use periods:

1. To end a declarative sentence, a sentence fragment or a request that is not really a question:

> The group will hike tomorrow.

> Good effort. Let's go.

> Will you please help her bring the boxes?

2. To follow abbreviations:

> Dr., M.D., etc., B.A., A.D. 1492, 31 B.C.

3. To indicate the omission of words, use three successive periods:

> When in the course of human events . . . we mutually pledge . . . our sacred Honor.

Semicolon:

A semicolon is a semi-stop in a sentence, not the complete stop of a period, but more of a separation than a comma. Use semicolons:

1. To separate independent clauses not joined by a conjunction:

> A smile is good; laughter is better.

> Don't fret about help; John is coming tomorrow.

2. To separate independent clauses that are joined by a transitional word or phrase:

> We were getting tired; however, we decided to press onward.

> She did well; after all, she was only eight.

> We ran hard; then raced for the water cooler.

3. To separate independent clauses that contain elements separated by commas:

> At the meeting we discussed books, short stories, poetry and cartoons; and listened to poetry submitted by Ellen, Jane, Jim and Fred.

Colon:

A colon is a mark of introduction. Something is to follow, like an exclamation, a list or a quotation:

There is only one thing to do: go forward.

Hiring Ben was a good decision: our profits doubled within a year.

The club's stated purpose was exercise, but the real purpose was different: social eating.

A partial list of words ending in *ence* follows: coherence, conference, inference, occurrence.

Here is an excerpt from chapter seven: Henry Ford had shaken up the business community in 1914 with the announcement of a minimum wage of five dollars a day . . .

The first word after a colon may be capitalized if the statement is a full sentence or if it is formal writing:

He saw the situation this way: Johnson will start and work through Wednesday, after which Peterson will take over.

The conference speaker began: It has come to my attention that the need for government assistance . . .

Phrases and informal statements after a colon need not be capitalized:

We will accomplish our goal this way: by starting each day at 7:00 A.M.

He suggested a possible problem: how can we raise the money by the early deadline?

Exclamation point:

Some writers love to overuse this punctuation mark. Some use two or three or even four in a row. This is overkill. In most writing, the words themselves should reveal the desired emphasis. Use this mark to emphasize a statement or an exclamation:

See the circus, the greatest event of the year!

Hurrah! Encore! Let's go!

Do not use exclamation points in business writing.

Capital letters:

Basically, use a capital letter for the first letter of a sentence and for proper nouns. A proper noun is a word referring to a *particular* place or person or class (group) of persons or things. There are, however, exceptions, and the use of a current dictionary is suggested when in doubt.

Here are the common uses of capital letters:

1. Even one-word sentences are capitalized:

   Go! Stay. Why?

2. Place names are capitalized:

Africa	Idaho Falls	Seattle
America	Lake Erie	Southwest
Dust Bowl	Milky Way	Washington
Hudson Bay	Russia	the West

3. Individual persons are capitalized:

Billy the Kid	President Kennedy
John Brown	Martin Luther King, Jr.
Buffalo Bill	Norman Rockwell
Gandhi	Colonel Sanders
Henry VIII	Queen Victoria

4. Particular classes or groups of persons are capitalized:

American Medical Assn.	Northern University
Americans	Polish
the Congress	Red Cross
Chrysler Corporation	a Shriner
the Democrats	United Parcel Service
Greek customs	United States Army
Ku Klux Klan	Yankees

5. Other proper nouns capitalized include:

   a. Days of the week, month and holidays:

   Monday, April, Independence Day.

   Names of seasons are *not* capitalized.

   b. Historical events:

Bill of Rights	Roaring Twenties
Boston Tea Party	Veterans Day
Labor Day	World War II

c. Religious words relating to a Supreme Being:

Baptist Church	Koran
Bible	Methodist
Christianity	Old Testament
God	Talmud
Jewish	Trinity

d. Professional titles are capitalized:

Senator Cain

Bob Jones, Regional Manager

Professor Smith

Doctor (or Dr.) A. C. Williams

Dash:

A dash indicates an abrupt change of thought, somewhat like a strong comma. Care must be taken not to overuse the dash or it will lose its emphasis.

1. The dash can be used to emphasize or indicate a sharp change of thought:

   There is no hope—unless we cooperate fully.

   Robert had hoped for complete happiness—but love passed him by.

   I know you find him hard to work for—who doesn't?

2. The dash is used to set off parenthetical, but strong, elements in a sentence:

   I would like to suggest—if I may have your permission—that this project be abandoned.

   He is fully aware of the consequences—he was a parachutist, you know—of jumping off that cliff.

   There was small hope—she must have been aware—of success.

3. The dash can be used to indicate the omission of letters and words:

   Mr. —— was the one.

   I'll be a —— if I know.

   "In that case, why don't you ——." He stopped abruptly and ran.

   She recited the alphabet, ABC —— XYZ.

Quotation marks:

Quotation marks are used to enclose direct quotations, to indicate words used in unusual ways and to enclose the titles of chapters or other divisions of a book. Note: periods and commas are placed inside the quotation mark; colons and semicolons are placed outside. Other marks are placed inside if they refer to the quoted section only, otherwise outside. Examples of quotation mark uses:

1. Direct quotations:

   Mary said, "Please get the potatoes ready."

   "Please make your bed," said Joan. "We're expecting company."

   Bob suggested, "Why not visit my cabin in the pines?"

   Why do they need "special treatment"?

2. Book chapter:

   He read, "Shaping Your Memo," a chapter in the book, *Put It in a Memo.*

   The fourth chapter is titled, "Failure at Night."

3. Unusual usage:

   Some business people have become "professional procrastinators": they consistently pay their bills thirty or sixty days late, thus operating with their suppliers' money.

   The referee was "down" on our center during the last game.

   The president's memo stated, "From February 19__ onward the Board will meet on the first Wednesday of each month."

   The president's memo changed the Board meeting to the first Wednesday of each month. (No quotation marks.)

4. With other marks:

   "What's that you said?" he asked again.

   Wasn't his last remark, "Didn't you hear me?"

   "No!" he exclaimed.

   He told us, "I lost my hearing trumpet"; surely *you* knew that!

Apostrophe:

The apostrophe has three uses: to indicate possession, to mark an omission and to form plurals of some words and symbols.

1. Possession. Most commonly used with an *s*:

Adam's	child's
Smith's	children's (plural)
righteousness' sake	ladies
Bob and Sue's house	ladies' (plural)
or Bob's and Sue's house	manager's

boy's	managers' (plural)
boys' (plural)	Jesus' disciples
anyone's	son-in-law's

2. Omission. To replace letters or numbers:

can't	hurricane of '88
don't	class of '69
didn't	he'd
John's good at that	it's
Vaughn's better	o'clock

3. Plurals. To form plurals of symbols and abbreviations:

Sol City B's

there are five *and*'s

your *I*'s look like *t*'s

make your *A*'s larger

sound your *th*'s

Omitting the apostrophe is preferred now when the added *s* doesn't form a new word or cause confusion:

5s, 10s, the 1960s

he has two PCs

the KKKs of the South

Parentheses:

Parentheses (   ) are used to enclose parenthetical (incidental) comments and to enclose numbers identifying items in a series. Commas set off closely related matter, dashes enclose material that is in abrupt contrast, and parentheses suggest an intimate contact between the writer and the reader. Note the following comparisons:

Robert had hoped for complete happiness, a longtime dream of his, and he is still waiting.

Robert had hoped for complete happiness (I have wished that for him too) and I understand he is patiently waiting.

Robert had hoped for complete happiness—but love passed him by.

Examples of parentheses in use:

We are waiting for FDA (Federal Drug Administration) approval.

We are waiting for Federal Drug Administration (FDA) approval.

Our group meets to discuss (1) our basic purpose, (2) meeting times, (3) election of officers and (4) agenda topics.

Note from the following four examples that (1) if the material enclosed is an independent sentence standing alone, it is punctuated that way within the parentheses; however, (2) if the material is included within the sentence, even if it could be independent, it does not start with a capital letter or end with a period, but it may end with a question mark or an exclamation point.

The Board of Directors met yesterday. (Their decision will not be published.)

Peaches (you can buy them fresh now) would be good for dessert.

After walking home (why did we walk?) we were exhausted.

We reinstructed our installers on Tuesday (although we certainly tried hard last week!) how they can save us one-fourth of the current cost.

Italics:

Italics are used to indicate emphasis and to distinguish certain elements such as book titles, foreign expressions and other conventions. In hand writing and typing, the words are underlined.

1. Titles of publications:
   a. Book: *Alice in Wonderland*
   b. Magazine: *Reader's Digest*
   c. Newspaper: *New York Times*
   d. Music: Grieg's *Peer Gynt Suite*
   e. Play: Shakespeare's *Hamlet*
2. Other uses:
   a. Ships, trains, aircraft: *Queen Mary*
   b. Scientific names: *Pereskia aculeata* (a variety of cactus)
   c. Foreign words not already accepted as English or American words:
      n'est-ce pas? (French, is it not?)
      Erin go bragh (Irish, Ireland forever)
      au fait (French, socially correct)
      s'il vous plaît (French, if you please)
   d. Words or letters discussed as such:
      He pronounces *th*'s funny.
      I can't distinguish the *o*'s from the zeros.

The word *loosen* means the same as the word *unloosen*: to release from restraint.

Virgule/slash:

The virgule or slash is used in many ways: to separate alternatives, to indicate omitted words and letters, to separate numbers in dates, to indicate numerical fractions, to tie words into one thought and to divide lines of poetry written in prose style.

The virgule or slash is a mark whose use rises and falls in cycles. In recent years its popularity has risen, to the chagrin of careful writers. Because it is so much in vogue, the slash is overused. The last part of this section provides several illustrations of how to clarify the meaning of words connected by a virgule.

In the opinion of this writer, the slash is too often used as a crutch by writers. For example, in the sentence, "We need heavy scarves and/or caps," do they need scarves *and* caps or scarves *or* caps or whichever you have? Scarves and caps serve different purposes. Is one needed more that the other? These are decisions the reader has to make. But it is incumbent upon the writer to say what he or she means.

The virgule, however, has some helpful uses and here are the common ones:

1. To separate alternatives:

   The host/hostess will provide the main course.

   I/we are interested in using the storage vault.

   We need heavy mittens and/or gloves.

   Dear Sir/Madam or Dear Madam/Sir may be used as a salutation if the gender is unknown.

   John's phone numbers are (000) 555-0762/2954.

2. To replace omitted letters or words:

   c/o (meaning in care of)

   our January/February issue

   60 ft./sec. (feet per second)

   60 miles/hour (per hour)

   The cost is $5.00/dozen (per or a dozen)

3. To separate numbers in dates:

   3/20/81

   07/04/96

   the years 1972/1973

4. To indicate numerical fractions:

   1/2, 2/3, 7/8, 31/32

   Forty and 27/100 dollars

5. To tie words into one thought:

   This heater/vent/air conditioning system has other advantages.

   Better: This heater, vent and air conditioning system . . .

   These groups average ten persons including the leader/facilitator.

   Better: . . . including the person who leads and facilitates the program.

   These are the address/phone changes.

   Better: These are the address and phone changes.

   The condominium leaders of Camelback/Camelback East and Snow-flake meet monthly at the Ridge Restaurant.

   Better: . . . leaders of the Camelback, Camelback East and Snowflake meet . . .

   The committee placed an HIV/AIDS discussion on the agenda.

   Better . . . an HIV and AIDS discussion . . .

   Mr. Watson demonstrated the organ's complete record/playback capability.

   Better: . . . the organ's complete recording and playback capability.

   We can't be no. 1 everywhere. We don't try to be. No one has a product line that extensive, a product/delivery schedule that precise, quality that high and pricing that low.

   Better: . . . a product line that extensive, product and delivery schedules that precise . . .

   Yes, I/we will attend.

   Better: Yes, I or we will attend.

   . . . Bruce Lindsey, who is taking on a new role as the president's political/legal counsel.

   Better: . . . as the president's political and legal counsel.

   . . . ; and a Low-Rate/No-Fee Credit Card List.

   Better: . . . ; and a Low-Rate, No-Fee Credit Card List.

   At the restaurant/piano bar, he saw a different side of Ryan.

   Better: At the restaurant's piano bar, . . .

   If you would like to play a social game of bridge either/and/or Tuesday or Friday afternoons at 1:00, please call . . .

   Better: If you would like to play a social game of bridge on Tuesday or Friday afternoons or both at 1:00, please call . . .

   He (she), he/she, s/he

   Better: He or she

Perhaps we should go back to using *he* as the universal, gender-neutral, non-sexist pronoun referring to a person of either sex. To quote *Merriam Webster's Collegiate Dictionary*, Tenth Edition, *he* is "used in a generic sense or when the sex of the person is unspecified (one should do the best he can)."

Hyphen:

Although a hyphen (-) is used to separate two parts of a word (co-op), it is more often thought of as combining two parts into a single word (anti-inflammatory, self-righteous, president-elect, ex-wife).

Because there is little logic and few clear rules identifying when a compound word is hyphenated and when it is not, consult a dictionary to determine if the word is one word (program), hyphenated (pro-family) or actually two words (pro forma).

Avoid, if at all possible, dividing a word at the end of a line because it makes reading more difficult, and the reader doesn't always know if it is a divided or hyphenated word.

The following are the most common uses of hyphens:

1. To form adjectives: (This is one of the most frequently overlooked uses. Use a hyphen to join two or more words used as a single adjective preceding a noun.)

   soft-spoken person

   fast-rising tide

   over-worked Moms

   high-powered engine

   a high-and-mighty ruler

   the out-of-work painter

   a down-to-earth fellow

Note, however, that these words are not hyphenated when *not* used as adjectives *before* a noun.

   that person is soft spoken

   the tide is rising fast

   most Moms are overworked

   the engine is high powered

   the ruler is high and mighty

   the painter is out of work

   that fellow is down to earth

2. To separate prefix and root (used especially when the root is capitalized):

> pre-Christian
>
> pre-Columbian
>
> pre-Renaissance
>
> pre-1900
>
> anti-Communist
>
> all-American

3. To avoid confusion (All these words are correct but have different meanings):

> reform, re-form
>> reform—means to improve
>>
>> re-form—means to form again
>
> recreation, re-creation
>> recreation—refreshment or diversion
>>
>> re-creation—to create again
>
> recover, re-cover
>> recover—to bring back to normal
>>
>> re-cover—to cover again
>
> redress, re-dress
>> redress—to set right
>>
>> re-dress—to dress again
>
> un-iced (not uniced)
>> better: not iced
>
> un-ionized (not unionized)
>> better: not ionized

4. To join words in phrases containing prepositions:

> falling-out
>
> father-in-law
>
> write-off
>
> over-the-counter
>
> Jack-of-all-trades
>
> good-for-nothing

5. To join the written compound numbers from 21 to 99:

> twenty-one
>
> one hundred fifty-five
>
> ninety-nine

6. To write out fractions:

   1/4—one-fourth

   9/10 or 0.9—nine-tenths

   However, when one part is already hyphenated, do not use another hyphen.

   1/32"—one thirty-second of an inch

   22/64—twenty-two sixty fourths

7. To replace *up to* or *through* in numbers (In this usage, both numbers are included):

   sections 27-36

   pages 102-156

   the years 1970-1990

   the years 1970-90

8. To join letters and numbers to another modifier:

   T-square

   S-curve

   U-turn

   F-sharp

   10-cent stamp

   12-minute quarters

   13-inch ruler

9. To serve as the words *to* or *versus*, indicating opposition:

   the Paris-London flight

   the Bay-Breakers annual run

   the old San Francisco-Los Angeles route

   won the tennis match 6-2, 6-2, 6-2

   defeated the Suns 98-88

   the Clinton-Dole debates

   the Lakers-Suns game

   the light rail-large bus controversy

10. To avoid repeating a vowel or tripling a consonant, and to add *like* as an adjective ending:

    re-echo

    re-enter

    pre-enrollment

    anti-inflationary

semi-invalid

cell-like

ball-like

thrill-less

Stalin-like

But: starlike

  businesslike

  priestlike

11. To combine some prefixes and suffixes—*ex, self, all, elect, quasi, half, odd*—with a base word.

  ex-wife

  she is an ex-governor

  self-confident

  Pete is self-educated

  the sale is all-inclusive

  all-knowing

  Mort is our senator-elect

  commissioner-elect

  quasi-legislative

  quasi-judicial

  the attempt was half-hearted

  half-completed project

  cross-eyed student

  a cross-check of the accounts

  forty-odd people came after the intermission

12. To connect combined units of measure:

  killowatt-hour

  degree-day

  light-years

Bracket:

Brackets [   ] are not likely to be used in business or informal writing but are used in professional and academic writings.

1. Brackets are used to enclose parenthetical material within parentheses:

  His most popular symphonic work was first performed in Munich in the early 1800s (and was reportedly composed just before his death [circa 1790]).

Eberly (a man I disliked [no, really hated] because he ruined my father financially) in his later years became a strong supporter of Indian mission work.

2. Brackets are used to make corrections not made by the author.

I amn't [*sic*] the one responsible.

"Last night we don't [*sic*] do it."

It was the work of [Joseph Patrick] Kennedy.

The phrase is quoted from chapter 6 [of section II].

Ben wrote, "We must make the rules sick [stick]."

It was early in the century [1803] that she wrote her most famous poem.

Our helpful friend [Chief Whitewater] had vanished into the woods.

The press stated that Caldwell's was by far the *most dynamic* presentation [italics added].

CHAPTER 12

Three Diverse Reports

Styles and Outlines

Reports can be formal or informal. An informal report can be a long memo, a letter or other organized composition. The length can vary from one to several pages. Formal reports can range from a few pages to bound documents exceeding a hundred pages. They may include a title page, a transmittal letter, a table of contents, a list of tables, a glossary, a statement of the problem, a conclusion and details supporting the conclusion. Detailed calculations, charts, graphs, illustrations and lists may be included with the detailed section or in a separate appendix.

Textbooks describing formal reports are available from bookstores and libraries. Here we will discuss and illustrate three variations of informal reports.

Before a report is written, certain steps should be taken:

1. Determine the purpose of the report.
2. Determine the scope of the report.
3. Determine the information sources.
4. Organize the data.
5. Outline the data in a logical order.

Whether reporting a telephone conversation, a basketball game, a procedure, a meeting or a recommendation, the following general outline is recommended:

1. State the problem and reasons for the report.
2. Give the conclusions and recommendations.

3. Provide the most important details.

4. Provide the less important details.

The first report illustrates a procedure. It is presented step by step.

Procedural Report

The office manager, Mr. Watson, says, "Bill, our printing die vendors are complaining that their bills are being paid 60 to 90 days late. So that I and every person involved knows what his or her duties are and how they fit into the picture, write a procedure for paying these bills on time."

To: T. C. Watson
From: W. P. Alieoto

Here is the procedure that must be followed if we are to pay our printing die invoices on time and also check their accuracy:

The corrugated box sales person works with the customer on the design of the box printing and obtains a pattern from the customer.

The die pattern is taken to the sales service clerk who coordinates the sales and production (manufacturing) departments. The sales service clerk enters the factory order number on the die pattern and sends it to the die-order clerk. The die-order clerk writes a purchase order for the die and sends it to the die vendor.

When the die is received, the plant receiving clerk writes a receiving record and forwards a copy to the die-order clerk along with the die. The die clerk checks the die against the order. He attaches the receiving record to the die order. He then notifies the sales service clerk, who notifies the production department so they can schedule the manufacturing process.

Vendor invoices received are sent directly to the die clerk who checks the invoice against the die order. The die clerk sends the invoices, receiving record and die order to the sales service clerk, who checks them against the original order for boxes. The sales service clerk initials the vendor invoice, indicating approval for payment. The invoice and attachments are sent to the accounts payable clerk.

The accounts payable clerk verifies any computations on the invoice, prepares an accounts payable voucher and sends all the papers to the office manager for a final review of the paperwork. The office manager then forwards the vendor invoice and the accounts payable voucher to the headquarters office where the actual check to the vendor is written. The recieving record and purchase order are retained at the local plant.

If each step is handled expeditiously, vendor invoices will be paid on time while putting accuracy first.

Cost Accounting Controls

The details of this company report are technical and not easily understood by one not familiar with the manufacture of corrugated boxes or with the relationship between a headquarters office and a plant operation that includes separate departments. In this report, the Bascom Box Plant is a department of the Bascom Mill. Headquarters has some staff (procedural and advisory) control over both.

A reading, or even a casual scanning, of this report reveals many areas in which accounting controls must be tightened.

Item 21 below, the dollar summary of the seven months operations investigated, might have had more impact if placed at the beginning rather that at the end.

Bascom Corporation

Attention: C. R. Winters   Subject: Bascom Study of Cost
          Plant Manager   Accounting Controls

                                            By: T. R. Brady
                                                Internal Auditor

Bascom Box Plant accounting functions are handled primarily by Bascom Mill accounting personnel based on information generated within the Bascom office or furnished by Box Plant personnel. As instructed, I conducted a study of the accounting records and procedures pertaining to the Box Plant in order to determine the adequacy of accounting controls and reliability of the financial and operating reports. Following is a report of my findings and recommendations:

1. In writing down exchange board to corporate cost, obsolete mill standard costs were used, which:

   a. Overstated integrated material costs $14,975 for the seven months ended July 31, 19__.

   b. Since these costs were used in building up the direct cost manual, board costs were overstated in the direct cost manual between 16¢ and 19¢/MSF, depending on the flute involved. The charge to Headquarters should be corrected for past and future 19__ shipments. The direct cost manual should also be corrected. The supplying mills should be asked to send new standards as published and Bascom Accounting should check quarterly to ensure that this is done.

2. Distribution of January 19__ leased truck costs to the box plant was overstated resulting in an excess charge to delivery expense of $3,886.

3. Freight is anticipated on each sales invoice by the billers when shipment is made. The total of these anticipations plus or minus any difference between payments and previous anticipations forms the basic charge to delivery expense. The freight bills are paid by Bascom Regional Office. These payments are not compared with the anticipations, creating several problems:

   a. Overpayments could go undetected such as a $76 overpayment on June shipment to General Mills, Idaho.

   b. Errors in rate schedules used by the billers and estimators are not recognized and investigated. This leads to:

      1) Incorrect cost estimating.

      2) Distortion between months in delivery expense. For example, July bore $775 of additional June costs whereas June received a May credit of $597, a net adverse variance for July of $1372.

   Bascom Accounting should investigate all of the major and some of the minor differences between anticipations and payments. Corrections required in billers' and estimators' rate schedules should be made.

4. Control sheets for recurring box plant entries for July were apparently not checked since the warehouse freight entry was omitted, overstating delivery expense $634.

5. The 2,271 pallets on hand at July 31, 19__ were valued at $1.47 each. A number of pallets were valued at the return freight cost of only 27¢ each rather than at the average unit cost, resulting in an overstatement of integrated material cost of $1,200.

6. Bascom mill profit transfers applicable to shipments to Consumer Products, Bascom Coated Papers Div. and Bascom Southern Plant were based on standard cost rather than actual mill cost. Bascom Box Plant integrated material costs were overstated $3,350 with a corresponding understatement of costs for the divisions receiving products shipped.

   Bascom Accounting should maintain board inventories at actual costs and base Bascom mill profit transfers on such costs.

7. Finished and in process inventories were priced at standard rather than actual Bascom cost for board. The July excess Bascom cost of $11,843 went directly to integrated material costs whereas $3,600 should have remained in inventory.

   Bascom Accounting should compute inventory values based on actual rather than standard cost of board.

8. In valuing board contained in finished and in process inventories, waste was computed at 6%, the overall divisional percentage, which does not give effect to the finish value of scrap allowed at Bascom. This overstated the July 31 inventory and understated integrated material costs $2,200.

   The Bascom Box Plant Manual of Accounts will be revised so that material values in inventory are computed using the waste percentage shown on page 9 of the Bascom Cost Estimating Manual for boxes with manufacturer's joint (currently 3.9%).

9. Adhesive on sheets and boxes in finished and in-process inventory is priced at 30¢, rather than the current cost of 33¢/MSF. This understated the July 31 inventory and overstated material costs $400.

   Bascom Accounting should use current costs in valuing finished and in-process inventories.

10. Tape received from Bascom Coated Papers Div. and ink received from Bascom Ink Division are recorded at cost rather that at market price in the materials statement. This has no effect on integrated material costs but understates materials at market and distorts cost estimating feedback reports.

    Bascom Accounting should change to established Bascom Box procedures wherein materials are charged for the market cost of tape and ink and Bascom profit is credited for the difference between market and corporate cost.

11. The breakdown of labor by center in the conversion cost statement supporting the statement of operations is based on a period from the 28th of the prior month through the 27th of the current month rather than the calendar month under report.

    The accountant of the Bascom Box Plant should use Bascom Box Form 2, Detail of Direct Labor, to prepare the conversion cost statement since the Form 2 covers the calendar month.

12. The statement of operations since June included a 4% reserve for the anticipated wage increase but Form 2 did not.

    The Bascom Box Plant payroll clerk should revise erroneous Form 2s by adding the 4% to each category. The accountant for the Bascom Box Plant should review Form 2s for errors in procedure and communication breakdowns.

13. That portion of the finished and in-process inventory value providing for finishing materials was improperly assigned to labor and fringe benefits, factory expense and administration expense with an offsetting $2,000 understatement of material costs at July 31, 19___.

    Bascom Accounting should follow the procedure outlined in the Bascom Box Plant Manual of Accounts.

14. Interplant transfers are not being priced in accordance with Bascom Box Plant Manual of Accounts revision issued in January 19___. Prior

to 19__, all plants had used the same pricing formula even though costs among plants are makedly different. The new formula provides for expected Bascom costs.

Tests of selected shipments indicated that transfers to other plants were substantially the same as those provided in the Manual of Accounts. However, established procedures should be observed to ensure realistic cost transfers in the future.

a. Bascom Accounting should price sheets in accordance with revised costs in Bascom Box Plant Manual of Accounts.

b. Headquarters should revise costs in the Bascom Box Plant Manual of Accounts:

   1) to provide for all extras currently being ordered by Bascom Southern Plant.

   2) to revise conversion and set-up charge in the Bascom Box Plant Manual of Accounts for amount the present Estimating Manual differs from actual cost: currently 15 % of conversion cost.

15. The cost of interdivisional shipments was not transferred in accordance with Bascom Box Plant policy, which requires that they be transferred at Class 16 less Bascom profit. Even though tests of selected transactions indicated that either method provided substantially the same result at the integrated level (after giving effect to the adjustments mentioned in items 16 and 17, and variances between expected costs provided in Estimating Manual and actual costs) the method in use overstates plant profit at market.

16. Cost estimates on interdivisional sales do not include the 25¢/MSF charge required for goods held awaiting customer pickup. This had no effect on integrated cost since it was offset by errors in Bascom Mill profit.

    Bascom Box Plant sales service should add this charge to future estimates.

17. Bascom Mill profit on interdivisional shipments was calculated at 10% of invoice value, or about $1.25/MSF, rather than the true Bascom Mill profit of $2.50/MSF.

    The accountant for the Bascom Box Plant should calculate actual Bascom Mill profit and transfer the cost of interdivisional shipments in accordance with established procedures.

18. The present financial statements mix costs controlled by Bascom Mill and Bascom Box Plant supervisors making it difficult to identify responsibility.

    It is recommended that in the future the factory expense statement be divided into two statements as follows:

a. Covering mill burden and shipping department costs by natural classification.

    b. Covering costs of the box plant proper. The costs covered in the first statement would be carried over as a one-line item on this statement, the total agreeing with the statement of operations.

    The same problem actually exists with the selling and administrative statements but to a minor extent, so separate statements are not considered necessary.

19. It was found that the control over finished and in-process inventories and the control over roll stock usage the box plant had decided to install in May 19__ were not being followed.

    a. In order to detect errors by the fork lift drivers in reporting board consumed, the planner was to continue comparing usage as reported with the amount of board that should have been required. This was apparently dropped the last two weeks in August 19__. Errors occurring during this period were failures to record butt rolls taken off the corrugator and additional errors in computing the report resulting in an overstatement of roll stock consumed of 75 tons. These errors were detected prior to the August closing. Corrections were made in August reports.

        It is recommended that:

        1) The present report comparing liner and medium usage against liner and medium apparently required be sent to the plant manager weekly.

        2) Corrugator operators report usage rather than the fork lift driver.

    b. The sales service manager was to have maintained a file of orders corrugated but not shipped for comparison with finished and in-process inventory as a control on the accuracy of the inventory. This comparison has not been made.

        Since this procedure was a compromise system at best, it is recommended that the normal Bascom Box procedure be installed. In this system, which is probably more economical and effective, the billing copy of the order is not sent to billing until corrugated. At month-end, unbilled orders can then be compared with the inventory to detect orders omitted from inventory or erroneously included in inventory as well as a check on the approximate quantity listed in the inventory.

20. Certain customers receive confidential discounts to meet competitive situations. Because of the need to restrict the knowledge of such discounts they have been recorded on an estimated basis rather than by actually computing the discount liability.

    About $73,000 in discounts had been charged to sales through July 31, 19__, but an additional liability of $16,500 should have been recorded. One-third, or $5,500, of this amount was picked up in August.

Headquarters recently devised a procedure that provides for the recording of such discounts in the month of sale. This procedure should be installed. The Bascom Billing Department should prepare the lists of invoices shown in Exhibit 1 on the first working day. If necessary the last day of the month could be included in the subsequent month. The accountant for the Bascom Box Plant then computes the liability and sets up a reserve based on rates supplied by the sales manager.

21. The net effect of these adjustments on the statement of operations for the seven months ended July 31, 19— may be summarized as follows:

| | Overstated (Understated) | |
	Amount	Per MSF
Revenue: Gross Sales	$16,500	$ .09
Expense:		
Delivery expense	4,596	.02
Materials (at cost)	21,325	.12
	25,921	.14
Pretax Income	$ (9,421)	$(.05)

Automation Study

In the third report illustrated, the problem is financial loss due to operations. Suggestions are made for reducing operating costs. The presentation is slightly more formal than the previous two reports.

Golden Paper Mills Corporation
Golden Container Division

October 29, 19—

To: P. Y. Emerson   By: A. B. Bashieni
    Plant Manager   Industrial Engineer

Subject

Golden Box Plant Automation Study.

Purpose

To review various proposals for cost reduction in the Golden Box Plant, and to indicate the savings possibilities and the attractiveness of the proposals.

Summary and Conclusions

Cost reduction proposals for the Golden Box Plant that offer substantial savings possibilities are:

	Annual Savings
1. Increasing plant efficiency to equal standard cost	$150,000
2. Pre-printing outer liner	250,000
3. Alternator-stacker for corrugator	50,000
4. Counter-ejector for folder-gluer	6,000
5. String tyer for folder-gluer	17,000
6. Automatic folder-feeder for stitchers	17,000
7. Bobst die cutting, creasing and stripping press	57,000
8. Reduced maintenance costs	46,000
9. Re-pulping additional waste at Golden Mill	71,000

These cost reduction proposals, and other areas of cost reduction, are particularly significant since the Golden Box Plant is losing approximately $150,000 a year with board at cost on a $5,000,000 investment in the Board Machine and the Box Plant.

Discussion

An analysis was made of the Golden Box operation to determine areas for potential mechanization and cost reduction. The result was a series of proposals or items to investigate that resulted from suggestions received from the supervisors concerned, from visits to other container plants, proposals by equipment suppliers and by the survey itself.

This report will analyze and give preliminary evaluations of these proposals so that efforts can be concentrated on the most attractive projects.

General

A review of the profit and loss statements for the Golden Box Plant operations was made to determine its economic position. On the basis of the first seven months of operation, the net loss was at the rate of over $900,000 per year if the paper mill received normal profit on board sold to the box plant or a loss of over $150,000 per year if the board were priced at cost.

Due to the substantial difference between the two figures, an estimate was made of the return on the investment in Golden Mill and Box Plant facilities if board were priced at market. An investment of approximately $5,000,000, composed of 20% of the cost of the board machine or $3,500,000 and the investment of $1,500,000 in the container plant, was used as a basis for the analysis. The difference between cost and market price for Golden Mill board would amount to $750,000 per year, based on the first seven months of 19___. If the container plant "broke even" when receiving board at market, this $750,000 figure would be the profit on the Golden Mill investment. The return on the $5,000,000 investment would be approximately 7%, or a 14-year payout. This would appear to be a minimum expected return on the investment.

Therefore, the first goal should be a cost reduction or profit improvement of the $900,000 per year the plant is losing when Golden Mill is priced at market. This appears to be a tremendous sum to achieve through plant cost reduction alone as the entire direct labor costs amount to only $667,000 per year. Although not within the limits of this study, it would appear that the costs of $580,000 per year in salaries should also be intensively studied to determine possible cost reductions. If, however, salaries, selling expenses, administrative expenses and material costs are considered "fixed," the remaining costs would have to be reduced by 65% to enable the plant to break even at market. If the selling price of containers were increased 10%, and the price of board did not rise, the loss would be reduced by $555,000 per year.

Startup of the Golden Mill's Cleveland box plant will have a definite effect on the Golden box plant. Some overhead will be distributed over two plants instead of one. However, the Golden box plant will probably lose some volume to the Cleveland plant.

Container Plant Operation Overall

The container plant labor force operates under a system of standards established by the local standards engineer. In recent months, direct labor cost has exceeded standard costs by:

August	31% or $13,000
July	33% or $13,000
June	28% or $11,000
May	30% or $13,000

or at the rate of $12,500 per month. This appears to be an excessive amount, approximately 30% over standard cost. Either the standards are wrong and they should be revised or abolished, or the efficiency is too low. A quick analysis shows that the corrugator consistently runs on, or slightly above, standard cost per operating hour. The finishing operations consistently exceed standard costs. It is interesting to note that the latter are portions of the operation which are given the least attention from a scheduling standpoint. While the corrugator is scheduled by a full-time programmer or planner, and the printing scheduling is done by the general foremen, the finishing operations are scheduled by the shift foremen as they come on shift.

This preliminary review would indicate that an investigation should be made of the feasibility of establishing a production planning function for the entire container plant. There is a good posibility this could be done with present personnel. At least one nearby plant has installed such a system. They feel that the production planning function has had a revolutionary effect on their productivity, overall plant efficiency and ability to meet shipping schedules.

Corrugator Operation

1. Alternator-stacker for corrugator: "Take-off" operating labor costs for the corrugator could be reduced $50,000 per year through installing an automatic alternator and stacker to replace the present three-man off-bearer crew. One company is developing a unit and hopes to construct the first model for a box plant in Portland. If they are not successful, our Machine Development Department should initiate the design of an automatic alternator and stacker. Such a unit could be installed on corrugators throughout the company. A simple stacking device could be used if there were no necessity for alternating "lifts" or "hands" approximately 7" thick when stacking the finished sheets. The alternating is done to retard warping in the sheets.

2. Preprinted outside linerboard offers a tremendous cost reduction potential to the corrugated container plant. In effect, the printer-slotter installation could be eliminated for a major share of the production. Slotting and flap cutting mechanisms could be installed on finishing equipment so that only certain specialty orders would have to be run on a printer-slotter.

Savings through pre-printing could run as high as $250,000 per year based on present Golden Box Plant capacity. A comparison of the Multiwall Department's Schmutz press operating costs and the printer-slotter operation indicates that labor and maintenance costs could be reduced by over $130,000 per year. Due to the greater accuracy of the register type cut-off on the corrugator, a waste reduction of $1\frac{1}{2}\%$ can be achieved by eliminating the end trim programmed into the machine. This would amount to another $44,000 per year. The pre-printing operation would have a negligible waste percent, based on Multiwall experience, so most of the waste now occurring on the printer-slotters would be eliminated for additional savings of approximately $80,000 per year. An additional reduction of waste on the corrugator would accrue through side register control devices installed as part of the pre-printing installation.

There are several disadvantages to pre-printing and considerable research and experimentation would have to be done. For instance, all waste on the corrugator would have a slightly higher loss due to the additional cost of pre-printing the outer ply. Factors such as width, size and type of printing press to buy would have to be analyzed while considering such items as corrugator trim, press operating efficiency, length of runs, roll diameter, offset problems and printing quality.

To date, Langston, a corrugator manufacturer, has two corrugator installations using its equipment to run pre-printed board. These installations consist of (1) a registering pre-printed liner control for the cutoff and (2) hydraulic web alignment equipment for the triplex slitting and scoring station and for the shaftless mill roll stand at the glue machine. They quote a price of $85,000 for these units. The printing press would cost in excess of $100,000. Most of the printer-slotters would be surplus after the installation.

One great advantage of pre-printing is the ability to obtain better quality printing than obtainable at present. Or, if aniline inks were acceptable, the press could use these inks and cut costs substantially.

Printer-Slotters

Considerable work is being done by Corrugating Supervision to increase the efficiency of this operation. However, to date approximately 40% of the printer-slotter time is still utilized for setup and make-ready. This will be reduced somewhat by recent installations of rapid cleanup attachments.

Currently one helper is assigned to each printer-slotter to feed stock into the machine. Development of automatic feeders, under investigation by one manufacturer, would permit a helper to feed two to four presses. The manufacturer will supply drawings and estimated prices in the near future.

Finishing Operations

The stitching, taping and gluing operations are in many respects the least automated of the corrugating operations. Considerable mechanization could be done in this area with equipment now on the market or which can be developed by our Machine Development Department.

The existing bostitch folder-fluer is not large enough to handle all of the boxes that could be glue-lapped. However, a previous study has shown that Sales cannot convert any substantial production volume from stitched and taped boxes to glue lap joints. Consequently, a new wide folder-gluer cannot be justified on existing or anticipated glued box business.

A. Bostitch Folder Gluer

The existing machine is essentially a high production piece of equipment when compared to stitchers and tapers, although crew requirements are quite high per machine hour. Reduced costs may be obtained through:

1. Counter-Ejector—An automatic device, commercially available, can re-place the present counter-ejector stacker girl on the machine. Savings of $6,200 per year would return the $7,500 investment in 2.7 years even if used on only 70% of the production. These units are presently in use in this area by several other box manufacturers. Supervisory personnel in these companies indicate the device works satisfactorily.

2. String Tyer—Bundles of glue-lapped boxes must now be string-tied by hand, requiring a crew of one to two additional people, depending on whether one or two strings are specified. Other companies have eliminated manual string tying by installing Saxmayer tyers after their folder-gluers. One company uses a two-man crew for their folder-gluer, including the palletizer. The palletizer looks after the counter ejector and string tyer, periodically inspects individual bundles and palletizes the bundles. Another company uses a two-man crew on their folder-gluer equipped with a string tyer. The second folder-gluer will be equipped with a Saxmayer tyer shortly. Installation of string tyers for the Golden Box folder-gluer would save $17,000 a year and pay out the $18,000 investment in slightly over two years.

3. Printing on Folder-Gluer—Several of the box plants in the Midwest are printing the freight stamp on their folder-gluer, thereby bypassing the printer-slotter operation.

B. Stitchers

The stitchers in the Golden Box Plant are classified as semiautomatic. This means that the stitching operation is automatic, but the folding and feeding operations are manual. Therefore, the operation is paced by the girl folder, not the machine.

1. Automatic Folder-Feeders—At least two companies in the Midwest are using automatic folder-feeders on their stitchers. Production rates are consider-ably higher than ours. One company averages 1500 pieces per hour on lettuce boxes and 3000 pieces per hour on can cases. Our average production is ap-proximately 800 per hour with the semiautomatic stitchers.

Installation of automatic folder-feeders would not only increase crew pro-ductivity, but would encourage further automation in the string tying and pal-letizing operations. The investment cost of $21,000 for only one folder-feeder and squarer would be returned in two and a half years with savings of $17,000 per year. This is on the basis one folder-equipped machine replacing two sem-iautomatics.

2. High Speed Stitcher—If long-range production forecasts for stitched boxes indicate continued business, then the Machine Development Department should investigate the possibilities of developing a high-speed stitcher.

C. Tapers

These are the least efficient group of machines in finishing. Average production is around 500 to 600 pieces per hour for stitchers and 4000 per hour on the Equalok folder-gluer. Although production is relatively small and growing smaller as production shifts to glue-lapped cases, over 10,200 operating man-hours were spent last year on this operation.

A new automatic feeder-folder-gluer could be purchased for the operation and reduce operating costs tremendously. In view of the trend toward glue-lapped cases, and the economics therein, acquiring or developing new equipment would be unwise unless surplus automatic feeders were available, or if Sales advises that we will continue to have a quantity of taped cases for a number of years.

D. Miscellaneous Finishing Operations

1. Die Cutting and Creasing—Installation of a Bobst automatic die cutter and stripper would save $57,000 in labor costs per year. With normal maintenance and overhead costs allocated to this machine, the $113,000 investment would be returned in 4.7 years.

2. Partition Slotting and Nesting—This is essentially a low-volume operation that is quite time consuming. The total direct labor costs of approximately $19,000 per year would be insufficient to justify a sizable investment in automatic machinery similar to that in use by some local companies. Should sales increase substantially, automatic equipment can be acquired. Efficiency on this operation is very low: 145% over standard in August, so the most effective and economical means of reducing costs would be to increase the efficiency.

Maintenance

Preliminary analysis of maintenance costs indicates that the Golden Box Plant's costs are high. A six-months cost comparison with Richmond, a comparable Golden Mills Corp. plant, reveals that Golden's maintenance costs averaged approximately 26¢ per M square feet compared with Richmond's 13¢ per M square feet. The two plants had comparable production during the periods covered. Golden's wage rates are approximately 35% higher than theirs. The maintenance cost comparison is based on only production center maintenance costs.

If Golden Box Plant's maintenance costs were comparable to Richmond's, maintenance charges would be reduced by $46,000 per year, taking into account the difference in wage rates of 35%. The big difference appears to lie in repair labor charges rather than in repair materials. Richmond maintains a ratio of $1 of repair labor to every $4.25 of repair material for production center maintenance. Golden's ratio is $1 of repair labor for every $1.20 of repair material, almost a one-to-one ratio.

Lift truck maintenance is known to be quite high. This field of maintenance is already the subject of another industrial engineering study. A report has just been distributed.

Waste

The Golden Box Plant sells about 1200 tons per year of wet strength waste and 2000 tons per year of regular waste board to outside customers. This is in addition to the 900 tons per year presently re-pulped at our board machine. Wet strength waste sells for only $20 per ton and regular waste for $30 per ton. This compares to pulp value at our board machine of approximately $50 per ton.

Recent improvements in handling procedures at our board machine pulper should increase capacity so that all nonwet strength box plant waste can be slushed. This will provide savings of $37,000 per year to the box plant by increased credits for waste, which replaces virgin pulp.

Studies are currently being made to determine the economics of installing a heat exchanger and auxiliary equipment on the pulper. If this is economical, the 1200 tons per year of wet strength waste can be re-pulped for our board machine consumption for additional savings of $34,000 per year.

This box plant waste can be used only as long as it is segregated between wet strength and nonwet strength and is not contaminated with foreign material. Considerable care must be taken to prevent board splinters, glass reinforced tape, waxed broke and similar materials from contaminating the waste. If possible, the material should be "hogged" and baled before being sent to our board machine as this will reduce handling time and increase re-pulping capacity.

The tabulation below indicates an improving trend in handling waste:

	Percent
1994 January	1.02
1994 July	.72
1995 January	.43
1995 June	.30
1995 July	.21

The waste caused by the Shipping Department in handling rolls from our board machine does not appear to be excessive.

Palletizing, Strapping and Baling

The Golden Box Plant standards engineer is working on a proposal to conveyorize production from the finishing equipment. Included in his proposal is a central steel strapping installation for unit loads. Savings through such an installation are sizeable.

Handling

A Pul-Pac palletless materials handling system was installed in the Golden Box Plant during the past year. For some time material damage appeared excessive when using this system; however, within the past few months, this problem has been substantially corrected. With the start of a planned driver training program throughout the plant, the drivers should become even more efficient with the Pul-Pac units. The whole Pul-Pac system should be re-analyzed in another three or four months to see if the anticipated savings are being made.

Acknowledgments of Assistance

Marshall Barker	Harold Beguhn
Gregory Peustow	William Radanovich
Samuel Johnson	John Graffius
Austin Stanwyck	Donald Kline
Carl Henning	Walter Troeller
Oscar Witowski	Thomas Phillips
John Beals, Richmond plant	Larry Collard, Headquarters Department Foreman

(With permission of Maurice W. Burke of M. W. Burke & Associates, Inc., Danville, CA 94526.)

CHAPTER 13

Confusing Words Clarified

This glossary of frequently confused words includes those I found most commonly misused in the worlds of business and writing. Some of the explanations follow the time-tested "correct" usage, some include a little of my personal preferences and some allow for recent changes in usage. You can use these explanations and examples as a guide that will be accepted by most writers and readers. The goal is to help you communicate clearly.

A/an

A is used in front of a word beginning with a consonant or hard sound.

Right: *a* horse, *a* cab, *a* donut, *a* historical, *a* heart, *a* headrest.

An is used before a vowel or soft sound.

Right: *an* onion, *an* honor, *an* apple, *an* heirloom, *an* hour, *an* heiress, *an* honest.

The general rule for words beginning with an *h* is that if the *h* is sounded when speaking, use *a*; if the *h* is silent, use *an*.

From a newspaper article: The church has a open membership and open communion.
Better: The church has *an* open membership and communion.
Better: The church has open membership and open communion.

Ability/capacity

Ability refers to the competence or power to do something.
Capacity refers to the capability or potential to hold or contain.

Right: John has the *ability* to be a baseball player.

Right: The stadium has a *capacity* of 34,500.

Accept/except

Accept means to receive or agree with.
Except means something is excluded.

Right: I will *accept* your offer.

Right: Everyone *except* me will attend today.

Adaptation/adaption

Adaption is a noun meaning *adaptation*.
Adaptation is a noun meaning an adjustment to environmental conditions or
a new form of a composition or, in general, the act of adapting, which in turn
means fitting into a new situation, often by change.
The use of *adaptation* is preferred.

Right: All *adaptations* or changes will be jointly worked out with the City
Planning Commission.

Right: She wrote an *adaptation* to the original melody.

Advise

As used in these "wrong" examples, *advise* is outdated and overworked "business jargon." In spite of that it is currently widely used, probably because it has
a slight ring of authority.

Wrong: Please be *advised* that tomorrow's meeting has been canceled.

Right: Tomorrow's meeting has been canceled.

Wrong: When can you come for an interview? Please *advise*.

Right: Please let me know when you can come for an interview.

Wrong: If you have any questions, please *advise*.

Right: If you have any questions, please let me know.

Wrong: Be *advised* that fees are charged by the advisers.

Right: Please note that fees are charged by the advisers.

Affect/effect

To *affect* is to influence. *Effect* is a result.

Right: The noise *affected* his ability to hear clearly.
Right: The *effect* of the hail was a damaged wheat crop.

Effect can also mean to cause.

Right: I am sure Doctor Jules will *effect* a cure.
Right: This procedure will *effect* a settlement.

All ready/already

All ready means all are ready.
Already means previously or in the past.

Right: The family is *all ready* to leave.
Right: The family *already* left for the trip.

All right/alright

All right is informal for *well* or *satisfactory*.
Alright is not accepted as a standard word.

Right: We are doing *all right*.
Right: That procedure is *all right* with me.

All together/altogether

All together means all are together.
Altogether means completely.

Right: The troop was *all together* when they started.
Right: The leader was not *altogether* pleased with their slow pace.

One way to check if *all together* is used correctly is to separate *all* and *together*. For example, in the first sentence above, you could say: *All* of the troop was *together* when they started out.

In the second sentence, you would not say: *All* of the leader was not *together* pleased with their slow pace.

Although/while

Although means in spite of the fact that.

While means during the time that, but it can also mean *although*. A problem arises when the context of the sentence does not clearly indicate the intended meaning of *while*.

Right: *Although* James was a slower runner, he was entered in the race.

Acceptable: *While* the two companies were competitors, they cooperated in many projects.

Better: *Although* the two companies were competitors . . .

Right: *While* John waited for the program to begin, he talked with Susan and Cedric.

Confusing: *While* the beaded belts were made in China, the largest sales were made in American Indian trading posts.

Better: *Although* the beaded belts were made . . .

Among/between

Among refers to three or more.
Between refers to only two.

Right: We were *among* the group of eight.

Right: We sat *between* Shirley and John.

Between can also be used when more than two things are referred to in a relationship.

Right: An agreement has been reached *between* these four nations.

Right: He paused *between* sentences to allow his ideas to sink in.

Right: *Between* his carpentry, plumbing, painting and electrical work, he had little time for designing new houses.

Amount/number

Amount refers to bulk or mass or sums, and is followed by a singular noun: *cash* in the example below.

Right: He carrys a large *amount* of cash.

Number refers to something that can be counted, and is followed by a plural noun: *boxes* in the sentence below.

Right: I have a *number* of boxes of pencils.

Right: The *amount* of wheat shipped to Russia was hard to imagine.

Right: The *number* of sockets in the low-priced wrench set has been reduced to eight.

And/but

And and *but* are most commonly used as coordinating conjunctions, joining words or phrases of equal rank within a sentence. But they are also used as the first word in sentences. Currently this usage is considered correct.

Two effects should be noted, however. First, starting a sentence with *and, but, for, nor, or, so* or *yet* slows the reading of the passage by inserting a transition into the readers's thoughts. Second, slowing the reader adds emphasis to the thought that follows.

This is a good stylistic device that should be used sparingly because overuse will lessen its power.

And/or

And/or is typically a shortcut expression that tends to confuse the reader. Do not use it in business communications or in formal writing.

Confusing: Will this change in the machine affect its speed and/or its precision?

Better: Will this change in the machine increase its operating speed, but perhaps reduce its precision?

Confusing: At college, Peter will study engineering and/or architectural design.

Better: At college, Peter will study engineering or architectural design or both.

Anticipate/expect

These words are often used as synonyms, but there is a distinct difference in meanings.

To *anticipate* is to give advance thought, to see ahead, and to prepare or act ahead of time.

Right: I *anticipated* his next move.

Right: I *anticipated* his next pitch would be a fast ball.

Right: I *anticipated* his criticism by rehearsing my replies.
Right: The teacher *anticipated* her pupil's questions.

Expect implies a degree of certainty and preparation ahead of time.

Right: I *expect* to complete the report by Thursday.
Right: I *expect* you home before midnight.
Right: You are *expected* to work harder tomorrow.

Apt/liable/likely

Apt and *liable* are often misused to mean *likely*.

Right: He is *likely* to be home by five o'clock.
Wrong: He is *liable* to be home late today.
Wrong: He is *apt* to be home early tomorrow.

Apt means unusually qualified or suited.

Right: She is *apt* in science studies.
Right: That is an *apt* quotation.

Liable is a legal obligation or responsibility.

Right: He is *liable* for damages.
Right: She is *liable* for a fine.

Likely refers to probability.

Right: We will *likely* have rain later today.
Right: Rain is *likely* today.

Likely also refers to suitable, credible and attractive.

Right: This is a *likely* place for us to live.
Right: He was a *likely* candidate for that position.
Right: She is a *likely* youngster.

As

As is an overworked and abused word. Use it sparingly.

Right: We will use bricks *as* a substitute.

Right: I will be happy to help *as* much *as* I can.

Do not use *as* as a substitute for *like, if, that, whether, because, since, while* or *when* in the following examples:

Right: *Like* her mother, she wore lace stockings.

Right: *If* we are going, let's go now.

Right: I doubt *that* I can do it.

Right: I don't know *whether* I can or not.

Right: You can help *because* you have done this before.

Right: *Since* it is raining, we will wait.

Right: *While* the sun is hot, we will stand in the shade.

Right: *When* we depart, John will go first.

Assume/presume

Assume implies a justifiable motive or taking something for granted.

Right: He *assumed* an attidude of helpfulness upon arriving at the scene of the accident.

Right: Dennis *assumed* his wife would phone if she were to be late.

Right: Clara *assumed* that, as usual, Don would come a quarter of an hour late.

Presume means to undertake without justification, to guess or to accept as true without evidence.

Right: We *presumed* we could get there on time even with our old clunker.

Right: I *presume* he will recover completely from his liver cancer.

Right: The gang was *presumed* innocent because they had not been proved guilty.

These two words should never be used in business communications. Business messages should be based on sufficient facts that nothing need be *assumed* or *presumed*.

Assure/ensure/insure

These words are interchangeable in the context of making sure or certain. They do, however, have different connotations or implied meanings.

Assure means to make safe against risk, to give confidence, to make certain, to provide positive information, to guarantee.

> Right: We can *assure* you there is no danger in proceeding with this project.
>
> Right: I *assure* you Jean is the best qualified.
>
> Right: I *assure* you there will be no conflict.
>
> Right: We *assure* you the quality will meet all the published standard requirements.
>
> Right: I can *assure* you of the accuracy of that statement.

Ensure means to make sure, certain or safe.

> Right: Wear these goggles when using the grinder to *ensure* that a piece of metal will not hit your eye.
>
> Right: He wore rubber boots to *ensure* against electric shock.

Insure means to make certain ahead of time. It relates to insurance, which is bought with the belief that you will not suffer a complete loss if you should need it.

> Right: Our house is *insured* against fire and theft losses.
>
> Right: This insurance company will not *insure* against flood damage.
>
> Right: I can *insure* my life against accidental death.

Augment/supplement

The difference between these two words is that *augment* means adding more of the same or adding intensity, while *supplement* means adding something different.

> Right: A large gift from his successful uncle *augmented* his already great wealth.
>
> Right: The company *augmented* its steel inventory by purchasing more from Japan.
>
> Right: The force of the report was *augmented* by its early arrival.
>
> Right: Dietary *supplements* improved her general health.
>
> Right: He later published a *supplement* to his first textbook.
>
> Right: The company *supplemented* its well-water supply by purchasing nearby canal water.

Average/mean/median/mode

Average generally means somewhere near the middle of two extremes.

Right: She is an *average* person.

Right: His height is *average*.

Right: John's grades are *average*.

Right: Sharon's musical skills are far above *average*.

More technically, *average* can be the exact midpoint between two numerical extremes. The *average* is then called the *mean*. For example, the *mean* between 40 miles per hour and 60 miles per hour is 50 miles per hour (40 + 60 = 100 ÷ 2 = 50).

The *average* can also be the *arithmetic mean* or the *mean* of a set of numbers. For example, the *mean* of 4, 5, 6, 9, 11, is 7, calculated this way: 4 + 5 + 6 + 9 + 11 = 35. Thirty-five (35) divided by the number of figures, five (5), = 7.

The *median* is the number placed so that there are as many figures below as above.

Using the previous set of figures: 4, 5, 6, 9, 11, the *median* is 6. There are two figures below 6 (4 and 5) and two figures above 6 (9 and 11).

The *mode* is defined as the most frequent value of a set of data.

A salesman of hi-fi equipment was explaining to me that many customers asked what the average cost of a hi-fi set is. He said, "We sell them from $1,000 to $50,000, and therefore the *average* is $25,500." What he failed to realize was that the customers weren't asking for the *arithmetic average* or *mean* but most likely for the *mode*: what most of his customers paid, or to paraphrase the definition, the most frequent value or price his customers paid.

There is also a *geometric mean*, but its definition involves square, cube and higher roots.

Bad/badly

Bad is an adjective meaning below acceptable standards.
Badly is an adverb meaning to an intense degree or in a bad manner.

Right: He had a *bad* experience.

Right: Her cough is *bad*.

Right: That is a *bad* plan.

Right: My sight is *bad*.

Right: I feel *bad*. (I feel sick or ill.)

Right: I feel *badly*. (My sense of touch is impaired.)

Right: John's hearing is *bad*.

Right: Pepo's speech is *bad*.

Right: Sandra has a *bad* sense of smell. (Her nose may be plugged.)

Right: Sandra smells *bad*. (She could use a bath.)

Right: Sandra smells *badly*. (Her nose may be plugged.)

Right: He wants the supervisory position *badly*.

Right: Eldon wrote *badly*.

Balance/remainder

In common usage, both mean what is left over.
Balance when used to mean the next or what remains is considered informal.

Informal: The *balance* of the work was left for Susan.

Formal: The *remainder* (or rest) of the work was left for Susan.

Informal: We hurried during the *balance* of the trip.

Formal: We hurried during the *remainder* (or rest) of the trip.

Informal: The *balance* of the trees will be cut next week.

Formal: The *remainder* of the trees will be cut next week.

Balance also has many technical meanings.

Technical: The ledger did not *balance*.

Technical: The *balance* in my account at the bank was incorrect.

Technical: The gold was weighed on a *balance* scale.

Technical: The decision was left hanging in the *balance*.

Technical: Watches have a *balance* wheel.

Technical: The height and diameter of a pillar must be *balanced*.

Technical: The painting had *balanced* colors.

Technical: He ran so fast he lost his *balance*.

Remainder also has technical meanings.

Technical: The number left after a subtraction is a *remainder*.

Technical: The undivided part left over from a division is the *remainder*.

Technical: A book sold as a publisher's close out is a *remainder*.

Because/since

Refer also to the word *as*, which is often misused for *because* and *since*.
Since properly relates to time; *because* relates to reason.
Since can mean from a specific time in the past until now.

Right: He has been a professsor *since* coming to London.

Since can refer to a prior period of time.

Right: That theory has long *since* been declared invalid.

Since can refer to something after a period in the past.

Right: He has *since* become a minister of the gospel.

Since can refer to past periods of time.

Right: He has had two full-time jobs *since* he retired.

Since can also mean *because*, but this usage is discouraged in formal and business writing.

Informal: *Since* he had more education, he was promoted first.

Because means for the reason that or the fact that.

Right: *Because* he had more education, he was promoted first.
Right: *Because* of her experience, she was chosen for president.
Right: Simon ran *because* he wanted to escape.
Right: He did not submit the report *because* it was incomplete.

Beside/besides

Beside means next to.
Besides can mean in addition to or also.

Right: Ben sat *beside* the slow moving stream to fish.
Right: *Besides* his stamps, he has a collection of coins.
Right: Jean didn't have money for the trip, and *besides* she had just
    sprained her ankle.

Bring/take

Bring means to convey or cause to come along with one toward the place where the action is taking place or being considered.

Take means the opposite: it means getting something away from the place being considered to another place.

The difference can be stated quite simply: *Bring* is from there to here; *take* is from here to there.

How often have I heard, "When you go to school this morning, be sure to *bring* your books," or, "I am packing for our vacation, but I haven't decided what all to *bring*"? I have also heard, correctly, "*Bring* your new friend home with you today." It is correct to *bring* a friend home (to our home) and later *take* the friend home (to his or her home).

Take also has myriad related meanings, mostly informal usage:

take a bath	take apart
take a back seat	take a powder
take account of	take care
take charge	take five
take hold	take for granted
take a hike	take it on the chin
take stock	take turns
take shape	take root
take your time	take advantage of
on the take	take the floor
take to task	take kindly to

Can/may/might

Can refers to the ability to do something.
May refers to possibility or permission.
Might also refers to possibility, and is less emphatic than *may*.
When referring to permission, *can* and *may* are generally interchangeable.

Right: John *can* do the rings exercise. (He is able.)

Right: John *may* do the rings exercise. (He has permission.)

Right: John *may* be able to do it later. (It is possible.)

Right: It *may* snow tomorrow. (Strong possibility.)

Right: It *might* snow tomorrow. (Weaker possibility.)

Right: You *may* be excused now. (Permission.)

Right: You *can* be excused now. (Permission.)

Right: *May* I ask who you are? (Permission.)

Right: *Might* I ask who you are? (Weaker permission.)

Capital/capitol

Capital has several meanings, but not building.
Capitol is an edifice or building.

Right: The beam was placed atop the *capital* of the column.

Right: A *capital* letter is the large one used at the beginning of a sentence as opposed to the small letter: A-a.

Right: *Capital* crimes are punishable by death, which is called *capital* punishment.

Right: His cost estimate included a *capital* error.

Right: He was captain of the fleet's *capital* ship.

Right: We now realize the *capital* importance of X's series of criticisms.

Right: They made *capital* of the situation.

Right: That is a *capital* idea.

Right: Our business needs more *capital*.

Right: Salem is the *capital* of Oregon.

Right: We saw the *capitol* building while in Salem.

Center/middle

Both of these words mean equidistant from two extremes. Sometimes they can be interchangeable.

Center, however, is generally a more precise term, as the *center* point of a circle or the exact midpoint of a defined length of line.

Middle can refer to a broader area, as a person's *middle* or the *middle* house on the west side of Oak Street.

Right: The parade went through the *center* (or *middle*) of town.

Right: The district was in the *center* (or *middle*) of a political battle.

Right: In politics, his views were those of the *center*.

Right: He held to the *middle* ground when thinking politically.

Chair/chairman

To *chair* a meeting or be the *chair* of an organization is correct, formal English. The attempted elimination of the word *chairman* to refer to a woman leader is the result of a movement to eliminate "sexist" language, even when the formal title of a position is "chairman."

Attempted substitutions for *chairman* include *chair, chairperson, chairwoman, presiding officer, head* and *moderator*. These words often sound awkward when spoken, and look out of place when written.

In my studied opinion, you have the choice of (1) using the word *chair* or (2) using whatever word you are comfortable with—or the least uncomfortable.

Compare/contrast

To *compare* is to seek similarities, and is used with the preposition *to* or *with*.

To *contrast* is to look for differences, and is also used with the preposition *to* or *with*.

Right: Please *compare* John's work *to* that of Jim.

Right: They *compared* the flowing music *to* a murmuring stream.

Right: Let's *compare* John's writing *with* the original work by Elliot.

Right: I had no one to *compare* you *with*.

Right: Please *contrast* the weight of steel studding *with* that of wood studding.

Right: The two nurses *contrasted* the work on the swing shift *with* that on the graveyard shift.

Right: What a *contrast* between sky diving and deep sea diving.

Right: She *contrasted* him *to* older men.

Right: He *contrasted* his blonde friend *with* redheads.

Professors who teach formal English and linguists such as Jacques Barzen, Henry Fowler, Theodore Bernstein and William Safire suggest that you use *compare to* when emphasizing similarities or when representing things as similar, and *compare with* when searching for similarities or comparing differences.

Right: The aborigines *compared* the airplane *to* a bird.

Right: We *compared* Webster's definition *with* that of Random House.

Perhaps if these confusing distinctions were clear to all of us, we could eliminate the phrase *contrast with*.

With informal usage, there is no significant difference between "This year's snow level *compared to* last year's" and "This year's snow level *compared with* last year's."

Complement/compliment

Complement means to complete.
Compliment is to approve or praise or flatter.

Right: The pearl necklace *complemented* her dress.

Right: We received our *complement* of lamps.

Right: She *complimented* him on his appearance.

Right: She blushed when I *complimented* her.

Continual/continuous

Continual means frequent but with interuptions.
Continuous means without interuption.

Right: It rains *continually* in that region.

Right: It rained *continuously* through the night.

A river (except in certain desert regions) flows *continuously*, but only in the best of times do the fish bite *continually*. A beautiful waterfall may splash and sparkle *continuously* but visitors watch it *continually*.

Convince/persuade

Convince means to overcome doubts.
Persuade means to influence or urge.

Right: I *convinced* him that this was the better course of action.

Right: You *convinced* me that John was right.

Right: You *persuaded* me to help you.

Right: He *persuaded* me to attend the concert.

One mnemonic device is to think of *convince* resembling *convict*, which is a more direct action than the reasoned movement of *persuade*; thus *convince* is to overcome, while *persuade* is to influence.

Council/counsel

Counsel is advice or a person who gives advice, such as a lawyer.
Council is an assembly or meeting, often administrative, to consult, discuss and advise.

Right: He *counseled* them against acting too fast.

Right: Jacob was *counsel* for the defense.

Right: The psychologist's *counsel* was helpful but expensive.

Right: The city *council* meets on Wednesdays.

Right: A *council* of Navajo chiefs was held.

Right: A *council* of citizens met to discuss street improvements.

Desert/dessert

Desert has two pronunciations and three definitions. With the accent on the last syllable, the word means to abandon.

Right: He chose to *desert* the group and strike out on his own.

Desert with the accent on the last syllable also means deserved reward or punishment.

Right: They got their just *deserts*.

Desert with the accent on the first syllable means arid and barren land.
Dessert, with the accent on the last syllable, is a sweet course or dish at the end of a meal.
Having lived in a desert region for many years, I am amazed at the number of educated people who spell *dessert* with only one *s*. Perhaps they could remember that *dessert* with two *s*'s tastes better than *desert* with only one *s*.

Different from/different than

Different from and *differs from* are acceptable whereas *different than* is not.
Differ with refers to disagreement. In rare instances, *different than* is acceptable, but to avoid confusion among your readers, do not use it.

Right: His opinion is *different from* mine.

Right: His opinion *differs from* mine.

Right: I *differ with* Joan.

Wrong: Because our system allows us to do things a bit *differently than* our competition, they don't understand how it works.

Right: . . . *differently from* our competition . . .

Disinterested/uninterested

Disinterested means impartial.
Uninterested means lack of interest.

Right: He took a *disinterested* view of the conflict.

Right: He was *uninterested* in the proceedings and dozed off.

Right: A referee should be *disinterested* in the game's outcome but certainly not *uninterested* in the conduct of the game.

With our ever-changing language, the word *disinterested* is beginning to mean a loss of interest.

Doubtful: I became *disinterested* in my exercise class.

Doubtful: My *disinterest* soon became obvious to my instructor.

Some editors now accept this meaning while others cling—perhaps hopelessly but desperately—to the classical distinction between *disinterested* and *uninterested*.

Disorganized/unorganized

Disorganized things were once organized.
Unorganized things were never organized.

Right: After the flood I found my records *disorganized*.

Right: Procedures were completely *unorganized*.

Due to

Due to is used frequently in business and informal writing as a preposition.

Iffy: *Due to* new procedures the report must be changed.

Iffy: The paper machine was down for seven hours *due to* lack of water.

Iffy: *Due to* a request from headquarters we changed the reporting date.

Iffy: *Due to* the railroad strike we are out of repair materials.

Iffy: School was closed *due to* the deep snow.

In more formal writing *due to* should be replaced by *because of* or *owing to* or *caused by*. Or, in many instances, it is better to revise the sentence.

> Iffy: *Due to* an increase in our cost, the sales price will have to be increased.
>
> Right: *Because of* an increase in our cost . . .
>
> Better: The sales price increase follows from our cost increase.
>
> Iffy: His loss of hearing was *due to* an illness.
>
> Better: His loss of hearing was *caused by* an illness.
>
> Iffy: Her high grades were *due to* her long hours of study.
>
> Better: Her high grades *resulted from* her long hours of study.

Eminent/imminent

> *Eminent* means outstanding.
> *Imminent* means likely to happen.

> Right: Mr. Walker is *eminently* qualified.
>
> Right: An explosion appeared *imminent*.

Enclosed please find

Please find is a hackneyed, outdated expression that is still commonly used because it is readily understood. It is "business jargon" and reveals that the writer lacks originality or cannot think of an ordinary, current expression.

> Iffy: *Please find* attached a copy of our paid invoice.
>
> Better: *We have attached* a copy of our paid invoice.
>
> Iffy: *Please find enclosed* my check for $50.00.
>
> Better: *I have enclosed* my check for $50.00.
>
> Iffy: *Enclosed please find* the letter you requested.
>
> Better: The letter you requested *is enclosed*.

Error/mistake

These words are often used interchangeably, but there are differences.
Error implies varying from a standard or procedure.

> Right: John made an *error* in procedure.
>
> Right: Missing an easy fly ball was an *error* against the right fielder.

Right: Watson made an *error* in calculating the tensile strength of one key
  bolt: the structure collapsed.

Mistake implies a less technical fault or a misunderstanding or common for-
getfulness.

Right: His *mistake* was quoting Shakespeare rather than the Bible.

Right: Sharon made the *mistake* of using a no. 4 pencil rather than a no.
  2 for marking the test.

Right: He made the *mistake* of setting his alarm clock for 6:30 A.M. rather
  than 6:00 A.M.

In business communications, the word *mistake* is rarely used, but the word
error is common. Although by definition, *mistake* is less serious than *error*, it
is also more personal. A report may contain a simple mistake such as a wrong
phone number or first name, but the person pointing out that mistake refers to
it as an *error* in research or analysis or reporting. The reasons are political.
Calling a mistake a mistake is a more personal attack that calling it an error.
The person who made the mistake may be or may become your boss. For the
sake of job security you will do all in your power to remain a team player and
not destroy personalities. An *error* is not a personal mistake but a variance from
procedure.

Explicit/implicit

Explicit means something expressed in a definite way.

Right: I gave him *explicit* instructions.

Implicit relates to *implied*. It refers to something not specifically stated.

Right: She made an *implicit* assumption.

Farther/further

Farther refers to measurable distance.
Further means more of something.
These two words historically have been more or less interchangeable, but the
trend now is to use *farther* only when referring to distance. *Further* is used
when referring to more of something.

Right: *Further*, he is better qualified in math.

Right: I am *further* along in my studies than James.

Right: No *further* data should be required.

Right: Let us go *further* with this project.

Right: We will send you *further* reports.

Right: I walked *farther* than John did.

Right: The oak tree is *farther* away.

Right: Boston is *farther* away than New York.

Fewer/less

Fewer applies to items that can be specifically counted.

Less applies to how much: less material in the drapes, less insurance coverage, less money in the bank, less grain in storage, less justice.

Wrong: I would like to see *less* photographs in the newsletter.

Right: We had *less* need to hurry.

Wrong: Women's earnings are *fewer* that last year.

Right: We picked *fewer* baskets of apples this year.

Exceptions:

Less is often used to modify plural nouns referring to small distances, small sums of money, and other small plural units.

Acceptable: *Less* than two miles.	*Less* than two percent.
Acceptable: *Less* than a quart.	*Less* than a handfull.
Acceptable: *Less* than 25 cents.	*Less* than six ounces.

Figuratively/literally

Figuratively means represented by a figure or emblem, or it may express one thing but really mean another, or it may be a "figure of speech," that is, not truly meaning what is said.

Right: *Figuratively*, he acted like a scared rabbit.

Right: Paul Bunyan was *figuratively* stronger than an ox.

Right: Speaking *figuratively*, playing computer games is becoming as American as Mom and apple pie.

Literally means actually or truly. It is often confused with and misused for *figuratively*.

Right: He took the message *literally* (to be true).

Right: Same was a hermit in the desert, and he *literally* (truly) walked the soles off his shoes.

Right: He was *literally* (actually) a remarkable man.

Finalize

This is a word often used in business and government to mean the end or completion of something. Although used since 1922, many readers object to its use because it is "business jargon." The meaning, however, is usually clear.

Iffy: When can we *finalize* the apple box project?

Better: When can we complete . . . ?

Iffy: Our work will be *finalized* by December 31.

Better: Our work will be done (or completed) . . .

Iffy: Our report cannot be completed until the subsidiary report is *finalized*.

Better: . . . until the subsidiary report is *finished* (or done or completed or received by us).

Some writers believe that if the meaning can be maintained with fewer syllables when *ize* is added to a word, the new word is acceptable.

Hospitalize could replace *put in a hospital*. Also *democratize* could replace *make it a democracy* or *change it to a democracy* or *encourage it to become a democracy*. Similarly, *weatherwise* has sometimes replaced *of the weather* or *about the weather* or *referring to the weather*.

I think the suffixes *ize* and *wise* are currently overused and misused. They tend to make our language "cute" rather than clear.

Flaunt/flout

Often *flaunt* is used when *flout* should be. One newspaper reported people *flaunting* new antismoking laws, and another mentioned *flaunting* tax laws.

Flaunt means to show off or display pretentiously or impudently.

Right: She *flaunted* her well-proportioned body.

Right: Fred *flaunted* his wealth with an expensive automobile collection.

Right: The officer *flaunted* his authority.

Flout means to disregard with scorn or contempt.

Right: Joe *flouted* the bedtime rules.
Right: He *flouted* the regulations the officer attempted to enforce.
Right: He *flouted* the dress code that required a tie and a jacket.

Good/well

Good is an adjective that implies faint praise, less laudable than *excellent* or *superior*.

Right: We had a *good* time.
Right: He is a *good* Methodist.
Right: She is a *good* speller.

Good can also be a noun meaning acceptable to others.

Right: These lessons are for your own *good*.
Right: The new medicine is *good* for you.

If the adjective describes the subject of the sentence, *good* is correct.

Right: Jean is *good* at arithmetic.
Right: Albert was not *good* at geography.

Well refers to a state of health, and can also refer to the efficiency of people or things.

Right: I don't feel *well* today.
Right: The football team did *well* this afternoon.

Comparisons:

Wrong: My car didn't run *good* this morning.
Right: My car didn't run *well* this morning.
Wrong: I don't *feel good* now.
Right: I don't *feel well* now.
Right: Mary is a *good* driver. (*Good* modifies *Mary*.)
Right: Mary does her work *well*. (*Well* modifies *work*.)

Got/gotten

Have got means have or have obtained.
Have gotten means only have obtained.

Right: They've *gotten* the popcorn. (They have obtained it.)

Right: I *got* the popcorn. (I purchased it and brought it with me.)

Right: I *have gotten* the popcorn. (I am the one who purchased it.)

Have gotten is not as common in American English as *have got*, but *have gotten* is preferred in formal writing.

Formal: I *have gotten* the supplies.

Informal: I *have got* the supplies.

Wrong: He *has not got* common sense.

Right: He *has no* common sense.

Iffy: I *have got* to go to the dentist.

Right: I *have* to go to the dentist.

Got is not a synonym for *have*.

Wrong: I *got* some new videos. (I have them.)

Right: I *have* some new videos.

Wrong: I *got* to go now.

Right: I *have* to go now.

Conversational: They *have got* together.

Conversational: They *have gotten* together.

Get and *got* are used frequently in colloquial expressions. For example:

I get you.	I got the blues.
I got rhythm.	That gets me.
Get going.	He got six months.
I get around.	She got over it.
Get after him.	Get a move on.
Get with it.	Get it together.
I got the picture.	Got it?
Get it?	Get moving.
He got away with it.	Oh, get along with you.
I can get away with it.	You got me.

Hopefully

When *hopefully* is used at the beginning of a sentence to mean *it is hoped* or *we hope that*, language purists consider it a misplaced adverb. Do not use it this way in formal writing. With informal writing, however, it has been used this way since 1932.

Wrong: *Hopefully* a site will be available that will be convenient to all our customers.

Right: *We hope that* a site . . .

Wrong: *Hopefully* the project will be completed by Friday.

Right: *It is hoped that* the project . . .

Right: Our *management hopes that* the project . . .

If/whether

If implies limited alternatives or simple conditions.
Whether implies doubt with the possibility of alternatives.

Right: *If* it is possible I will attend.

Right: We will go *if* we earn the bus fare.

Right: I asked *if* the conductor had arrived.

Right: I don't know *whether* I will attend or go to the office.

Right: *Whether* we win or lose, we will have played our best.

Infer/imply

Infer is to draw a conclusion from something.
Imply is to suggest something, to hint at.
The distinction in meanings is somewhat blurred, with *infer* used to mean suggest. In formal writing do not substitute *infer* for *imply*.

Right: I *inferred* from his statements that he is educated.

Right: Based on her past record, it was easy to *infer* that Rosa would represent us well.

Right: She *implied* that she would be here next week.

Right: Dorothy *implied* that she knew more than she had told the prosecutor.

Its/it's

Its is a possessive pronoun: something belongs to something else.
It's is a contraction of *it is* or *it has*.

Right: The horse put *its* head out the door. (The horse's head.)

Right: *It's* my horse. (It is my horse.)

Right: *It's* been a beautiful afternoon. (It has been a beautiful afternoon.)

Last/latest

These words are frequently confused because *latest* is often used correctly to mean the last available or most up to date.

Right: This dress is the *latest* fashion.

Right: This is the *latest* Ford out.

Right: She demonstrated the *latest* dance steps.

These words are also confused when *last* is used to mean the *latest*.

Uncertain: *Ironwood* was his *last* book. (His latest written or the final book he will write?)

Better: *Ironwood* was his *latest* book.

Uncertain: The *last* event was the best. (The most recent or the final event?)

Better: The *latest* performance was the best.

Last applies to something that comes at the end of a series, but does not necessarily imply that the series has ended.

Right: The *last* page of this book was revealing. (There may be more books.)

Right: That phone call was the *last* we heard of him. (We may hear more later.)

Right: He was given *last* rites.

Right: She was *last* in her class.

Right: She was the *last* person to fall for him.

Right: He read the *last* issue of *Time*.

Better: He read the *latest* issue of *Time*.

Lay/lie

These words are confusing because *lay* is the present tense of the verb *lay* and also the past tense of the verb *lie*.

Right: I *lay* the book down. (I am putting the book down now.)
Right: Janet *lay* on the bed earlier. (She rested or reclined.)

Lay, meaning to put down:

Lay in this usage must always have an object. Remember that the humble hen *lays* an egg in her nest. In the following four examples, the object is *pencil*:

Right: Now I *lay* (or *am laying*) the pencil down.
Right: I *was laying* the pencil on the desk.
Right: I *laid* the pencil down.
Right: I *have laid* the pencil down.

Lie, meaning to recline:

Right: I *lie* (or *am lying*) on the sofa.
Right: I *lay* (or *was lying*) on the sofa. (past tense)
Right: I *have lain* on the sofa.

Lie, meaning not telling the truth:

Right: I never tell a *lie*.
Right: Sandra *lied* to me about her past.
Right: Josie never *has lied*.

Common errors:

He has *lain* (should be *has laid*) the package on the table. (put)
The package *has laid* (should be *has lain*) on the table all day. (reclined)
The cat *was laying* (should be *was lying*) on the window sill. (reclined)
I *lied* (should be *lay*) in bed all morning. (reclined)
I *have laid* (should be *have lain*) in bed until now. (reclined)
Lay down (should be *lie* down) pussycat. (recline)
The trailer *was laying* (should be *was lying*) on its side. (reclining)
The valley *lays* (should be *lies*) before us. (reclines)

Lineal/linear

The first definition of *lineal* is *linear*. We are concerned here with *linear measure*, but *lineal* also refers to heredity and lineage. *Linear*, too, has many other meanings: they relate to mathematics, vegetation leaf construction and sequential development.

I once worked for a company that manufactured rolls of paperboard, many of which weighed over 5,000 pounds. It was sold by the thousand square feet, thus we had to know the width ordered by the customer and the length of each roll. Some old timers in the industry referred to the length as *the lineal*, while others called it *the linear*. *Lineal* was first used in the 1300s, and *linear* in the mid-1600s. In my written messages, I used *linear* because my subconscious seemed to say that *linear* referred to a finite length, but that *lineal* ran on forever. Regardless of which word was used, there was no confusion.

Method/methodology

These two words are often confused by business writers who haven't learned the distinction or by those who think the longer word makes the writer sound more educated.

Method implies an orderly, logical and effective procedure usually broken down into steps.

Right: Ms. Lawrence uses a new training *method*.

Right: He used the approved *method* for calculating variances.

Right: His chemical analysis was done by the standard *method*.

Right: Peter's cost analysis was done by the Xavier *method*.

Methodology applies to a set of procedures or a body of methods or an analysis of procedures in a field of inquiry.

Right: In his analysis he followed the *methodology* of of chemistry.

Right: He followed the *methodology* set forth by the Internal Audit Department.

Myself

Do not use *myself* as a subject replacing *I* or as an object replacing *me*.

Wrong: Please notify Kathy or *myself*.

Right: Please notify Kathy or *me*.

Wrong: Please contact your supervisor or *myself*.

Right: Please contact your supervisor or *me*.

Wrong: Make out a work order and send it through Fred or *myself*.

Right: Please make out a work order and send it through Fred or *me*.

Wrong: My partner and *myself* are attorneys.

Right: My partner and *I* are attorneys.

In the following sentence, *myself* is an intensive personal pronoun; it intensifies or emphasizes the subject *I*:

Right: I, *myself*, will go with you.

Of

This word is often overused.

Wordy: Most *of* the ways *of* doing this job consist *of* several steps *of* concentrated work.

Better: This work requires concentration with each step.

Wordy: We are proud *of* the way you have *of* working with children.

Better: The way you work with children makes us proud.

Wordy: Many *of* the reasons *of* why you have to work so late are because *of* the way you have *of* planning your procedures.

Better: You have to work late because your procedures are not planned.

Wordy: Please join us and plan to enjoy a couple *of* hours *of* good fellowship.

Better: Please join us and plan to enjoy a couple hours *of* good fellowship.

Wrong: He walked off *of* the sidewalk.

Right: He walked off the sidewalk.

Wrong: He could *of* walked faster.

Right: He could *have* walked faster.

Only

Only is an adverb that is so often out of place that many writers accept the misplacement of this modifier, especially in speech.

ABC newscaster Peter Jennings said, "President Clinton is *only* making one stop." It should be *is making only one stop*.

Dr. Robert Schuler said in a sermon, "You *only* hear about it from others." It should be *you hear about it only from others*.

Columnist Ellen Goodman wrote, "Well, you show me a woman who *only* wants to be thin for her health and I'll show you a man who buys *Playboy* just to read the interviews." It should be . . . *a woman who wants to be thin only for her health*. Then in the next paragraph Ms. Goodman writes correctly, "Nevertheless, it's a turning point when a pitchwoman for a diet company is reluctant—embarrassed?—to admit that she's dieting *only* to improve the way she looks."

The use of the word *only* is discussed in more detail in the section "Misplaced Modifiers" in Chapter 3.

Oral/verbal

Oral, to quote *Webster's*, means "uttered by mouth or in words."

A synonym is *spoken*, which means "delivered by word of mouth." Oral can also relate to the mouth itself.

Verbal means relating to or consisting of or involving *words*, rather than actions.

The problem is that the *words* included in the definition of *verbal* can be spoken, as in the definition of *oral*, or they can be *written*.

Attempts by language experts to explain the difference between *oral* and *verbal* get bogged down in what the experts would *like* each word to mean. They would like any statement or agreement that is spoken to be *oral* (or spoken) and anything written to be *verbal* (or written). That would clarify the difference, but common usage does not support that wish. The context of written material will tell the reader whether *verbal* is used to mean *spoken* or *nonaction*.

Acceptable: She took an *oral* exam for her certificate of proficiency. (spoken)

Acceptable: The dentist made an *oral* examination. (mouth)

Acceptable: He made an *oral* acceptance. (spoken)

Acceptable: The foreman gave *verbal* instructions. (nonactive)

Acceptable: The group made a *verbal* protest. (spoken)

Acceptable: My neighbor said he would sell me his house for $100,000. Can I enforce this *verbal* agreement? (spoken)

Acceptable: Even if you have witnesses to this *verbal* conversation, it is unenforceable. (Arizona Revised Statute 44-101) (spoken)

Acceptable: The principal problem with *oral* contracts is that they cannot be proved, and therefore can be unenforceable. (spoken)

Precede/proceed

Notice the spelling difference in the word endings. The beginnings of these words are Latin prefixes: *pre* means before or in front of; *pro* generally means forward, especially from a point or after a pause.

Right: Four other speakers *preceded* Lorenzo to the platform.

Right: I will *precede* you as we walk down the aisle.

Right: In that book, the preface *precedes* the table of contents.

Right: After stopping for water, we will *proceed* to the foothills.

Right: We were advised by our financial adviser how to *proceed* with our investments.

Right: You have been taught; now *proceed* with the action.

Principal/principle

Principal refers to money or to the main, top, or chief person or thing.
Principle refers to fundamental guidelines or to a high standard of conduct.

Right: The interest on our *principal* is 6%.

Right: Mr. Ward is the school's *principal*.

Right: The *principles* of sociology will be studied soon.

Right: The football coach has high *principles*.

Right: The *principal* reason for the rule is to maintain discipline.

Stationary/stationery

Stationary means fixed.
Stationery is paper, pencils, ink and supplies used in the process of writing or in the operation of an office.

Right: The heavy machine is *stationary*.

Right: We need more *stationery* supplies for the office.

That/which/who

When referring to persons, *who* is generally preferable to *that*.

Right: My husband *who* is an artist can give you a professional's viewpoint.

Right: The house *that* is yellow will be repainted next year.

Which is correctly used to introduce nonrestrictive clauses.

Right: Stories, *which the children enjoyed*, will be read again tomorrow.

In the sentence above, the clause is nonrestrictive. The sentence states that stories will be read tomorrow. The clause adds the *parenthetical* information that the children enjoyed the stories, but does not limit what stories will be read tomorrow.

Notice the lack of commas in the two sentences that follow. The second sentence has a restrictive clause. We are stating the specific stories to be read tomorrow.

Wrong: Stories *which the children enjoyed* will be read tomorrow.

Right: Stories *that the children enjoyed* will be read tomorrow.

As a general rule, if the clause is to be set off with commas (because it is parenthetical) use *which*, otherwise use *that*.

Wrong: The query is primarily a sales tool *which helps authors* sell their articles before writing them.

Right: The query is primarily a sales tool *that helps authors . . .*

Unique

Unique means one of a kind, sole, without equal. It expresses absoluteness in the same way as do the words *round* and *square*. Something unique cannot be compared.

Right: This is a *unique* design.

Right: The Chinese juggling act is *unique*.

Language changes, however. *Merriam Webster's Collegiate Dictionary*, tenth edition, includes the above description of *unique*, but also adds, "distinctively characteristic" and "unusual." This change permits the following sentences to be acceptable:

Acceptable: Our program is fairly *unique*.

Acceptable: This is a very *unique* set of earrings.

Acceptable: This is the most *unique* minivan available today.

Who/whom

Who is a subject. *Whom* is an object. The key to whether *who* or *whom* is correct is how the word is used in its *own* phrase or clause.

Another key: substituting *he* or *she* for *who*, and *him* or *her* for *whom*, clarifies which word to use.

Right: *Who* could teach the class?

Key: Who (or she) could teach.

Right: *Who* is the new driver?

Key: Who (or he) could drive.

Right: James is one *who* we think could teach this class.

Key: Who (or he) could teach. Don't let the inserted phrase, "we think," confuse you.

Right: Ginger is a person *who* we know is helpful.

Key: Who (or she) is helpful. Don't be confused by the inserted phrase, "we know."

Right: George is a person *whom* we know.

Key: We know whom (or him).

Right: For *whom* did the directors vote?

Key: For whom (or him) did the directors vote?

Right: I told him *whom* to call.

Key: I told him to call whom (or her).

Right: Vote for the presidential candidate *whom* you prefer.

Key: You prefer whom (or him).

Right: Vote for the presidential candidate *who* you think is the best.

Key: Who (or he) is the best.

Right: *Who* do we help?

Key: This use of *who* is so common in colloquial use that it is acceptable in informal conversation.

Right: *Whom* do we help?

Key: Do we help whom (or her)? *We* is the subject; *whom* is the object.

Whose/which

Although *whose* usually refers to people, it can also refer to things and animals. This usage avoids some awkward sentences.

Right: The city invited local fish processors to use the sewer to dump fish remains, *whose* easy removal enabled Washington's arbitrary demands to be met.

Awkward: . . . fish remains, the easy removal *of which* would enable . . .

Right: We loved the orange blossoms, *whose* scent was strong in the evening.

Awkward: . . . the orange blossoms, the scent *of which* was strong in the evening.

CHAPTER 14

Glossary of Terms

This chapter defines many of the terms used throughout the book. The terms are words some readers may have forgotten or never understood completely.

Action Verb

An action verb tells what the subject does. It is also called a transitive verb, and it takes a direct object.

Doris *reads novels.*

Alvin *sawed* the *board.*

Bob *caught* a *fish.*

Add-on Sentence

See Cumulative Sentence.

Adjective

A word that modifies, that is, describes or limits nouns and pronouns.

Adverb

A word that modifies verbs, adjectives, other adverbs or complete sentences. It usually tells how, how much, how often, when, where and why.

He walked *slowly*.

Sue was *somewhat* hungry.

Sandy *frequently* swam in the mornings.

I wish to swim *now*.

They walked *outside*.

The purse tore because it was *poorly* made.

Agreement

Nouns and pronouns must agree in number, person and gender.

Number: foreman/his; foremen/their
Person: I/my; you/yours; we/ours
Gender: boy/his; girl/hers; house/its

Alliteration

The repetition of close consonants:

click and clack; willy-nilly

Ambiguity

Having more than one possible meaning. (noun)

Ambiguous

Having more than one possible meaning. (adjective)

Antecedent

A word or words replaced by a pronoun.

Tabbi lost *her* ring. (*Tabbi* is the antecedent of *her*.)

Like *their* coaches, *athletes* can be pushy or whimpy. (*Athletes* is the antecedent of *their*.)

Apostrophe (')

Used to indicate possession, to mark an omission and to form plurals of some words and symbols.

The *cat's* paw.

We *can't* go now.

She had difficulty pronouncing her *l*'s and her *this*'s.

Appositive

A noun placed near another noun to rename or supplement its meaning and that has the same grammatical use.

Our guide, *Carlos*, spoke good English.

Johnston, *the detective*, was slovenly but sharp.

The perfectionist, *Peter*, finally made one tragic mistake.

Article

The words *a, an* and *the* are a type of adjective called articles.
Indefinite articles: *a* and *an.*

We visited *a* university.

She added *an* egg to the batter.

Definite article: *the.*

I rode in *the* truck yesterday.

Auditory Learning

Learning by hearing sounds.

Auxiliary Verb

A verb used to help another verb (most commonly a form of *to be*, but also *have, do, can, shall, should, will, must, ought*).

He *is* running, *has* run, *had* run, *does* run, *can* run, *shall* run, *should* run, *must* run, *ought* to run.

Brevity

Making the writing as short as possible while still providing the necessary information.

Capital Letter

The first letter of a sentence or of a proper noun:

Africa, Seattle, George Washington Bridge.

Case

The form of a noun or pronoun showing its relationship to other words in a sentence.

Subjective case words, *his, she, he, you*, relate to a subject.

Objective case words, *you, him, her*, refer to objects of a verb.

Possessive case words, *man's, his, hers*, refer to possession.

Clarity

A statement is clear to the reader when it can be understood after the first reading.

Clause

Unlike phrases, clauses have subjects and verbs.

Phrase: to supply the required energy.

Clause: *Bob walked home today* after he took his exam.

Independent clause: Bob walked home today.

Dependent clause: after he took his exam.

Nonrestrictive clause: She read stories, *which the children enjoyed*.

Restrictive clause: She read stories *that the children enjoyed*.

In the nonrestrictive clause, she read stories, the children enjoyed the stories. In the restrictive clause, she read only stories she knew the children would enjoy.

Coherence

A piece of writing is coherent when all sentences of a unit clearly relate to one another, when they flow smoothly and logically, when the reader never strains to put the separate sentence thoughts together. (*See also* Transition.)

Collective Noun

A noun that denotes a group, and the group is treated as a single unit.

flock	orchestra
batch	committee
jury	public enemies
band	army

Colon (:)

A mark of introduction. Something is to follow: an exclamation, a list or a quotation. The word following may or may not be capitalized. It is capitalized when the material following is one or more complete sentences.

Comma (,)

Commas are used to clarify the meaning of a sentence, also to slow the reader, to replace intentionally omitted words, to introduce, to enclose, and to separate.

We made a change of course.

We made a change, of course.

She went to her home, I to mine.

Commas must be used to:

introduce direct quotes

separate thoughts at the end of a sentence

indicate the omission of words

separate first and last names listed in reverse order

separate names from a title

set off a direct address

Comparative

The form of an adjective used to indicate a higher degree of quantity, quality or manner; but not the highest degree (*see* Superlative).

big—bigger   good—better

high—higher   fast—faster

active—less active

Complement

The part of the predicate of a sentence that completes the idea presented by the verb.

Jean was a *tutor*.

Peter sold his *car*.

The cook became the *hero*.

Tim's dog is *obedient*.

Sean painted their house *yellow*.

Completeness

Writing all that needs to be said from the point of view of the reader.

Compound Predicate

Two or more predicates of the same subject.

Our troop raised money for the elderly poor and started a junior club for preteens.

Compound Sentence

A sentence containing two or more main clauses and no subordinate clauses.

Rolo went shopping for a new car, and Alex went shopping for a ski jacket.

Compound Subject

Two or more subjects of the same verb.

Pam and Ethel went shopping.

Concise

Using as few words as possible while being clearly understood.

Conjunction

A word joining two independent clauses.

We hiked all morning, *but* they waited until evening to start their hike.

Connotation

A feeling of what the word implies beyond what it explicitly names or describes.

A home is more than a house.
From him she received a bouquet of red roses.

Consonant

A letter that is *not* a vowel: a, e, i, o, u, y.
Consonants usually have hard sounds: *C*ut, *d*on't, *K*entucky.

Contraction

Words with an apostrophe replacing some letters.

cannot/can't	it is/it's
do not/don't	they are/they're

Coordination

The joining of two separate thoughts of equal importance.

Our favorite basketball team won today, and they will win tomorrow.

Cumulative Sentence

The main idea is stated at the beginning and is amplified or explained with additional information.

It was a difficult climb because we stumbled over rocks, scrambled over fallen trees and sank into bogs, hoping to reach the top before nightfall.

Dash (—)

Used to indicate an abrupt change of thought.

There was no hope—surely she was aware of that.

Denotation

A straightforward, dictionary explanation or definition of a word.

A house is a building that serves as living quarters for one or more families.

Dependent Clause

See Clause.

Editing

Preparing for publication; checking and removing errors; rearranging in a more meaningful or easily understood way.

Exclamation Point (!)

A mark used to emphasize a statement or an exclamation.

We won! Whee!

Use this mark sparingly.

Expletive

A fill-in word usually signifying that a meaningful subject will follow.

It is Joan whom we want on our team.
There will be an ice cream social Wednesday at 3:00 P.M.

Formal Writing

The language of literature, textbooks, essays, dissertations, the professions and business letters.
Phrases from formal to slang:

He is a well-dressed gentleman.
He's a nice-looking man.
He's cool!

Fragmented Sentence

A group of words punctuated as a sentence—with a capital letter and a period—but which is lacking a subject, a verb or an independent clause.

Fixing his old Model A.

Because he likes to tinker.

Such as coils and sparkplugs.

Which helps him forget his troubles.

Future Tense

See Tense.

Gender

Refers to feminine, masculine or neuter.

he/her   he/him   it

Gerund

A verb form ending in *ing* and used as a noun.

Walking is good exercise.

Swimming is better exercise some people say.

By *running*, he got there first.

My first love is *boxing*.

Hyphen (-)

A link, tying two parts of a word together or connecting two or more words.

co-opted   son-in-law

twenty-two   well-lighted room

pages 10-23   four- or six-cylinder car

Imperative Mood of Verbs

See Mood.

Independent Clause

See Clause.

Indicative Mood of Verbs

See Mood.

Indirect Object

See Object.

Infinitive

A verb form used as a noun, but can also be used as an adjective or adverb.

To fly was fun.

Shane was about *to go*.

Esther was happy *to write* the play.

We didn't dare *let* her go alone. (*to* is implied but not expressed)

Interrupters

Data added to a sentence, or within a sentence, that adds special interest. Dashes add emphasis; parentheses subtract emphasis.

Care givers—especially older ones—need time off now and then.

Driving through an amber light is dangerous (you and I know that), but Pepo finds it exciting.

Intransitive Verb

See Verb.

Italics

Used to indicate emphasis and to distinguish certain elements such as book titles; foreign expressions; names of ships, aircraft, spacecraft; special use of words. In handwriting and typing, italics is indicated by underlining.

Jargon

A special, and sometimes highly technical, language used by occupational groups. It is often a shortcut language among those who understand it.

Metaphor

A figure of speech implying a comparison of two things.

Her eyes are sparkling diamonds.
Jerry's girl friend is a doll.

Modifier

A word or phrase that changes, describes or limits other words or phrases.

The *house* is *red.*
Andy *walked slowly.*
She was *first.*
My *tomatoes* are *smaller.*
He is *partly right.*

Mood

The form of verbs indicating manner.

Imperative: shows command or request.
    Go now. Please come back later.
Indicative: shows straightforward actions or facts or questions.
    Pedro caught the ball.
    Ismael won the foot race.
    Did Haskell enter the race?
Subjunctive: expresses ideas that are contrary to fact:
    Suppose he were here now.
    If it were to rain, the picnic will be held in Bolton Hall.
Or supposition with improbability:
    He talks as if he were to become the elected Speaker.
    If I were you, I wouldn't enter the race now.

Or doubt:

> He swaggers as if he were innocent.
>
> The motor sounds as if it were about to stall, but it keeps running.

Or formal motion:

> I move that his nomination be accepted.
>
> I move that the ammendment be approved by unanimous acclamation.

Or wish:

> I wish I were stronger.
>
> It is our wish that Johnson be accepted into membership.

Motor Learning

Learning by writing words repeatedly until their spelling or meaning becomes "automatic."

Nonrestrictive Clause

See Clause.

Noun

A word that names a person, place, thing, idea or condition.

> *Rosa* attended church last Sunday.
>
> *Sacramento* is the capital of California.
>
> Her *basket* held our lunch.
>
> Insurance *coverage* was the guide's suggestion.
>
> *Illness* was common among the refugees.

Number

Refers to singular or plural. Singular is one; plural is more than one.

Object

A noun or pronoun or phrase used as a noun that receives the action of a verb or completes the meaning of a preposition.

> Direct object: Receives the direct action of a transitive verb.
>
> > Pepo hit the *ball*.
> >
> > He brought the *needed equipment*.
> >
> > I walked for *charity*.

Indirect object: States for whom or to whom the verb acts.

I told *him* my story.

Frank went to the store for *her*.

Objective Case

See Case.

Outline

A condensed treatment of a subject, revealing the order of topics discussed and their relative importance to each other.

Paragraph

A complete thought, usually a group of sentences all of which are related to a central topic or idea.

Parallel

Referring to words or ideas in the English language, it means equal construction, balanced ideas, repetition of form, or a rhythm of thoughts.

Parentheses ( )

These are used to enclose parenthetical (incidental) comments and to enclose numbers identifying items in a series.

John Lang (the father of Joe Lang) was being considered for the presidency.

We need (1) wood chips, (2) barbeque sauce, and (3) starter fluid.

Parenthetical Inserts

Inserted comments or interruptions placed within parentheses in a sentence to indicate subordinate thoughts or observations of the author. These are "asides" by the author and not part of the author's commentary.

Participle

A verb form used as an adjective. Do not confuse with a gerund, which is a verb form used as a noun. Both gerunds and present participles end in *ing*.

Present: *Running* water is safer than standing water.

Past: *Filtered* water is even safer.

Present perfect: Tobby, *having filtered* the water, can now drink it.

Passive Verbs

The subject receives the action rather than directing the action.

Passive: The train *was stopped* by the landslide.

Active: The landslide *stopped* the train.

Perfect Tense

See Tense.

Period (.)

Used to mark the end of a sentence, to follow abbreviations, to follow an individual's initials and to follow numbers indicating divisions.

We walked home slowly.

Mrs., Dr., etc.

J.C. Smyth, C.M. Watson

1. length, 2. breadth, 3. height

Person

First person is the person speaking: I, we.

Second person is the person spoken to: you.

Third person is the person or thing spoken about: he, she, they, it.

Phrase

Normal: A related group of words that modifies another word in a sentence and has no subject or verb.

He decided *to walk home*.

Dangling: An inappropriate phrase tacked onto the end of a sentence.

The toast burned *while drinking orange juice*.

Misplaced: He walked *for breakfast* into the kitchen.

Correct: He walked into the kitchen for breakfast.

Plural

More than one.

Possessive Case

See Case.

Predicate

The part of a sentence that contains the verb. It tells what is said about the subject.

Simple predicate: Alfred *runs*.

Complete predicate: Alfred *runs twice daily to build up strength and sta-mina for the big June event.*

Prefix

A letter or letters placed in front of a base word to change its meaning.

*pre*disposed	*out*cast
*over*work	*in*decent
*un*cover	*counter*plot

Preposition

A word showing relationship between a noun or pronoun and other words in a sentence. It must be followed by a noun or pronoun object.

at the house	*in* the barn
over the rocks	*under* the porch
with his friend	*for* him

Present Tense

See Tense.

Pronoun

A word that takes the place of a noun and functions like a noun.

She and *I* will go

Sandra is one *who* cooperates.

We will help *them*.

I *myself* witnessed the event.

Those are better.

Who said that?

What's wrong?

Prose

The ordinary way of writing and speaking, distinguished from poetry with its rules of rhythm and sometimes rhyme.

Punctuation

Written symbols such as periods, commas, hyphens, dashes, colons and question marks, which in conversation are demonstrated by physical movements and vocal inflections.

Purple Prose

Exaggerated or ornate descriptions. A style of writing often used by reviewers of artistic performances to enhance the reputations—and perhaps the egos—of the performers.

Quotation Marks (" ")

Used to enclose direct quotations and to indicate words used in unusual ways.

He said, "Please stay awhile."

This is a "specified" situation.

Redundancy

A part of a writing that can be eliminated without loss of meaning; duplicating a word or thought's meaning.

His new walking shorts are red *in color*.

A proposal was discussed and voted on, but the discussion continued *to be discussed*.

Report

An organized presentation of data to serve a specific purpose. Formal reports are usually more complex, more lengthy and more detailed than informal reports.

Restrictive Clause

See Clause.

Root

The base word to which prefixes or suffixes are added.

dis*agree*	*ir*regular
out*cast*	*in*decent
*slow*ly	*accept*able
*care*ful	*outrage*ous

Semicolon (;)

A semi-stop in a sentence, not the complete stop of a period, but more of a separation than a comma. It is used to separate independent clauses and also to separate phrases that include commas.

Running is hard work; it requires stamina.

The fruit consisted of apples, pears, peaches and apricots; and the vegetables of carrots, beets and lettuce.

Sentence

A single thought containing a subject and a verb.

Simple sentences:

Horses run.

Horses and chickens run.

Horses and chickens walk and run.

Compound sentences contain two or more main clauses but no subordinate clauses:

The horse walked, and the chicken walked.

Betty made jam, but Ellen made clear jelly.

Simile

A figure of speech comparing two things, usually introduced by *like* or *as*.

Her eyes sparkle like diamonds.
He is as cuddly as a teddy bear.
Her complexion is like peaches and cream.

Singular

One of a thing.

Slash (/)

A slash (virgule) is used:

to separate alternatives; and/or
to replace a word: April/May issue
to divide dates: 04/06/96
to indicate fractions: 1/2, 3/4
to represent the word *per*: five/dollar
to tie together: the address/phone changes

Subject

The person or thing in a sentence that acts or is acted upon.

John went to school.
The *paper* flew out the window.
The *branch* was broken by the wind.
She is ill.

Subjective

See Case.

Subordination

Giving one thought lesser importance than another thought.

We all liked Cedric, although he was difficult at times.
Please give her the book, the red one.
The family, including Tim, went together.

Suffix

A letter or letters added at the end of a base word.

accept*able*	care*ful*
force*ful*	homestead*er*
leader*ship*	real*ism*

Superlative

An adjective or adverb form expressing the highest degree.

big, bigger, *biggest*
good, better, *best*
fair, good, excellent, *superior*

Tense

The form of the verb that indicates the time of action.

Present: I *go*
Past: I *went*
Future: I *will go*
Present perfect: I *have gone*
Past perfect: I *had gone*
Future perfect: I *will have gone*

Topic Sentence

A sentence that states the subject matter and presents subtopics or themes that will support the topic. It thus limits the range of a paragraph or composition.

This is a study of birds native to Arizona.
The purpose of this report is to suggest ways to reduce machine operator overtime in the Lakeside plant.

Transition

A word or phrase that ties two ideas together.

Direct transitions include such words as *again, also, in addition, however* and *likewise*.
Reference transitions repeat a word or use a similar word to relate the current thought to a previous or following thought.

Transitive Verb

See Verb.

Unity

Sticking to one idea, one focus, one part of a subject and one unit that can be summarized in a topic sentence.

Verb

A word denoting action or a state of being. All sentences have a verb, either stated or implied.

Stated: Garcia *hit* the baseball.
Implied: Who is going? You and Pete. (You and Pete *will go*.)

Transitive verbs require an object:

Garcia hit the *baseball*.

Intransitive verbs do not require an object:

We *fished* in Lake Powell.
She *played* hard.

Verbal

A verb form consisting of a gerund, participle or infinitive.
See also Gerund; Infinitive; Participle.

Viewpoint

One person's observations or thoughts on a subject. Each sentence, paragraph and composition should have only one point of view. When the viewpoint is changed, use a transition to warn the reader that a viewpoint change is to be made.

Virgule (/)

See Slash.

Visual Learning

Learning by seeing, that is, by observing.

Voice

Indicates whether the subject does the acting or is acted upon.

Active: I *climbed* the tree.
Passive: The tree *was climbed* by me.

Vowel

The letters a, e, i, o, u, y. Vowels usually have soft sounds: *a*n, *o*ld, *y*ou.

Wordiness

Writing that uses long, flowing sentences replete with adjectives, adverbs and excess explanatory words. Writing concisely is more difficult because it requires more thinking, but the result is better understanding by the reader.

Bibliography

Andrews, Clarence A. *Technical and Business Writing*. Houghton Mifflin, 1975.

Bailey, Edward P. *The Plain English Approach to Business Writing*. Oxford University Press, 1990.

Bailey, Edward P. *Plain English at Work: A Guide to Business Writing and Speaking*. Oxford University Press, 1996.

Barnes, Cynthia A. *Model Memos for Every Business Occasion*. Prentice Hall, 1990.

Barnes & Noble, eds. *Word Speller and Divider: A Guide to Correct Spelling and Word Division*. Barnes & Noble, 1997.

Barton, Judi and Rosenblatt, Nate. *The Only Personal Letter Book You'll Ever Need*. Round Lake Publishing, 1997.

Bellafiore, Joseph. *Words at Work*. Amsco School Publications, 1968.

Bettinhaus, Erwin P. and Cody, Michael J. *Persuasive Communication*. Harcourt Brace Jovanovich College Publishers, 1987.

Blake, Gary and Bly, Robert W. *The Elements of Business Writing*. Macmillan, 1991.

Bonet, Diana. *Clear Writing: A Step by Step Guide*. Crisp Publications, 1991.

Booher, Dianna Daniels. *Would You Put That in Writing? How to Write Your Way to Success in Business*. Facts on File, 1993.

Bower, Peter. *The Superior Person's Book of Words*. David R. Godine, 1985.

Brock, Susan L. *Better Business Writing*. Crisp Publications, 1988.

Brock, Susan L. *Writing Business Proposals and Reports*. Crisp Publications, 1992.

Brusaw, Charles T., Alred, Gerald J. and Oliu, Walter E. *The Business Writer's Handbook*, 5th ed. St. Martin's Press, 1997.

Buckley, William F., Jr. *The Right Word*. Random House, 1996.

Burchfield, R. W., ed. *The New Fowler's Modern English Usage*. Clarendon Press, 1996.

Carroll, Lewis. *Alice's Adventures in Wonderland*. The Modern Library, 1947.

Cazort, Douglas. *Under the Grammar Hammer*. Loewell House, 1997.

The Chicago Manual of Style. University of Chicago Press, 1993.

Corbett, Edward P. J. and Conors, Robert J. *Style and Statement*. Oxford University Press, 1999.

Cresci, Martha. *Complete Book of Model Business Letters*. Parker Publishing Company, 1976.

Cutter, Martin. *The Plain English Guide: How to Write Clearly and Communicate Better*. Oxford University Press, 1996.

Cypert, Samuel A. *Writing Effective Letters, Memos, Proposals, and Reports*. Contemporary Books, 1983.

Davis, Polly. *English Structure in Forms*. Newberry House Publishers, 1977.

De Vries, Mary A. *The Complete Word Book: A Guide to Anything and Everything You Need to Know About Words and How to Use Them*. Prentice Hall, 1991.

De Vries, Mary A. *The New American Handbook of Letter Writing: And Other Forms of Correspondence*. Wings Books, 1988.

Dowis, Richard. *SPELL Member's Handbook: Society for the Preservation of English Language and Literature*. SPELL, 1995.

Dumaine, Deborah. *Write to the Top*. Random House, 1989.

Elgin, Suzette Haden. *The Gentle Art of Written Self-Defense: How to Write Your Way Out of Life's Delicate Situations*. MJF Books, 1993.

Elser, Arthur G. *Writing from Scratch: For Business*. Rowan & Littlefield, 1990.

Encyclopedia Americana. Americana Corp., 1974.

Feierman, Joanne. *Action Grammar: Fast No-Hassle Answers on Everyday Usage and Punctuation*. Simon & Schuster, 1995.

Ferrara, Cosmo F. *Writing on the Job: Quick, Practical Solutions to All Your Business Writing Problems*. Prentice Hall, 1995.

Fielden, John S. *Bottom-Line Business Writing*. Prentice Hall, 1984.

Fielden, John S. *What Do You Mean I Can't Write?* Prentice Hall, 1984.

Fine, Edith and Josephson, Judith P. *Nitty-Gritty Grammar: A Not-So-Serious Guide to Clear Communication*. Ten Speed Press, 1998.

Flesch, Rudolph and Lass, A. H. *A New Guide to Better Writing*. Warner Books, 1989.

Frank, Marcella. *Modern English: A Practical Reference Guide*. Prentice Hall, 1972.

Frank, Milo O. *How to Get Your Point Across in 30 Seconds—or Less*. Simon & Schuster, 1986.

Freeman, Morton S. *The Wordwatcher's Guide to Good Writing & Grammar*. Writer's Digest Books, 1990.

Gabel, John B. and Wheeler, Charles B. *The Bible as Literature*. Oxford University Press, 1990.

Gorenstein, Helm. *Put It in a Memo: A Practical Guide to Persuasive Business Writing*. Houghton Mifflin, 1992.

Grave, Robert and Hodge, Alan. *The Use & Abuse of the English Language*. Morlowe & Company, 1995.

Hayakawa, S. I. *Choose the Right Word: A Contemporary Guide to Selecting the Precise Word for Every Situation*. HarperPerennial, 1994.

Heller, Bernard. *The 100 Most Difficult Business Letters You'll Ever Have to Write, Fax or E-Mail: Clear Guidance on How to Write Your Way Out of the Toughest Business Problems You Will Ever Face*. HarperBusiness, 1994.

Hodges, John C. and Whitten, Mary E. *Harbrace College Handbook*. Harcourt Brace Jovanovich, 1986.

Hook, J. N. *The Appropriate Word: Finding the Best Way to Say What You Mean*. Addison-Wesley, 1990.

John Wiley & Sons, eds. *A Concise Guide to Clear Writing*. John Wiley & Sons, 1975.

Johnson, Edward D. *The Handbook of Good English*. Facts on File, 1991.

Judd, Karen. *Copy Editing: A Practical Guide*. Crisp Publications, 1990.

Kelsch, Thomas and Mary Lynn. *Writing Effectively: A Practical Guide*. Prentice Hall, 1981.

Kierzek, John M. and Gibson, Walter. *The Macmillan Handbook of English*. Macmillan, 1963.

Kilpatrick, James J. *The Writer's Art*. Andrews, McMeel, & Parker, 1984.

Kramer, Melinda G., Leggett, Glen and Mead, David C. *Prentice Hall Handbook for Writers*. Prentice Hall, 1995.

Krohn, Robert. *English Sentence Structure*. University of Michigan Press, 1971.

Lamphear, Lynn. *Shortcuts to Effective on-the-Job Writing*. Prentice Hall, 1982.

Lannen, John M. *The Writing Process: A Concise Rhetoric*. Scott, Foresman, 1989.

Lederer, Richard. *Crazy English: The Ultimate Joy Ride through Our Language*. Pocket Books, 1989.

Lederer, Richard. *The Play of Words: Fun and Games for Language Lovers*. Pocket Books, 1990.

Lederer, Richard and Dowis, Richard. *The Write Way: The SPELL Guide to Real-Life Writing*. Pocket Books, 1995.

Lesiker, Raymond V. *Business Communication: Theory and Application*. Richard D. Irwin, 1976.

Lutz, William. *The New Doublespeak: Why No One Knows What Anyone's Saying Anymore*. HarperCollins, 1996.

Maggio, Rosalie. *How to Say It: Choice Words, Phrases, Sentences and Paragraphs for Every Situation*. Prentice Hall, 1990.

Markel, Michael H. and Lucier, R. J. *Make Your Point*. Prentice Hall, 1983.

McKeown, Thomas W. *Better Business Writing*. Clear Communications Press, 1990.

McKeown, Thomas W. *Powerful Business Writing: Say What You Mean, Get What You Want*. Writer's Digest Books, 1992.

McKernan, John. *The Writer's Handbook*. Holt, Rinehart and Winston, 1988.

McQuain, Jeffrey. *Power Language: Getting the Most Out of Your Words*. Houghton Mifflin, 1996.

Merriam-Webster's Collegiate Dictionary: Tenth Edition. Merriam-Webster, 1993.

Meyer, Harold E. *Lifetime Encyclopedia of Letters*. Prentice Hall, 1998.

Miles, Robert and Bertonasco, Marc. *Prose Style for the Modern Writer*. Prentice Hall, 1977.

Moore, Robert Hamilton. *Effective Writing*. Rinehart & Company, 1959.

Myers, Alfred Stuart. *Letters for All Occasions: The Classic Guide to Social and Business Correspondence*. HarperPaperback, 1993.

Newman, Edwin. *A Civil Tongue*. Galahad Books, 1976.

Newman, Edwin. *Strictly Speaking*. Galahad Books, 1974.

Oliu, Walter E., Brusaw, Charles T. and Alfred, Gerald J. *Writing That Works: How to Write Effectively on the Job*. St. Martin's Press, 1988.

Opdycke, John B. *Harper's English Grammar*. Harper & Row, 1966.

Paxson, William C. *Principles of Style for the Business Writer*. Dodd, Mead & Company, 1985.

Pei, Mario. *The Story of Language*. Lippincott, 1965.

Perlman, Alan M. *Writer Choices: New Options for Effective Communication*. Charles C. Thomas, 1989.

Pinckert, Robert C. *Pinckert's Practical Grammar: A Lively, Unintimidating Guide to Usage, Punctuation and Style*. Writer's Digest Books, 1986.

Plimpton, George, ed. *Writers at Work: The Paris Review Interviews*. Viking Penguin, 1986.

Poor, Edith. *The Executive Writer: A Guide to Words, Ideas and People*. Grove Weidenfeld, 1992.

Princeton Review staff. *Grammar Smart: A Guide to Perfect Usage*. Villard Books, 1993.

Proctor, William. *The Terrible Speller: A Quick and Easy Guide to Enhancing Your Spelling Ability*. William Morrow and Company, 1993.

Reid, James M. *Effective Letters: A Program for Self-Instruction*. McGraw-Hill, 1978.

Robinson, Adam. *Word Smart: How to Build a More Educated Vocabulary*. Villard Books, 1993.

Rockwell, F. A. *How to Write Non-Fiction That Sells*. Regnery, 1975.

Roddick, Ellen. *Writing That Means Business*. Macmillan, 1984.

Roget's International Thesaurus, 5th ed. HarperCollins, 1992.

Safire, William. *Coming to Terms*. Doubleday, 1991.

Safire, William. *Language Maven Strikes Again*. Doubleday, 1990.

Safire, William. *Take My Word for It*. Times Books, 1984.

Safire, William. *Watching My Language: Adventures in the Word Trade*. Random House, 1997.

Safire, William. *You Could Look It Up*. Times Books, 1988.

Schell, John and Stratton, John. *Writing on the Job*. New American Library, 1984.

Shaw, Harry. *Errors in English and Ways to Correct Them*. Harper & Row, 1986.

Sitzmann, Marion. *Successful Business Writing: A Practical Guide for the Student and Professional*. National Textbook Company, 1983.

Smith, Leila R. *English for Careers*. Prentice Hall, 1992.

Strumpf, Michael and Douglas, Auriel. *Painless, Perfect Grammar: Tips from the Grammar Hotline*. Monarch Press, 1985.

Strunk, William, Jr. and White, E. B. *The Elements of Style*. Macmillan, 1972.

Tarshis, Barry. *Grammar for Smart People: Your User-Friendly Guide to Speaking and Writing Better English*. Pocket Books, 1992.

Tietz, Robert and Tietz, Elaine. *Complete Book of Effective Personal Letters*. Prentice Hall, 1984.

Troyka, Lynn Quitman. *Simon & Schuster Handbook for Writers*. Prentice Hall, 1987.

Usris, Auren. *Memos for Managers*. Thomas Y. Crowell, 1975.

Walpole, Jane. *The Writer's Grammar Guide: Easy Ground Rules for Successful Written English*. Simon & Schuster, 1984.

Weiss, Allen. *Write What You Mean*. Amacom, 1977.

Williams, Joseph M. *Style: Toward Clarity and Grace*. University of Chicago Press, 1990.

World Book, ed. *The World Book Complete Word Power Library, Volume 1*. World Book, 1981.

Zinsser, William. *On Writing Well: An Informal Guide to Writing Nonfiction*. HarperCollins, 1991.

Index

About the Author

HAROLD E. MEYER was Senior Accountant at Crown Zellerbach Corporation. With an accountant's dedication to accuracy and clarity, he wrote the unmatched book on letter writing, *Lifetime Encyclopedia of Letters*. He is also a former newsletter editor. During over thirty years in business, Mr. Meyer collected, analyzed and rewrote numerous vaguely written letters and reports that crossed his desk. He became aware that many writers needed help. To assist readers who want to write clear, understandable letters, memos and other written communications, he brought together his years of study and research to write this book.